THE MAKING OF THE INCLUSIVE SCHOOL

There is a new inclusive mood at large in society. It has created a demand for schools to find ways of including and teaching *all* children – even those who at one time would have been sent to special schools.

Society's readiness for inclusion coincides with the accumulation of more and more evidence about the limitations of special education. But although the arguments for inclusive education seem overwhelming – ethically and empirically – the move to inclusion has been painfully slow.

After exploring the arguments for inclusion, this book examines the international evidence of children's well-being and academic progress in inclusive schools. It also describes how those who are in the vanguard of inclusion have gone about developing their practice.

The second part of the book presents a detailed case study of one special school's confrontation with exclusion and its transformation from a special school into an inclusion service – a project which involved closing the special school and moving its children to a group of mainstream partner schools.

Gary Thomas is a professor of education at the University of the West of England, Bristol and directed the research project on which this book is based. **David Walker** is residential policy and practice adviser with NCH Action for Children, having formerly been the headteacher of Princess Margaret School. **Julie Webb** is the researcher who undertook most of the fieldwork for the project, and she currently works as a freelance journalist.

THE MAKING OF THE INCLUSIVE SCHOOL

Gary Thomas, David Walker and Julie Webb

London and New York

First published 1998
by Routledge
11 New Fetter Lane, London EC4P 4EE

Simultaneously published in the USA and Canada
by Routledge
29 West 35th Street, New York, NY 10001

Typeset in Garamond by Routledge
Printed and bound in Great Britain by Creative Print and Design
(Wales), Ebbw Vale

British Library Cataloguing in Publication Data
A catalogue record for this book is available from the British Library

Library of Congress Cataloguing in Publication Data
Thomas, Gary, 1950–
The inclusive school / Gary Thomas, David Walker, and Julie Webb.
Includes bibliographical references and indexes.
1. Inclusive education–Great Britain. I. Walker, David.
II. Webb, Julie. III. Title.
LC1203.G7T56   1996
371.9'046'07973–dc21   97–13798
CIP

ISBN 0–415–15559–2 (hbk)
ISBN 0–415–15560–6 (pbk)

CONTENTS

Part II From special schools to inclusion services

ILLUSTRATIONS

FIGURES

TABLES

PREFACE

This book has two themes. One is about a general move to inclusive schools; the other is about the actual experience of a specific group of schools in moving to inclusion. The book grew out of a research project funded by the children's charity Barnardos into a unique 'natural experiment' being conducted by staff in one of its special schools. The staff of this school, the Princess Margaret School (PMS) in Somerset, England, had decided to close the school and return all its children to be educated in the mainstream. Although the decision was a principled one and based on good evidence about its likely success, there were several people – in the school and outside it – who were apprehensive about it, for the existing system seemed to work well and the proposed change meant a trip into uncharted waters.

It was inevitable, therefore, that the mooted venture would be contentious and that there would be many uncertainties along the way. It was clear, however, that lessons would be learned in this brave experiment, which is why Barnardos contracted the research: given the novelty of this project it was important to extract every ounce of information which came from the experience.

So this is a book in two parts. The first part is about inclusion in schools and inclusivity in society – it makes a case for inclusion, and examines its provenance and its practice. It seems to us that a time is coming – if indeed it hasn't already arrived – when the institutions of society, notably schools, will recognise the importance of including everyone, irrespective of their ability or background, in their endeavours. Merely to say that, though, is easy and empty rhetoric without guidelines on how to conceptualise and manage such inclusive endeavour, and we have therefore tried in the first part of the book to bring together evidence on the ways in which it has been thought about and done to date. The second part gives in detail the findings of the research into the Somerset Inclusion Project and discusses these findings in the context of the debate in the first part of the book.

The ideas behind the closure of the school and the development of its replacement – the Somerset Inclusion Project (SIP) – were conceived in June 1991. The closure of PMS finally happened in July 1996. What happened at

PMS over the intervening five years was extraordinary and affected everyone connected with it – pupils, parents, staff, volunteers, managers, colleagues, friends and supporters from all over England and beyond. There are many people to thank for helping to develop the ideas and make theory turn into practice. In particular, Dave Walker, as manager of the project, would like to thank Steve Connor, his manager, who first persuaded him that he could lead the school through the change and whose steady support and vision was unswerving and vital; the PMS senior management team – Vivian Upton, John Morris, Peggy Anderson and, later, Barbara Street – who shared the pain and the joys and whose support was a rock; and Carol Bannister who took her class out of PMS and into 'West Hill' School, thus becoming the first bridge to the future. Sue Rickell, who was consultant to the school through much of the process and whose experience and skill gave so much, is due special thanks. Tribute and thanks must also go to those parents who, despite many anxieties and misgivings, put their confidence in the project and its staff.

Acknowledgements are almost too numerous, since the production of this book has depended on the work of so many others. On the research side, acknowledgements must go to all the children and young people in all of the schools in which we have worked for their patience in putting up with our observations, questions and our intrusive presence in their lives. Acknowledgement and thanks must equally go to their parents for their generosity of ideas and time; to all of the teachers, headteachers and assistants who have suffered cheerfully and uncomplainingly our presence in their classrooms and have freely given of their time, reflections and suggestions; and thanks are especially due to the teacher-co-ordinators; to Paul and Vivian Upton for their essential and dedicated part in the inception of the project, their advice and their commitment to inclusion; to Barnardos and Tony Newman for enabling the project to happen; to the steering group; to Judy Sebba for her energy, enthusiasm and invaluable advice; to Mark Vaughan, co-director of the Centre for Studies on Inclusive Education (CSIE) in Bristol, for his meticulous comments on drafts of parts of the book and for his generosity in sharing the invaluable resources and connections of the CSIE; to Lyn Cooke and Cynthia Britton for their friendly efficiency and their proficiency in typing; to colleagues at the University of the West of England for their support and many ideas. Last but not least to our families for their support and forbearance.

We are grateful to the Audit Commission for permission to reproduce part of their 'Checklist for Action', to the Council for Exceptional Children for permission to reproduce part of their '12 Principles for Inclusion', and to David Skidmore for his kind permission to republish the World Wide Web inclusion list.

As we write, the future for the Somerset Inclusion Project looks uncertain. It is likely that the project will transfer from Barnardos to Somerset

Local Education Authority in September 1997. How it will grow and develop from there is unclear. What is clear is that the establishment of the Somerset Inclusion Project has been a success and has had implications far beyond one special school.

Gary Thomas
Dave Walker
Julie Webb

Bristol, 1997

ABBREVIATIONS

Although each abbreviation or acronym is spelt out in full the first time it is used in this book, the casual 'dipper-in' may have difficulty with the wide range of abbreviations used, especially as their provenance is increasingly international. Some definitions are therefore given here for an international audience.

CEC   Council for Exceptional Children – based in the USA

CoP   Code of Practice: under UK legislation schools must 'have regard' to the CoP, which lays down guidance about how children's special needs should be met

CSIE   Centre for Studies on Inclusive Education: see Appendix

DES   Department of Education and Science – now called the DfEE (see below)

DfE   Department for Education – now called the DfEE (see below)

DfEE   Department for Education and Employment: the UK national government department responsible for education

EBD   Emotional and behavioural difficulties

FC   Facilitated communication

GCSE   General Certificate of Secondary Education: the examination taken in different subjects at 16 by nearly all pupils in England and Wales

GEST   Grants for Education Support and Training: money provided to schools from the DfEE via the LEAs

IEP   Individual Education Plan: a plan that has to be written for each child with special needs under guidelines laid down in the Code of Practice; similar to its US equivalent

LEA	Local Education Authority: the body in the UK responsible for the regional administration of education
LSA	Learning support assistant: assistants who are appointed usually with the purpose of supporting children with special needs
NC	National Curriculum: introduced in Britain in 1988 and specifies the subjects which have to be taught by state schools
OECD	Organisation for Economic Co-operation and Development: an internationally respected organisation, which has funded several studies into inclusion.
PL 94-142	Public Law 94-142: the American law which encourages special provision in the 'least restrictive environment'
PMS	Princess Margaret School: the special school which closed in order to re-form as the Somerset Inclusion Project (SIP)
PSE	Personal and social education
SAT	Standard assessment task: tasks children have to undertake as part of National Curriculum assessments; similar to the American equivalent
SEN	Special Educational Needs: a widely used official term in the UK
SENCO	Special educational needs co-ordinator: a teacher with specific responsibilities for co-ordinating special needs provision in each school
SIP	The Somerset Inclusion Project, which involved the closing of PMS (see above) and its transformation into an inclusion service for local mainstream schools
Y1–Y11	Year 1 to Year 11: these are the years of the compulsory school career in England and Wales; Y1s are 5–6 years old; Y11s, 15–16

Part I

INCLUSION IN SCHOOLS

Inclusion is a buzzword of the 1990s. Politicians now stress their commitment to inclusion and social justice – not competition. The new inclusive mood has created a growing demand for mainstream schools to find ways of including and teaching *all* children – even those who at one time would certainly have been sent to special schools. In the first part of this book we examine the arguments for inclusive schools and the evidence for the success of inclusion; in Part II we proceed to examine ways of making inclusion happen, based on the experience of a group of schools which have – in the Somerset Inclusion Project – embraced the inclusive ideal.

This first part of the book looks at society's readiness for inclusive institutions and notes the coincidence of this readiness with the accumulation of more and more evidence about the ineffectiveness of special education. It is odd that although the arguments for inclusive schools seem overwhelming, ethically and empirically, the move to inclusion has been painfully slow. We examine reasons for this slow move to inclusion and look at what is needed to make inclusion happen. We also examine the international evidence about children's progress in inclusive schools.

After examining the provenance of inclusion as an ideal and the rationale for it in today's schools, Part I proceeds to look at a number of issues in detail. These include the way support is provided by assistants and teachers in the inclusive classroom; the ways in which the curriculum can be adapted to enable true inclusion; the challenge to produce a congenial social environment for children in moves to inclusion; and, particularly where children have physical disabilities, the logistic and physical challenges that confront an inclusion project. Throughout, we have tried to distil the lessons of the Somerset Inclusion Project and other projects where these have been reported in the literature.

1

INCLUSIVE EDUCATION
The ideals and the practice

FROM SEGREGATION TO INCLUSION

Inclusion is not a new idea. Although recent concern about inclusion can be traced to the civil rights movements of the 1960s, the ideals behind inclusive education have much deeper roots in liberal and progressive thought. If we research the shaping of the current school system a century earlier, we can see that two avenues were then open. One was inclusive, the other segregative.

A significant body of opinion at the turn of the century – perhaps exemplified best in the work of the child welfare pioneer Elizabeth Burgwin – saw neither purpose nor virtue in segregation. Those who shared these views did not even seriously consider segregated schooling. Instead, in thinking about the needs of children with disabilities, they thought automatically of adaptations that could be made to ordinary schools. It is quite possible that this inclusive thought might have prospered and provided the philosophical and organisational foundation for the school system of the twentieth century.

Another body of opinion, however, considered that children could be categorised according to their difficulties and suggested that different, 'special' schools be established to cater for children who, in the words of the School Board for London (1904), could not be taught 'in ordinary standards or by ordinary methods'. (The origins of the special system are discussed in detail by Potts, 1982; Tomlinson, 1982; Copeland, 1995; Copeland, 1996; and Scott, 1996.)

It is possible that this segregative body of opinion might have lost the argument against the progressive opinion of the day. However, the segregative conviction was reinforced greatly by the burgeoning 'science' of psychometrics and associated ideas on eugenics. These suggested that 'misfits' should be removed from the genetic pool; it needed only a minor extension of this logic to propose that defectives and degenerates be removed from society's mainstream institutions, notably schools. When Cyril Burt was appointed the first psychologist for London in 1911 further momentum was added to this body of opinion. His growing reputation, his fondness for

3

psychometrics and his commitment to the idea that intelligence was inherited and more or less immutable all combined to give great stimulus to a segregative education system based on the categorisation of the child. This was especially so as Burt was one of the principal architects of the 1944 Education Act insofar as it related to special education. The 1944 Act constructed a highly segregative post-war education system with its ten categories of handicap for which special schools would cater.

It became received opinion that special schools provided a sensible way of meeting the needs of a minority of children, at the same time as safeguarding the efficient education of the majority in the mainstream. Indeed, it seemed more than just sensible: it was self-evident fact that special schools were appropriate. Pijl and Meijer (1994) go so far as to suggest that the system of special schools was widely accepted throughout western Europe. They even suggest that it was one of which society as a whole was proud. Since the facts as to its utility were plain, evidence to support it was unnecessary. This orthodoxy became so firmly embedded in the individual and institutional consciousness that no serious challenges were made to the idea until the mid-1960s.

It took the world-wide push for civil rights to begin to challenge this orthodoxy. The changing world-view liberated people with disabilities to give voice to their anger about the stigma, degradation and curricular and social limits imposed by the segregated education to which they had been subjected. Simultaneously, evidence about the surprising lack of success of the segregated system (surprising, that is, given the generous resources allocated to it)[1] began to accumulate with such consistency that it could not be ignored (e.g. Christophos and Renz, 1969; Galloway and Goodwin, 1979; Lipsky and Gartner, 1987; Reynolds et al., 1987; Reynolds, 1988; Anderson and Pellicer, 1990). All this built on evidence (e.g. Dunn, 1968; Birch et al., 1970; Mercer, 1970) which showed that the special system selected disproportionately children from ethnic minorities and children from lower socio-economic groups. Moral arguments and empirical evidence came together to result, towards the end of the twentieth century, in a consensus which sees inclusion as an appropriate philosophy and a relevant framework for restructuring education.

Looking back on this history, however, one realises that the seeds of an integrative philosophy existed many years ago. The segregated system, which a few years ago seemed so manifestly right (and still seems natural to some), can be seen as simply one possible method of organising the education system. It succeeded in providing the blueprint for the school system for the great part of this century because of the psychometric and eugenic views that prevailed before the Second World War. However, it is now recognised that segregation by no means offers a common-sense or natural way of organising education.

An inclusive philosophy has ultimately risen again and prospered. It has

4

been able to succeed because it chimes with the philosophy of a liberal political system and a pluralistic culture – one that celebrates diversity and
promotes fraternity and equality of opportunity. Inclusion must be at the
heart of any society which cherishes these values and at the heart of a truly
comprehensive education system.

EVIDENCE FOR INCLUSION?

So, although inclusion has won partly because of evidence from educational
research showing that special schools are not as effective as one would expect
or wish, it has won mainly because it is *right* that it should have done so.
Arguments for inclusion are principled ones, stemming from concern for
human rights. As Fulcher (1993) points out, these principles drive policy.
Now, this creates problems for evaluation, for values cannot be evaluated.
Fulcher goes on to say that value-driven policy 'cannot be evaluated by an
ecological-systems model, nor by rich databases, nor by looking at the inter-
dependence of elements of the system' (1993: 128).

Newman and Roberts (1996) support Fulcher's case. They point out that
many pioneering developments in welfare for children (such as the shipping
of children to Australia for a 'new life' at the turn of the century) seemed
right and proper at the time. However, it is now recognised that these were
often disastrous in their consequences. There are indeed several contemporary detractors who pick up this theme and warn that an inclusive
philosophy is an inappropriate and misleading one to follow. Within the
deaf community, for example, Mason (1994) suggests that inclusive dialogue
has stressed political, economic, bureaucratic, professional and administrative issues, rather than the effects of inclusive education on individual
children.[2] Gerber argues that special education should be valued because it
has always been subversive. It has ever striven, he suggests, to accommodate
children with 'extreme individual differences' (1996: 156) within a wider
educational system which tacitly seeks to exclude them entirely. And Dorn *et
al.* (1996) warn that by focusing on inclusion the positive action accumulated over decades in favour of children with disabilities and learning
difficulties may evaporate.

They have a point. The move to inclusion must be monitored to ensure
continuity of services. Special provision in special schools has always been
made on the axiom that resources should be provided in direct ratio to need,
heeding (albeit unconsciously) Rawls's (1971) advice on the redistribution of
resources to achieve social justice. But a gradual attrition of provision is
possible if the critical mass of the special school does not exist to ensure the
survival of advantageous provision. And if principles cannot be evaluated for
their veracity nor ethics for their truth, it is crucial that the consequences of
the principled policy decision to provide inclusive education are rigorously
monitored, especially as recent evidence concerning the academic, social and

emotional benefits of integrative programmes are nowhere near as clear-cut as earlier evidence promised. For instance, Hegarty, in summarising a major international review of the literature on integration for the Organisation for Economic Cooperation and Development (OECD), suggests that 'research has failed to establish a clear-cut advantage in either direction' (1994: 197), partly due to the methodological problems of comparing non-comparable groups receiving different kinds of education. He emphasises that integration and segregation are not sharply defined and that integration can take numerous forms, some of them overlapping with segregation. These problems in definition make comparison extremely difficult. Moreover, there are important differences between organisational structures of schools and integration schemes which exaggerate the difficulties of comparative research. Further, any matching of variables in the comparisons of groups do not (presumably because of the small numbers generally involved) extend beyond age, sex and IQ. The corollary of all this, Hegarty says, is that 'the body of research comparing integration and segregation has a limited validity' (*ibid.*).

Steinberg and Tovey (1996), reporting mainly on American research, concur with Hegarty, pointing to the heterogeneity of disabling conditions which make matching difficult or impossible for control grouping. They also emphasise the difficulty of comparing outcomes of inclusion versus special education where there is bound to be selection bias – that is, the tendency to select 'harder to teach' children for special class placement and 'easier' children for inclusion programmes. Despite the difficulties of comparison, many researchers feel able to offer their findings. Baker *et al.* (1995), for instance, report from three meta-analyses that there is a small-to-moderate beneficial effect of inclusive education on social and academic outcomes of students with special needs. And Lipsky and Gartner (1996) summarise over twenty recent studies which report academic and social benefits arising from inclusion.

The problems of selection bias do, however, remain and are even present in the largest longitudinal study of outcomes for students placed in mainstream schools (the US National Longitudinal Transition Study of Special Education Students), which is tracking the post-school progress of 8000 young people. This shows that students with physical disabilities who had received mainstream education were 43 per cent more likely to be employed post-school than counterparts who had attended special placements. Although selection bias must have existed, it is reassuring to note that children with different disabilities were separated in the analysis and that the analysis was sensitive enough to show better outcomes for certain of these groups, notably those with physical disabilities (see Woronov, 1996, for a report).

As Hegarty concludes from the existing research, 'While [the inadequacies of comparative research] means that any inferences drawn must be tentative, the absence of a clear-cut balance of advantage supports integration' (Hegarty, 1993b: 198). Hegarty appears to be saying that unless evidence relating to children's progress and happiness at school is unequivocally unsupportive of integration, then the principles we have used to guide the current practice toward inclusion should be used to determine the direction of policy.

More than this, given that the move to inclusion is a principled one, it is important also that research should focus on ways of making inclusion work. It should illuminate good practice and investigate problems in such a way that obstacles can be recognised and overcome. This is what the research reported in Part II of this book is about.

INCLUSION IN SOCIETY

Most educational discussion on inclusion concentrates on curriculum, pastoral systems, attitudes and teaching methods, but there is a further dimension to inclusion which goes beyond these narrowly school-based considerations. It is the wider notion of inclusion in society – for the notion of inclusion is not unique to education. Indeed, the recent popularity of inclusion as an idea in education probably rests at least in part on its consonance with this wider notion of inclusivity in society – of a society in which each member has a stake. Commentators (e.g. Hutton, 1995; Kay, 1996; Plender, 1997a) have begun to discuss the meaning of this new inclusiveness. There is an interesting notion of reciprocity in their discussion – a recognition of *mutual* obligations and expectations between the community and institutions such as schools, in such a way that these institutions are reminded of their responsibilities and public duties.

To illustrate the point, Kay notes from etymological research that many ideas which seem unrelated to us now – for example the notions of owing and owning – share a root which reveals that there was once a bond between the notions. The bond between *owe* and *own* rests in an expectation of duty, sharing and a concern for others who are weaker. Thus, *owning* always carried with it some implication of *owing* – some bearing of obligations. Only relatively recent usage has separated the two. The ethic of a stakeholding, inclusive society implies a renewed bonding of these ideas.

Now, while Kay draws this distinction in the context of large companies and their obligations to their employees and their customers, the lessons learned from this analysis are surely valid also in relation to schools in their willingness to become inclusive. For there is an injunction in the inclusive, stakeholding ethic, says Plender (1997b), to take account of social costs and benefits that are not explicitly priced in the market. In this process the role of state and individual are downplayed while the role of intermediate institutions (companies, unions, schools, etc.) is reinforced. In an inclusive society, entrustment to governors and headteachers of large amounts of capital and the futures of many children must be accompanied by an obligation to find ways of making inclusion happen. And these obligations must not merely be to the parents of high-achieving children.

So, aside from the curricular and social principles which educationists may wish to see embodied in the policy and practice of a school which claims to be inclusive, one might also include a broader set of principles, imposed not only by the direct stakeholders in the school (teachers, parents and students), but also by those in the local community and society at large and recognised by politicians and the legislature. If this were the case, some further inclusive principles for schools might therefore incorporate, in Mason's (1995) term, the 'intentional building of community'. Such intentional building might include (to paraphrase Hutton and Kay) the following expectations:

- governors and school managers, being entrusted by local communities to run schools, have obligations to run those schools inclusively;
- an effective school is recognised to be one where all members are included and have a stake, not simply one which achieves high scores on academic criteria.

This notion of inclusivity now emerging is in contrast to the individual, instrumental ethic of the 1980s, which was legitimised by the political rhetoric of the time and given academic credence by the economic doctrine of Hayek and others. It was acceptable, fashionable even, to be selfish. Writing at the beginning of the 1980s, Hargreaves (1982) saw this as the efflorescence of *egoism*, which – as Durkheim noted – has deep roots in northern European thought. The aggressively meritocratic, individualistic and competitive thought associated with that tradition clearly provides ample rhetorical justification for segregation. By contrast, in the new philosophy which sees all members of society as stakeholders it is natural to see schools as places where all are welcomed – and duty is felt to all.

Durkheim's ideas are relevant here and perhaps shed some light when examining the difficult question of adopting a particular moral stance. Looking at the failures of the past (such as the shipping of children to Australia for a new life), it is easy to be seduced by a relativist moral stance wherein there are no markers by which one can measure the moral correctness of a position. However, if the ethic which guides our culture is one of collective responsibility and belonging, the words of Durkheim are helpful:

Everything which is a source of solidarity is moral, everything which forces man to take account of other men is moral, everything which forces him to regulate his conduct through something other than the striving of his ego is moral, and morality is as solid as these ties are numerous and strong.

(Durkheim, 1933, quoted by Hargreaves, 1982: 107)

8

This theme of collective belonging is linked by Tawney (1964) with the question of inequality in a civilised society and his reasoning is relevant when thinking about the organisation of education. Tawney did not deny that people were born with different abilities. However, he asserted that a truly civilised society strives to reduce the inequalities which arise from these 'givens' and from its own organisation. The organisation of society's institutions, such as schools, should lighten and reduce those inequalities which arise from birth or circumstance, rather than exaggerate them:

> while [people's] natural endowments differ profoundly, it is the mark of a civilised society to aim at eliminating such inequalities as have their source, not in individual differences, but in its own organisation, and that individual differences, which are a source of social energy, are more likely to ripen and find expression if social inequalities are, as far as practicable, diminished.
>
> (Tawney, 1964: 57)

Some might query this passage's use in support of inclusion. Those who favour an education system incorporating and employing special schools might argue that special schools (as opposed to inclusive mainstream schools) do indeed succeed in diminishing circumstantial differences, as Gerber (1996) has reasoned. But existing inequalities between children – in what they can do with their bodies, or in their 'cultural capital'[3] – cannot be compensated for simply by the physical and personnel resources they are given at school. For those inequalities lie more importantly in opportunities to do the same as other children: to share the same spaces as other children and to 'speak the same language'[4] as other children. Reducing inequality is thus about more than providing money and better resources: it is about providing the chance to share in the common wealth of the school and its culture.

Redistribution on its own, then, is not enough. Rawls (1971) argued for the elimination of inequality through the redistribution of resources in his *Theory of Justice*, saying that in general there should be an equal distribution of social resources, but that there should be a bias in this distribution in favour of those who are 'disadvantaged'. However, Rizvi and Lingard (1996) make the point that redistribution by itself is insufficient to achieve social justice. The thesis they propound is that redistributive logic on its own obscures and thereby perpetuates injustices in existing institutional organisations. For emphasising redistribution could merely mean shifting resources into special education and this would not achieve the structural changes required for social justice. Roaf and Bines (1989) make an allied point: that an emphasis on *needs* in special education detracts from a proper consideration of the *rights* of those who are being educated.

Social justice cannot therefore be achieved simply by redistributing resources based on assessment of need. Achievement of social justice does not come simply through removing inequality.

Tawney disentangles the knot of inequality and social justice further by examining a quotation from Matthew Arnold – which, incidentally, looks remarkably prescient in the context of the current debate: 'On the one side, in fact, inequality harms by pampering; on the other by vulgarising and depressing. A system founded on it is against nature, and in the long run, breaks down' (quoted in Tawney, 1964: 33). There are thus two sides to inequality, and Arnold and Tawney's warnings of the consequences of inequality seem clear in the context of schools. First, inequality has effects arising from the wholly unreal situation which mainstream schools encounter when their rolls are shorn of a significant minority of pupils. This 'pampering' of mainstream schools has its effects in a more academic curriculum (as Postman, 1995, has indicated), in less flexible pastoral systems and in a pupil population which is less familiar with and less accepting of difference and diversity. And second, the removal of children disheartens and depresses those who are removed and it socialises them, as Oliver (1995) asserts, into long-term dependency. Accounts of those who have left special schools attest to this (see, for example, Rieser and Mason, 1990; Shelling, 1996). As Matthew Arnold said, an unequal system is 'against nature' – and in education we are now witnessing its breakdown.

INCLUSION OR INTEGRATION?

The evaluation reported here is about an inclusion project. It is worth at the outset examining what is meant specifically by 'inclusion', and in particular how inclusion may differ from 'integration', a term which has been used – and is still used – to describe the process of transfer of children and young people from special to mainstream schools.

Ten years ago the term 'inclusive education' was not used. It is only since the late 1980s that 'inclusion' has come to supersede 'integration'. Whether the two words can be said to describe different processes in schools is open to question, and has been discussed by a number of commentators (e.g. Booth, 1995, 1996; Sebba and Ainscow, 1996).

Where attempts have been made to draw a distinction between inclusion and integration, the emphasis is usually on how well the curricular and pastoral systems of the school can be said to make comprehensive education meaningful for all children. (A comprehensive education system which does not include all children is in any case surely a misnomer.) Ainscow (1995b), for instance, suggests that whereas integration is about 'additional arrangements' in schools which are essentially unchanged, a move to inclusion on the other hand implies a more radical set of changes through which schools come to embrace all children.

Booth (1996), however, warns against investing too much in the notion of

10

inclusion, suggesting that the word is being used to describe an ideal, unrealisable state. He goes on to say that that there is a temptation to think that there is some practice of inclusive education which can be studied, and that this is a chimera. He suggests elsewhere (Booth, 1995) that his own understanding of 'integration' is of 'comprehensive community education' which has its own cultural and political history linked to battles over selection and local participation. His interpretation therefore rejects the distinction drawn by Ainscow, which ignores the social and political struggle which has been part of the integration movement.

Booth's rejection of the more limited interpretation of 'integration' is supported by earlier discussion about the term. Hegarty *et al.* (1981) in their seminal work on early integration programmes in the UK pointed out the various ways in which integration might be used, noting that there had been a temptation to think predominantly about what the minority group needed to do to become absorbed into the mainstream. Lipsky and Gartner (1996) make a similar point about the American legislation on integration, which they say is based on a 'readiness' model; in other words, students must prove their readiness for an integrated setting, rather than presuming such a setting as a norm.

Hegarty and his colleagues contrast this approach with a standpoint which sees school and children in a 'synthesising process involving all parts in a mutually adaptive interaction'. Interestingly in the light of the Princess Margaret School (PMS) project, they further include in their definition of integration a role for the special school; they say that integration can be 'a process whereby an ordinary school and a special school interact to form a new educational whole' (Hegarty *et al.*, 1981: 15). This sees a powerful role for the special school which is not covered in some of the more recent discussions of the definition of inclusion, although Paul and Ward (1996) in asserting the importance of the inclusion movement acknowledge the need to combine the best features of special education into the new enterprise.

Despite the recent changes in word-usage, many researchers and commentators (e.g. Jupp, 1992; Meijer *et al.*, 1994; Vislie, 1995) continue unashamedly to use 'integration' and 'inclusion' as though the terms describe identical processes. In effect, the terms are used as synonyms. The views outlined above indicate that there is no reason why this should not be done, though it is probably correct to say that the use of 'inclusion' does eliminate some of the less helpful notions – more to do with assimilation than true integration – which used to accompany 'integration', as Hegarty *et al.* (1981) acknowledge.

Inclusion versus exclusion

Most discussion about inclusion stresses its contrast with *segregation* – in exactly the same way that distinctions are drawn between integration and segregation. But an important distinction between integration and inclusion concerns inclusion's status as the opposite of *exclusion* (as separate from segregation), as Booth (1995) notes. Segregation and exclusion are currently thought of as somewhat different processes: segregation is usually associated with children with learning difficulties, sensory impairments or physical disabilities, whereas exclusion is usually of children whose behaviour is found difficult. Integration – perhaps because of its focus on the child – does not define what is to be done instead of segregation, as Flynn (1993) notes, and thus it has been possible for the processes of segregation and exclusion to continue to be thought of separately. Using *inclusion*, however, specifically shifts the focus onto the school rather than the child when thinking about excluded pupils.

Many of the unashamedly market-oriented education policies implemented by national governments in recent years (for example, the publication of 'league tables' of examination results) have had clear consequences in the reduced willingness of schools to accept children regardless of ability or background. Schools are now wary of accepting children who might, through their own low attainment or through their effects on others, depress mean exam or standard assessment task (SAT) scores. This has a potential effect not merely on admissions policies but also on exclusions. The significant increase in exclusions in recent years (see OFSTED, 1996a) testifies that this is the case. One hopes that the greater acceptance of the ideas embodied in an inclusive, stakeholding society augurs a reversal of this trend.

Inclusion as international descriptor

Another feature of 'inclusion' is its present status as an international descriptor of a particular marriage of ethos and practice. This is a further reason to prefer its use to that of 'integration'. While 'integration' was used in the UK, Australia and New Zealand, the preferred term in the USA and Canada was 'mainstreaming' (e.g. Strain and Kerr, 1981). The understanding of inclusion, however, is international.

Inclusion as a new set of classroom practices

Some of the earliest and most original thought on inclusion has come from Canada (e.g. Forest and O'Brien, 1989), and indeed it was Forest and O'Brien who through their proselytising of work in Canada provided much of the impetus for the Somerset Inclusion Project (SIP). The significance of national and regional law, particularly that of New Brunswick (see New Brunswick, 1994) and simple, devolutionary funding in providing stimulus to inclusive practice is described interestingly by Porter (1995), who also provides an excellent summary of differences between what he calls the traditional approach (which may include 'integration') and an inclusionary approach. The main distinctions he draws are summarised in Table 1.1.

It is worth noting that Walker (1995), as one of the architects of the Somerset Inclusion Project, produces a similar typology, an adapted version of which appears in Table 1.2.

Porter's exposition of the New Brunswick approach is particularly interesting since the procedures and systems which he outlines marry with many of those established in the Somerset Inclusion Project. One of the main differences he outlines between traditional and inclusive approaches is that the traditional approach requires a child's referral to an expert. The message inherent in this process, he says, is that 'mainstream teachers are not qualified or competent enough to provide education to a student with a significant learning problem' (1995: 302). 'Expertism' (Troyna and Vincent, 1996) and professionalism (Tomlinson, 1996) have abounded in special education: experts and professionals have in the past promoted the idea that only those with special qualifications are equipped to assess, teach and make decisions about children who are significantly different from others. In the middle decades of this century a three-way symbiosis developed among mainstream education, special education and the experts wherein more difficult-to-accommodate children were categorised by professionals, removed from the mainstream and placed in the special system, to the satisfaction of each party. Special education and the professions surrounding it burgeoned and mainstream education was relieved of the need to accommodate children who added administrative and curricular burdens.

The legitimacy of this process and the premises underlying it have, of course, been contested by many researchers and educators (e.g. Skrtic, 1991; Thomas, 1995b). Indeed, Baker *et al.* go so far as to assert, 'There is no separate knowledge base for teaching children classified as mildly retarded or learning disabled' (1995: 14). The new notion central to inclusion is that exceptional students belong in the mainstream; mainstream classteachers must believe this and have confidence that these young people will learn

Table 1.1 Porter's (1995) comparison of traditional and inclusionary approaches

Traditional approach (which may include integration)	Inclusionary approach
Focus on student	Focus on classroom
Assessment of student by specialist	Examine teaching/learning factors
Diagnostic/prescriptive outcomes	Collaborative problem-solving
Student programme	Strategies for teachers
Placement in appropriate programme	Adaptive and supportive regular classroom environment

Table 1.2 Walker's (1995) contrast of inclusion and integration

Integration emphasises	Inclusion emphasises
Needs of 'special' students	Rights of all students
Changing/remedying the subject	Changing the school
Benefits to the student with special needs of being integrated	Benefits to all students of including all
Professionals, specialist expertise and formal support	Informal support and the expertise of mainstream teachers
Technical interventions (special teaching, therapy)	Good teaching for all

there. A central aspect of an inclusion project must therefore lie in the deconstruction of the idea that only special people are equipped and qualified to teach special children. It must convince mainstream staff of their competence. This presents quite a task, of course, since for the last one hundred years special educators have been saying the opposite – that there is a set of teaching procedures which is especially appropriate for a segment of the child population. The system built around this idea has been reinforced and buttressed by a whole range of investments, from school buildings to professional careers.

Another important component of a successful inclusion project, according to Porter, is the 'district-based student services team', in which competent district-based educators act as consultants and provide support for headteachers, teachers and other staff. They can also help in gaining access to additional resources and provide advice in monitoring and programme development. In view of the discussion above, their role is additionally to teach the mainstream about its competence. This team is a key component of the inclusion project being evaluated in Part II of this book.

Inclusion and assumptions about difference and 'special need'

Another key difference between inclusion and integration lies in assumptions about difference. 'Integration' was usually used to describe the process of the assimilation of children with learning difficulties, sensory impairments or physical disabilities to mainstream schools. In fact, the use of the term 'special educational needs' has usually specifically excluded other children – for example, children whose first language is not English – following the specific exclusion in legislation of these children from the 'special' definition. The key aspect of inclusion, however, is that children who are at a disadvantage for any reason are not excluded from mainstream education. This represents a redefining and modernising of the term 'special needs' which is surely more consistent with the spirit (if not the letter) of the Warnock Report (DES, 1978). The Warnock Committee talked about a fluid definition of special need, whereby categories would be abolished and a child's needs would be defined as and when they arose. It was thus surely inconsistent then to go on to define special needs purely in terms of the constructs of learning difficulty and disability by which they had tradition-ally been defined.

For children's special needs may arise from a multiplicity of factors related to disability, language, family income, cultural origin, gender or ethnic origin, and it is inappropriate to differentiate among these.[5] As Young makes clear, the mere existence of supposed groups of this kind forces us to categorise, and the categories encourage a particular mindset about a group, while in reality the 'groups' in question are 'cross-cutting, fluid and shifting' (1990: 45). Assumptions about disadvantage and oppres-sion rest on these categorisations where in fact they may not be warranted. Meekosha and Jacubowicz (1996) make a similar point: that there is no discrete class of people who are disabled. In fact, they argue, people with disabilities are as heterogeneous as people in general, and the agglomeration of all disabilities alienates disabled people from other minorities. And the stressing of a minority status – in disability or in any other area – empha-sises the presumed weakness and vulnerability of the group in question rather than the inadequacies of the supposedly supportive system.

The notion of inclusion, therefore, does not set parameters (as the notion of integration did) around particular kinds of putative disability. Rather, it is about a philosophy of acceptance; it is about providing a framework within which all children – regardless of ability, gender, language, ethnic or cultural origin – can be valued equally, treated with respect and provided with equal opportunities at school. In short, accepting inclusion means moving from what Roaf has called an 'obsession with individual learning difficulties' (1988: 7) to an agenda of rights.

KEY ASPECTS OF INCLUSION IN PRACTICE

Many definitions have been written of inclusion. One of the least prescriptive is provided by the Centre for Studies on Inclusive Education (CSIE, 1996). This suggests that an inclusive school contains the following elements:

- it is *community based*: an inclusive school reflects the community as a whole. Membership of the school community is open, positive and diverse. It is not selective, exclusive or rejecting;
- it is *barrier-free*: an inclusive school is accessible to all who become members – physically in terms of the buildings and grounds and educa-tionally in terms of curricula, support systems and methods of communication;

- it promotes *collaboration*: an inclusive school works with, rather than competitively against, other schools;
- it promotes *equality*: an inclusive school is a democracy where all members have rights and responsibilities, with the same opportunity to benefit from and take part in the education provided by the school both within and beyond its premises.

The Council for Exceptional Children (CEC, 1994) has a list of twelve principles for successful inclusive schools, and many of these are similar to the CSIE's list. However, it also states that the inclusive school has the following:

- a *vision* of equality and inclusion, publicly articulated;
- *leadership* which publicly espouses inclusion and equal opportunities;
- an *array of services* that are co-ordinated across and among education and agency personnel;
- *systems for co-operation* within the school: inclusive schools foster natural support networks across students and staff. Strategies are implemented such as peer tutoring, buddy systems, circles of friends, co-operative learning and other ways of connecting students in natural, ongoing and supportive relationships. In addition, all school personnel work together and support each other through professional collaboration, team teaching, co-teaching, teacher and student assistance teams and other collaborative arrangements;
- *flexible roles* and responsibilities: there will be changed staff roles and responsibilities arising from inclusion;
- *partnerships with parents*: parents are involved in the planning and implementation of inclusive school strategies.

Stainback and Stainback (1990) have developed a similar list for schools and local administrators which emphasises *strategies* for promoting inclusive schooling. It includes the following:

- establish a school *philosophy*;
- follow the principle of natural proportions – in other words *neighbourhood* schools should be sought for inclusion (as distinct from schools which are out of the child's local area);
- have an inclusion *task force* in the school which gathers information on inclusion, organises information sessions and establishes a plan which sets objectives for inclusion;
- maintain *flexibility* in the face of false starts; treat the move to inclusion as a problem-solving exercise and don't assume that it will be an easy ride.

All this advice has been important for the Somerset Inclusion Project, as the analysis reported in Part II of this book will show. In particular, the questions of leadership, co-ordination and flexibility of role seem crucial for the success of inclusion in any given school and it will be important for any project promoting inclusion to influence them.

To the points made above, we would add the following on the basis of the foregoing discussion:

- de-professionalisation: an inclusive school is one where there is an assumption amongst staff (shared by students) that all staff share in the contribution they make to children's learning;
- democracy: an inclusive school is one in which all members – students, staff, parents and governors – share in the development and management of the school;
- communication: in an inclusive school, there is an assumption that all members will have a voice which will be heard, and there will be systems for ensuring that this voice is heard.

These last two points – communication and democracy – combine to form the need for *self-advocacy*, and it is this important facet of inclusion which is discussed next.

SELF-ADVOCACY AND INCLUSION

Children with disabilities have been (and still are) particularly susceptible to benevolent, but often misguided, attempts to plan for them, as noted by Newman and Roberts (1996, discussed above). But in an education system which aspires to be inclusive, it is important that discourse does not exclude the perspectives and interpretations of children, particularly the perspectives of those children with disabilities. If planning is informed by stereotypical images of disability or outdated models of childhood the risk is that marginalisation and exclusion will continue.

For children – and particularly children with disabilities – have habitually been excluded from discussion about their education (or, indeed, other aspects of their lives). The results of this exclusion are seen in the anger of adults with disabilities over the education that was planned for them when they were children. The tacit assumption has been that children will be neither sufficiently well informed nor sufficiently articulate or rational to contribute to such discussion. It has been assumed that it is somehow illegitimate to seek or to accept the views of children. And where children are disabled, discussion has predominantly taken place about disabled children by professionals and academics (see, for example, the critique offered by Rieser and Mason, 1990).

Alongside this systematic exclusion, there has been an awakening to the realisation that the views of certain people in society are discounted because they are, as Foucault (1980) put it, 'naive' or 'insufficiently elaborated'. The example Foucault gives is the discounting of the accounts of psychiatric patients or delinquents. He points out, though, that these accounts are just as legitimate and valid as the account of any other person. Foucault's analysis applies with equal validity to children and especially to children with disabilities. Their voices have been systematically ignored as reason has been delegated to professionals (psychologists, administrators, teachers and social workers) working on their behalf. Alongside this exclusion of voice, or perhaps because of it, educational planning has often been guided by stereo-typical images of the needs of certain children involving passivity, vulnerability or weakness (Kitzinger, 1990). Indeed, such stereotypes emerge in part from the traditional models (such as the Piagetian model – see Thomas, 1997) within which childhood has been constructed (see also James and Prout, 1990).

To be both a child and disabled therefore conjoins characteristics which are doubly disadvantaging as far as having one's voice heard is concerned. Disabled children are people for whom it has seemed only too self-evident that rights about self-determination should have been taken away and important life decisions taken instead by someone else who 'knows better'. And these others who know better are guided by models of childhood which elevate adult rationality, diminish child rationality and relegate the child to the status of onlooker.

Why should we not regard the opinions of children, including those with disabilities and learning difficulties, as valid and legitimate in themselves? The Warnock Committee (DES, 1978) gave official recognition to the idea that the *parental* contribution to the discussion of children's education is useful and important (Vaughan, 1989) and the committee's position has been validated by the evidence of parental advocacy in practice. The time is now, therefore, surely right for a similar revolution in thinking about the contribution of the children themselves. Indeed, it is only by drawing on such sources of knowledge that educational environments may be developed in ways which are meaningful and important to children.

To take this stance is important for the research reported in Part II of this book for two main reasons. First, it is an assumption on which inclusion is based in the definitions above that an inclusive school is one in which communication is open and all-embracing; in other words, the views of all school members (including the children and including those children with disabilities) are considered and acted upon. This principle is therefore one against which the activities of the Somerset Inclusion Project and its 'partner schools' must be judged. Second, in the research itself, it is a key assumption that the views of the children and young people themselves are gained. This is discussed further in Chapter 6.

On the question of how schools can move towards achieving self-advocacy for the children they educate, Garner and Sandow (1995) make some useful practical suggestions. They note the value of various aspects of school life which can promote self-advocacy, such as an effective school council, appro-priate rules and open and regular communications with parents. But they also warn of the danger of tokenism and suggest ways of making sure that views of children are not merely articulated, but are also taken further by the management forums of the school.

THE COMPREHENSIVE IDEAL: MOVING TO INCLUSION

The comprehensive ideal has a long tradition. As Booth (1995) has noted, one cannot separate the struggles of those who were at the forefront in promoting integration from this comprehensive tradition. Many of the integration struggles were about individual children – to integrate a child with Down's Syndrome here, or a child with cerebral palsy there. They continue to this day, and the Special Educational Needs Tribunal was established partly to resolve the tensions which have emerged between local education authorities (LEAs) and parents over children's placement, with many parents taking their children's cases to the tribunal because they want integration,[6] contrary to the general LEA defence that this would be inefficient or uneconomic.

These struggles of individual children, their parents and advocates are akin to guerrilla warfare against a system which still defends the need for substantial segregation, even of children with only 'moderate' learning difficulties or physical disabilities. But the broader aim of helping schools to become more inclusive demands that there are responses from schools and local authorities which are of a more significant scale. For true inclusion, the change has to be systemic as well as individual.

The changes currently required are of the same scale as those facing schools in the 1960s as they prepared to move from selective to comprehensive schooling. They are not only of the same scale, but they are also similar in nature. The emerging comprehensives faced many of the problems with which inclusive schools now contend. Systems, curricula and the fabric of the school then had to be re-thought (and were re-thought with varying degrees of success) to enable schools to cater for children of a broader range of ability. Plans had to be implemented to effect the change – and the transformations varied in their success.

Similarly with inclusion, changes are being made with varying degrees of success. Some local authorities are, in effect, implementing only *re-placement* policies (where a child is moved from special school to the mainstream, perhaps with the support of a learning support assistant). The term 'main-dumping' has been used in the US (see, for example, Stainback and Stainback, 1990) to describe the worst examples of this process – wherein children are moved from special schools to mainstream schools with inadequate preparation or resourcing. Many schools, in fact, have accepted disabled children only on the basis of 'assimilation' – that is, children are welcome only if they can benefit from what is already on offer.

Other local authorities have more sophisticated schemes in which 'outreach' support is provided by specialist teachers who visit mainstream schools. Sometimes, under the guidance of a forward-thinking headteacher, a special school has decamped from its special location and reformed on the premises of its local neighbourhood school. There are a few published accounts of such developments: Wilson (1990), for example, the head of a school for children with severe learning difficulties, gives an interesting account of such a development, and in *Bishopswood* (CSIE, 1992) there is an account of a school for children with severe learning difficulties which moved in its entirety to mainstream institutions.

One forward-thinking local authority, Newham, has planned the closure of all its special schools. This has involved the integration of all children in mainstream schools with varying degrees of support, as described by Jordan and Goodey (1996). A controversial aspect of the programme of closure has been (at least in the short term) the placement of the transferred children to 'resourced schools' – that is, schools which are especially resourced to take a group of former special school pupils. The consequence of this compromise policy is that children do not necessarily attend their neighbourhood schools. Staff of the special schools were offered transfers to the resourced schools or to the authority's learning support service.

However, the most sophisticated and creative example of inclusion planning comes with the planned dismantling of the special school in such a way that the school is reconstructed as a service, as in the Somerset Inclusion Project. In effect, the school is closed, children move to local schools and the personnel who taught them now work in those schools. This carries significant advantages over the mass provision of a support service, not least of these being the retention of a nexus of committed staff who know the students involved in the programme and who have solidarity and direction as a small team.

Whatever the advantages, such a major change creates very significant organisational challenges and there are many imponderables which face those embarking on such a journey. Part of the task of the research reported in this book is to examine these organisational challenges and to begin to answer questions concerning the likely outcomes for the children and young people who are part of the enterprise. Some of the forms of organisation and reorganisation taken by the move to inclusion are summarised below:

- **re-placement**: moving individual children to the mainstream with varying degrees of support, and varying levels of success for the children involved;
- **de-camping**: moving a special school, with its students and staff, into the mainstream;
- closing special schools and providing **resourced schools** – that is, schools which are especially resourced to take a group of former special school pupils;

- closing special schools and providing a **support service** – comprising support teachers and learning support assistants, usually from the former special schools;
- providing an **inclusion service** – that is, converting a special school to a service, whereby ex-special school staff restructure and work in neighbourhood schools.

The various changes outlined can be contrasted with integration, wherein the emphasis is only on 're-placement'.

Contemporary arrangements for integration in the UK include (and are probably still dominated by) the movement of individuals or *re-placement*. However, there is now an increased awareness of the need for major structural change in order to free up the resources to enable real inclusion. The result has been the introduction of a range of innovative and essentially experimental schemes wherein the skills and resources of the once-existing special school are delivered in the mainstream. Here, money follows children and there is no dilution of resource provision as children move from special school to mainstream school. The research reported in this book examines one of these projects.

FINANCING AND IMPLEMENTING INCLUSION

The changes of the 1980s concentrated on moving individual children to special schools, and – with varying degrees of success – simultaneously arranging whatever support could be afforded in the mainstream. This movement of individuals presented serious difficulties to funding the integrated placements, since in the absence of 'new money' from central government to fund integration, the fixed costs of existing special schools did not diminish sufficiently to liberate the necessary resources to make those integration arrangements satisfactory. This problem is well documented in the UK by the Audit Commission (1992a). There are similar problems in the US, where Hehir (in conversation with Miller, 1996) points out that despite legislative commitment to inclusion in many states, money does not follow children as they move to inclusive placements. The solution, he suggests, is for states to change their special education financing formulae, and thirty-five states are at the time of writing being instructed by the US Department of Education to change their funding systems.

The Audit Commission (1992a) also found in the UK that inclusion was being held back by the financial systems operating in local government. The commission found that local authorities were reluctant to delegate more money to schools to enable inclusion because, the authorities said, they could not be confident that the delegated money would be used wisely or correctly. However, the local authorities at that time had no way of monitoring how well schools were performing with special pupils, so they would not know whether this assertion was true or not. There was also a problem, the commission found, in that an authority – knowing that an inclusive placement would be expensive – would have 'an incentive . . . not to specify what is to be provided because they thereby avoid a long-term financial commitment' (Audit Commission/HMI, 1992a: 25).

Of the four underlying causes for a slower-than-acceptable move to inclusion identified by the commission, three concerned financial matters surrounding the organisation of the school system by the local authority. These were:

1 'the LEA is legally in the position of the person representing the child's educational interests. However, it is also the provider of education through special schools. There is no separation of the role of the client, who purchases services, and the contractor, who delivers them. Hence the LEA is in the position of monitoring itself' (1992a: 31). In this situation, decisions about possible school transfer would usually be left to the special school headteacher, who would rarely advise on a transfer, due to (3), below;

2 there is a 'financial disincentive' for authorities to move pupils from special schools to the mainstream as they then have to fund the ordinary school place as well as an empty special school place;

3 there is no incentive for special school heads to pursue programmes of transfer of pupils to mainstream schools, since the consequence could be a loss of viability for their own schools.

Even though the number of pupils with special needs being educated in ordinary schools is rising, the number of teachers employed in special schools has not declined in line with that trend. The commission found that if special schools had indeed reduced in size (or if they had restructured themselves in some way, through for example enabling teaching and support staff to do outreach work), £53 million would have been released to support special pupils in mainstream schools over the period 1986–1991. This, however, is an underestimate of the potential redirection of funds, since it includes the redirection made only through the reduction in numbers of teachers; it does not allow for redirection of the substantial fixed costs of maintaining and running the special school. The commission found that different authorities, and different schools within one authority, varied greatly in their success in 'releasing' teachers to work in the mainstream, and the ability to release teachers did not seem to relate to the size or type of special school.

But there are political and professional hurdles also to be overcome in effecting transfers of resources, for there are formidable interests in maintaining special education. There are some genuinely held professional beliefs about the benefits of maintaining segregation. There are many parents who are cautious about inclusion and prefer a special school place for their child. There are advocacy groups – for example, for hearing impaired children and dyslexic children – who argue for separate provision. In these circumstances, local authorities, aside from any financial considerations, have pressures imposed upon them to maintain an establishment of special schools. The solution, the OECD suggests, is to confront the issue and take difficult decisions (as opposed to avoiding these decisions) about the 'desired moves' to inclusion and to press ahead with organisational changes which will effect the principled decision. It gives the example of how Somerset reduced the percentage of the school population in special schools from 2.3 to 1.6 in four years in the 1980s by 'pushing ahead with a firm policy in the face of opposition (for example, that of the association representing dyslexics, who wanted special classes)' (OECD, 1994: 43).

Given that it is so difficult to redirect these substantial resources, the Audit Commission/HMI (1992b) have produced helpful guidelines on the kind of structure which will support a move to inclusion. An abbreviated version of these guidelines is given in Table 1.3.

Table 1.3 Redirecting special school resources: a checklist for action

Action by LEA	Action by special schools	Action by both
Number of teaching and non-teaching assistant hours, if any, to be released from each school is identified		
	Surplus staff time is released	
		Decision is made on whether staff can be reallocated immediately or whether they should temporarily remain in special schools, with the surplus time identified spent in ordinary schools
		Use of special schools as approved suppliers of specialist services to ordinary schools is considered
Scheme for the recoupment of costs of services provided by special to ordinary schools is established		

(adapted from the Audit Commission/HMI, 1992b: 67)

Despite this very clear advice on the desirability and nature of this kind of action, the Audit Commission/HMI (1994) disappointingly found in follow-up through local audits two years later that few authorities had made the changes in special school staffing levels which were needed. The 'opportunity cost' of failing to have made the necessary changes amounted to nearly £500,000 per LEA. Instead of making these changes, LEAs have concentrated their efforts on complex audits of provision *within* the mainstream schools (in other words, excluding the moneys allocated to special schools from the analysis). This may marginally enhance the fairness of fund-allocation (Fletcher-Campbell, 1996a) but it does little to address the central issues behind funding inclusion, which concern the redistribution of the whole special education budget.

As long as this impasse – this avoidance of difficult issues – continues, the cost is a perpetually underfunded inclusion system. In such a system, local authorities will continually be hedging their bets, as they produce policies on special educational needs which are inclusive in name only. The strategic use of words like 'usually' in policies will allow existing practices to continue unchanged. Vaguely written statements of special need will continue to result in teachers who teach children with statements in the mainstream being forced to operate with artificially low levels of resourcing.

The case study examined in the second part of this book displays in miniature many of the tensions which we have just discussed. The staff of a special school have voluntarily (and most unusually) opted to reconfigure themselves into an inclusion service and therein close the school. Although the LEA at first has given its support to the project, it has subsequently – under the pressures outlined – found it necessary to withdraw a large part of that financial support. In effect, it seems likely that children will be supported in their new schools only at the level provided historically for children with statements. The higher level of support (which would be calculated on the basis of the redistributed costs of educating the children in the special school) will not, it seems, be forthcoming. At the time of writing, final decisions are still to be taken by the LEA on this issue.

This hiatus, this uncertainty, in the project's development highlights the importance of partnership between policy-makers and practitioners in effecting change. Neither policy on the one hand nor imaginative initiatives from practitioners on the other can succeed on their own. It is not sufficient (as the current uncertainties in the SIP show) for practitioners to embark on change without the contractual agreement of policy-makers that systems will exist to support the innovation. But neither is it sufficient only to have inclusive policy 'from the top' – from politicians and policy-makers. The correct policy will not magically induce inclusive practice. Many case studies and analyses (e.g. those of Weatherley and Lipsky, 1977; Fulcher, 1989; Loxley and Thomas, 1997) show that the best intentions can be subverted at local level if the conditions are not right – if people are not prepared for and committed to the change at the 'chalk-face'. Fullan (1993) says that school reform efforts have often failed because they have been imposed from the top without input from and partnership with those who do the work. In words which are strikingly similar to those of Weatherley and Lipsky (1977), who indicated the problems which come from initiatives in special education emerging from 'street-level bureaucrats', Fullan says that the assumptions behind reform efforts often simply express a desire by some politicians to want to be seen carrying out a reform agenda.

As Fullan says, both bottom-up and top-down strategies are necessary. Initiatives must come from the bottom – from the schools – but legal and financial structures must be in place to support the initiatives and enable them to succeed. The message, then, is that change to inclusion will have to be a partnership among those at national, regional and school levels. At the national level legislation has to provide the ground-rules and at regional level there have to be real money-follows-child accounting systems available to those groups of schools who wish to move to inclusive practice. But ideas and initiatives for change must come from those who do the work in the schools.

Before looking in detail at the results of the research into the operation of the project, the next few chapters examine and discuss particular aspects of inclusion:

- What does inclusion mean for support arrangements and how should these be provided?
- Does inclusion mean the curriculum will need to be adapted, and if so, how?
- Are there insurmountable social difficulties which face children and young people as they are included in the mainstream?
- Are there physical and logistic challenges which confront an inclusion project, and if so, how can these be overcome?
- And how can we best find out from children themselves what *they* want? How can we help them to become their own advocates?

2

USING SUPPORT IN INCLUSIVE CLASSROOMS

The effective delivery of support is crucial for successful inclusion, yet surprisingly little attention has been paid to the ways in which support works in classrooms. There is widespread acceptance of the central role which support assistants and support teachers play in meeting children's special needs yet few commentators have given thought to the changes which might occur when these extra people move into the domain of the teacher and how their potential contribution might be maximised. There seems to have been the assumption that support personnel will effortlessly and seamlessly slide into the classroom to work alongside the classteacher in inclusive arrangements; that simply to provide 'help' for the teacher will automatically be a Good Thing. Unfortunately, the evidence shows that it isn't: often it can be a burden rather than a help if the people involved are not able to work as teams (see Thomas, 1992).

The arrangements in which teachers and learning support assistants (LSAs) are finding themselves in inclusive classrooms mean involvement in teamwork, but *good* teamwork is notoriously difficult to achieve. Evidence for the difficulty of teamwork in classrooms is provided by the history of team teaching. Team teaching began in the late 1960s with high hopes of success. It has, however, failed. Many studies, both in the UK and in the USA, have shown that only a fragment of the original team teaching edifice remains (see, for example, Cohen, 1976; Geen, 1985; Hatton, 1985). It appears that teamwork in classrooms is more difficult to accomplish than many had anticipated.

Indeed, looking at the history of teams in classrooms one could quite justifiably claim that classrooms provide an especially uncongenial environment for teamwork. One important finding on classroom teams is that the presence of extra people in class does not automatically improve the situation for the children: having assistants in the class does not generally free the teacher for more time with pupils but rather results in the 'host' teacher spending more of her time *without* pupils (see, for example, DeVault *et al.*, 1977; McBrien and Weightman, 1980; Thomas, 1992). The finding is surprising yet consistent. It can perhaps be explained by the complex set of

26

interpersonal and professional uncertainties which are introduced when extra people work alongside the classteacher.

In short, support is more difficult to achieve than one might anticipate; this chapter, therefore, looks at the issue in some detail. Support can take many forms and some of these were reviewed in chapter 1. Support arrangements involve a range of personnel and organisational changes. The particular personnel being focused on in this chapter are learning support assistants (LSAs) and to a lesser extent specialist teachers, since it is these people who will be offering the bulk of day-to-day support to teachers and children. Given the significance of the support dynamic, much of the analysis undertaken in the Somerset Inclusion Project study (see Part II of this book) focuses on the proper role of the LSA.

A number of issues frame the debate about how LSAs and support teachers should work. These include:

- Should LSAs and/or support teachers concentrate only on the 'designated' child, or should they work with the rest of the class, as available and as necessary?
- Should children be withdrawn from the classroom for special work, should all support be provided in the classroom, or should there be a combination of withdrawal and support?
- Who is the LSA supporting – the child or the classteacher?
- What sort of training do LSAs need?
- How can staff from non-education agencies be included fully in the support process at school?

These questions can be addressed by examining the following issues.

THE RELATIONSHIP BETWEEN SUPPORTERS AND CLASSTEACHERS

Hrekow and Barrow (1993), examining support in the context of attempts to prevent exclusion of 'disruptive' pupils, developed a typology involving three sorts of support: tutorial/counselling, in-class and family support. Their conclusions about support are relevant across a range of special difficulties: 'School-based support cannot simply be for the benefit of a variety of individual children, even if it does focus on the notion of the "whole child". It must also support [classroom] teachers' (Hrekow and Barrow, 1993: 11).

Flexibility was considered to be an important feature of provision, since the need for support could arise at short notice and be unpredictable in its duration or intensity.

The issue of expertise is an important one to resolve before it can be said that the school is inclusive. If school staff assume that certain educational needs are only soluble in the presence of specially trained experts, then movement to inclusion will be slow. The CSIE suggest that 'the "white-coat" image of special needs begins to disappear as teachers realise that meeting difference is an extension of their existing skills and expertise' (CSIE, 1995: 5).

Inglese (1996) examined the reciprocal perceptions of supporters and classteachers concerning the role of the other. A situation was revealed which was far from CSIE's ideal. Very few of the classteachers questioned had had any training for working with support staff, almost all of them regarded the support staff as possessed of special non-transferable skills (which did not, however, include much knowledge of curriculum requirements) and 'many found advisory suggestions difficult to incorporate in the classroom' (Inglese, 1996: 85).

The Canadians O'Brien and Forest (1989) have tried to counteract this perception of the role of professionals in inclusion by developing the notion of *inclusion co-ordinators*, and this concept has been important for the Somerset Inclusion Project (see chapter 9). These co-ordinators carry out much of their work prior to the arrival of the child in the classroom. Their role is to act as an intermediary between family and classteacher, preparing and advising both parties but steering classteachers in the direction of making their own assessments of the child's strengths and weaknesses, rather than relying on that of specialists. There is thus an element of the 'barefoot doctor' here – a notion that generic skills are more important than supposed specialist expertise.

An understanding of teachers' concerns, such as increased work-load, is crucial to this process, but it must be accompanied by a recognition that practical involvement is more effective than any amount of training in over-coming initial resistance and developing commitment (Janney et al., 1995). Wolery et al. (1995) found that classteachers who regarded their attempts at inclusion as unsuccessful often felt they had received less personal support than they needed.

Best (1991) analyses the role of the support teacher working alongside the classteacher, as opposed to providing co-ordination and advisory services. He tackles the productivity question, which may be a concern of senior manage-ment, particularly if the supporter appears to be doing nothing during long 'chalk and talk' sessions. He points out that one beneficial effect of the support teacher's presence in the classroom, if support is used across the whole class where necessary, is to increase the pupil–teacher ratio by 100 per cent. He characterises the ideal classteacher/support teacher relationship as based on mutual trust and perception of equal status, long experience of each other's ways of working, excellent two-way briefing and planning, and constructive evaluation of each lesson.

Thomas (1992), however, is less sanguine, having examined the role of the support teacher and the learning support assistant in a range of class-rooms and schools. He concludes that the personal and professional tensions created by support teaching are difficult to overcome. They generate the need for advanced planning and team teaching, which the exigencies of the support teaching situation often seem to conspire against. Likewise with support provided by a learning support assistant. Here the problem is that neither teacher nor supporter has been trained in how to work with other adults and the communication failures which often ensue from this deficiency result in inappropriate support provision. For instance:

- classteachers may make invalid assumptions about the preference of the LSA to work solely with the 'designated' individual;
- they may assume academic expertise held by the LSA which the latter does not in fact possess (particularly in the secondary school);
- the LSA may, because the classteacher is 'in charge', be inhibited from making suggestions about appropriate ways of working.

As a result of these misunderstandings, the classteacher and supporter/s develop a 'fraternity' – namely, a superficial 'getting along' in which confusions and misperceptions are submerged as participants concentrate on not alienating each other (see Thomas, 1991). In this environment, there is little opportunity for resolution or development.

Thomas concludes with a number of recommendations about the classroom teams which arise from classteacher-plus-supporter relationships, and these stress the importance of planning and ongoing evaluation:

- The opportunity should exist from the outset for discussion about the pedagogic, professional and affective concerns and expectations of team members;
- Planning for teamwork should involve all team members;
- Individuals' strengths and weaknesses should be identified in planning;
- A clear definition of the tasks and activities to be undertaken in the inclusive classroom needs to be identified during planning;
- The team needs to meet regularly to discuss and evaluate the way that they have been working. (Thomas, 1992: 204)

Thousand and Villa concur on the need for communication and shared responsibilities in the teaching team. Having concluded a review of team effectiveness, they assert that 'the distribution of responsibility among team members for planning, instruction, and evaluation' (1990: 153) is the most important facet of team success – a finding which has consistently been made over the years (see also DeVault et al., 1977, for a thoroughgoing analysis and review). Given this need for a clear understanding of role, Thomas (1985) has described the use of *room management* as a way of organising the work of LSAs (and, indeed, support teachers or parents) alongside the classteacher. In room management, specific roles are allotted to each adult in the class. This has been shown to work in primary classrooms and, with the advent of Individual Education Plans (IEPs), offers a useful way of making individualisation more of a real possibility, and more meaningful when it does occur. Essentially, it involves the following:

- One person (teacher or LSA) takes on the role of an individual helper, concentrating on the work of individual children, working intensively with them for short, specified periods of time. A programme of children to be worked with is established before the lesson. The individual helper would thus be responsible for managing the teaching element specified in the IEP;
- One person (again, teacher or LSA) takes on the role of activity manager, working with the rest of the children, and concentrating on their work in groups. This is at a less intensive level, and the activity manager will also take on responsibility for managing the routine and control of the class, dealing with interruptions and other matters.

Room management provides a good way of meshing the sometimes conflicting demands of individualisation and differentiation in the inclusive classroom. Cowne (1996) provides a good account of how it might be used in a classroom and supplies a useful planning sheet (adapted in Table 2.1) for specifying the work of individuals and groups.

The *inclusion co-ordinators* of O'Brien and Forest (1989, and see above) – paralleled perhaps by the teacher-co-ordinators of the Somerset Inclusion Project – could play the key role in ensuring that the kind of planning, communication and ongoing development necessary for room management, or any other means of organisation, are in place and monitored.

These co-ordinators also have a key role in developing and co-ordinating the work of agencies from outside education (such as speech therapists and physiotherapists) who may be unfamiliar with the notion of classroom support. There may also be disagreements or teething troubles associated

Table 2.1 Planning for teamwork in class

	Group 1	Group 2	Group 3	Group 4	Group 5
Task; Resources; Intended learning outcomes					
Role of activity manager					
Role of individual helper					

with the move to a new style and place of work and there is an important role here in organising and managing change.

THE RELATIONSHIP BETWEEN SUPPORTERS AND STUDENTS

Best (1991) examines the roles which support teachers can play in relation to the pupil, the most interesting of which is that of co-learner (where the support teacher has little knowledge of the subject):

> In order to accomplish the set task, the support teacher has to take the individual pupil through the learning/reasoning/problem-solving process rather than try to explain it as a fait accompli. Moreover, the child may see that even teachers make mistakes and struggle with some things, and that this is not an occasion for shame.
>
> (Best, 1991: 30)

Nolan and Gersch (1996) describe the use of learning support assistants in Waltham Forest. These are employed, trained and supervised by the Education Psychology Service rather than by individual schools (and are therefore in a similar position to Barnardo's LSAs in that they are effectively serving two management systems), and are responsible to an educational psychologist whom they meet once a term for discussion on aspects of the job such as record-keeping and working with teachers, and, on a day-to-day basis, to the school co-ordinator for special educational needs (SENCO), who arranges support for individuals and tries to ensure that teachers work effectively with their LSAs. Close communication and co-operation, and a clear understanding of responsibilities, are crucial to the success of such partnerships between schools and outside agencies, as discussion of the Somerset Inclusion Project research findings in Part II of this book will show.

LSAs frequently find themselves in one of the roles outlined by Best's support teachers (see above): for example, acting as the child's servant, rushing up to help at the first sign of difficulty; or as a kind of foreman, pushing children to meet the teacher's production targets. Booth describes how the combination of these roles can be detrimental to the child's full involvement in an inclusive classroom:

> I observed Carol, who has Down's Syndrome, in several lessons. Because of the level of support she received 'she' always completed the work, though some activities had little meaning for her. However, I only saw her as a full participant in a classroom, caught up in the general chat, when she was supported by a special needs assistant who claimed to have hated school and joined in the general flow of fun and mild disruption herself.
>
> (Booth, 1996: 96)

Grey areas may exist in the definition of the LSA's role, simply because no one has made explicit what an LSA is expected to do. Particular problems exist in specifying the LSA's responsibility for discipline and differentiation.

Where physically disabled students are concerned, there is additional confusion due to the supporter's job evolving out of responsibility for personal care. Now, in an inclusionary ethos, a more educational role is expected (Lovey, 1995). Unless classteachers, assistants and students are clear about what is expected, a productive relationship can be hard to establish.

WHO TO SUPPORT: CHILD OR WHOLE CLASS?

Jones (1987) explains why the relationship between the supporter and the child with special needs should not be an exclusive one. First, it can be bad for the child, in that s/he may become over-dependent on the supporter socially, academically and/or physically. Second, it can prevent classteachers from getting to know children well enough to plan for their inclusion in curriculum activities. Third, as we observed earlier, the generalised use of support can be of significant benefit to the rest of the class. Jones suggests that many classteachers feel uncomfortable at first about the presence of another adult in the classroom, but comments that those in her school had eventually 'found that the experience of working with a colleague was a rewarding and useful one for themselves and all the children' (1987: 176).

Bayliss (1995) describes how a middle school benefited from the adoption of whole class support in terms of opportunities for all staff to rethink their understanding of how children learn best. He reports that the students themselves were better motivated, and produced more positive outcomes, when receiving general class support than in individual or group withdrawal situations.

Others concur on the need for whole class support rather than the supporter being restricted to one or two children (e.g. Bines, 1986; Thomas, 1992; Jordan, 1994). Indeed, Jordan sees the teacher who insists on the supporter working only with the designated individual as being wedded to a 'restorative' approach to special education – in other words, an approach which sees the special supporter as someone who will restore the child to normal, in contrast with a preventative approach which is more consistent with inclusion.

Putnam (1993) goes a stage further and says that there is no evidence for the benefits which are supposed to reside in withdrawal. She reviews a wide range of research which supports in-class support. This is consistent with the integrative thrust of special education policy; there is little point in de-segregating by reforming special schools, if the new practices operated in the mainstream segregate even more conspicuously in the new environment (see also Thomas, 1986, for a discussion of this issue).

TRAINING

It seems clear from the discussion above of the varied roles, relationships and expectations, and from a consideration of assistants' varied backgrounds, that a more developed system of training of support staff and teachers who work with them would be beneficial. But Jupp (1992) questions the wisdom of a general course for support assistants, on the grounds that this constitutes indoctrination with the kind of knowledge which may be counterproductive to getting to know the individual personally and responding on the basis of that individual's need. His comments suggest the need for inclusive practice, though it is surely not too much to expect that such 'getting-to-know' practice will be fostered by a course. The solution to avoiding bad practice is surely not to abandon training, but to produce training courses which fit the needs of children.

Nolan and Gersch (1996) describe an induction course which focuses on the twin themes of, first, the relationship of the assistant to other staff, and second, the equal opportunities context of their work. The education psychology service he describes provides ongoing training for the assistants, which is evaluated by them and covers topics such as building children's self-esteem and behaviour management. They have their own form of certification covering this training, as do some further education institutions which provide courses for learning support assistants (such as the City and Guilds' 'Certificate in Learning Support'). Fox (1996), however, suggests that although a national training policy would be helpful, training is best carried out through SENCOs working in their own schools, auditing the specific training needs of their assistants and bringing in professionals from outside agencies where appropriate. She concludes that if SENCOs take time 'to ensure assistants are clear about their job – what to do, when to do it and how to work – and to provide training to develop their skills – these investments will result in a more effective learning experience for the child and a motivated and committed team of assistants' (Fox, 1996: 51).

PARENT AND PEER SUPPORT

There is another dimension to support which should not be understated, and this is the support which is given by peers, parents and community volunteers. Tizard and his colleagues demonstrated some time ago (Tizard et al., 1982) how parental involvement in helping children to read can produce remarkable improvements in reading ability. Their 'low-tech' approach is consonant with the spirit of inclusion for two reasons. First, specialist assessment and curricular 'treatment' are played down while the value and legitimacy of simple pedagogy is reinforced. And second, the contribution of the parent (and other volunteers) is given credence. Tizard's findings killed the assumption that there is a special set of pedagogic skills accessible only to those highly qualified in education. Even more important, it laid to rest the idea that children who were experiencing difficulties at school needed an extra-special set of pedagogical skills and methods to help them.

It is not only parents who can provide extra support, but also peers. Leyden (1996) stresses that all children, even those with significant special needs, can benefit from peer and collaborative learning experiences, and suggests that adult and peer support is complementary. He reviews evidence which demonstrates the wide range of benefits – curricular and social – which can come from peer tutoring and other forms of peer support and collaborative learning. These successes arise not only when the tutor is the mainstream student, but also when s/he is a 'learning disabled tutor' (1996: 52).

Topping (1988) gives helpful advice on structuring such peer tutoring. In brief, he gives ideas on:

- how partners can be matched;
- the nature of the materials being used;
- the time, place and duration of peer tutoring sessions;
- teaching techniques to be adopted;
- participant training methods;
- monitoring, evaluation and feedback.

Pugach and Johnson (1990) give helpful advice on how the teacher can share expertise with peers and parents, separating the strategic thinking and planning from the 'doing'.

FUTURE DIRECTIONS FOR SUPPORT PROVISION

Following this review, some guidelines emerge about the use of support to foster inclusive arrangements. It is perhaps useful to relate these to the questions set at the beginning of this chapter, namely:

- *Should LSAs and/or support teachers concentrate only on the 'designated' child, or should they work with the rest of the class, as available and as necessary?* It is consistent neither with the ethos of inclusion nor with the evidence as to its efficacy in practice that supporters should work only with designated children. They should be able flexibly to provide support to anyone who appears to need it insofar as this does not result in the neglect of the designated child or children. Furthermore, other kinds of support – from parents, peers and volunteers – can be encouraged. There is no special set of pedagogic skills which cannot be shared with these other potential supporters. Any combination of people can have their work structured using a simple system of organisation such as 'room management' (described in this chapter).
- *Should children be withdrawn from the classroom for special work, should all support be provided in the classroom, or should there be a combination of with-*

drawal and support? An inclusive ethos implies that all children should be educated together for curricular and social reasons. There is no evidence that withdrawing them for particular periods is beneficial.[1]

- *Who is the LSA supporting – the child or the classteacher?* The evidence is that there is inadequate communication between team participants in support arrangements. Communication and planning would improve if the supporter were to be seen working as part of a team with line-management responsibilities to the classteacher.

- *What sort of training do LSAs need?* Expectations of LSAs are often made on judgements about their role which centre around care. These may be appropriate in some cases, but not in all, and even when children do have care needs, the job of the LSA in a school must be centred on educational needs rather than those care needs. LSA training is therefore needed in differentiation, teaching and learning and the National Curriculum. There are also training needs for mainstream teachers, support teachers and LSAs in communicating with others, responsibilities and relationships in the inclusive classroom, and planning.

The *inclusion co-ordinator* has a clear role in facilitating these developments. While most integration schemes do not have anyone in this role, there is an analogue here in the Somerset Inclusion Project in the role of the teacher-co-ordinator.

On the difficult-to-resolve question of inter-agency collaboration in inclusion, the inclusion co-ordinator also has a role, though consistent change probably requires unified Special Educational Needs (SEN) budgets and single children's departments at local authority level. The professional and policy hurdles to be overcome here make this a distant goal.

3

CURRICULAR INCLUSION

The physical presence of students in classrooms is no guarantee of their involvement in class and school activities: 'integration' may happen but this is not necessarily 'inclusion'. If this is true, then it is especially so because of the curriculum. It is through the curriculum that messages are sent by the school staff – and received by the students – about the values held by the school. If some students are seen to study a different curriculum from others then complex messages are being transmitted about their status in the school, and indeed about their status as learners and people.

For this reason, the curriculum has often greatly exercised special educators. Should all children study the same curriculum? Should some children study a different curriculum or a 'watered-down' curriculum? Legislation has resolved some of the surface questions, since all children now have to study the National Curriculum, whether they are in a mainstream school or a special school. But serious questions still confront the special educator, since the new system has brought with it a vocabulary of 'access' and 'differentiation', technicist concepts which suggest that the curriculum is a discrete, finite thing which can be processed and regulated like a machine. They imply that with the pulling of a lever or the turning of a knob 'the curriculum' will become available – 'accessible' – to children who have hitherto experienced difficulty with their schoolwork.

The analogy which Swann uses for the absurd notion of 'access to the curriculum' is that of support teachers 'prising open the doors of a department store for the benefit of the masses. "The curriculum" is there for the taking, if the key can be found' to enable the access (1988: 98). This is not much different, Swann feels, from deficit theory. In other words, it now sometimes seems to be assumed that what 'special' children are lacking is the appropriate filling of curriculum, where previously it was assumed that they lacked enough IQ points. As Swann makes clear, the curriculum is more usefully seen 'not as knowledge to be conveyed but as a set of teaching and learning relationships by which that knowledge is conveyed' (*ibid.*).

Swann's insightful analysis also reminds us that the new shibboleths of entitlement and access should not be straitjackets when it comes to inclusion.

36

In a case study of a profoundly and multiply disabled girl in a vibrant primary classroom he shows how the girl is included by being accepted on the basis that she was able to learn at her own pace. Her inclusion came only because she had been *exempted* from the curriculum and from normal expectations.

Inclusion does not, then, come through the formulaic use of techniques or procedures, nor through fundamentalist adherence to a principle such as 'entitlement'. Rather, it lies in providing the opportunities for all children to learn.

CAN EFFECTIVE MANAGEMENT BE USED TO PROMOTE CURRICULAR INCLUSION?

Recent literature has emphasised the place of school effectiveness in the promotion of inclusiveness, concentrating on the way that whole school approaches to teacher development and organisational change can affect the delivery of the curriculum. The encouragement of mixed-ability grouping, co-operative and active learning, and planning for the class as a whole as opposed to planning for individuals, has been seen as not only beneficial in terms of initiating more inclusive practice but as a way of changing the general culture of the school in the direction of greater appreciation of diversity (Sebba and Ainscow, 1996).

Ainscow emphasises the importance of two factors: the opportunity to consider new possibilities, and the availability of support for experimentation and reflection. Material resources, Ainscow asserts, are of less importance, and emphasis on them could displace attention from an often overlooked resource, the students themselves: 'Within any classroom the pupils represent a rich source of experiences, inspiration, challenge and support which, if utilised, can inject an enormous supply of additional energy into the tasks and activities that are set' (1995a: 149). He comments that attempting to change teaching practice in ways that increase inclusion entails a difficult balance between respecting the innate conservatism of schools and acknowledging the need to develop in order to respond to new challenges.

The effectiveness research referred to by Ainscow and others examines ordinary schools and classrooms, in the main using statistics to make generalisations about the characteristics of schools which are successful in predefined outcomes. The emphasis in this research has been on general achievement and behaviour, and although much of the American research on this theme emphasises the achievement of children from minorities and the urban poor (e.g. Edmonds, 1979; Neisser, 1986; Hallinger and Murphy, 1986), the major UK research has stressed the achievement of children in general (e.g. Rutter *et al.*, 1979; Mortimore *et al.*, 1988).

Although more recent work has attempted to examine differential school effectiveness on pupils of different initial attainments (Jesson and Gray,

1991; Sammons *et al.*, 1993), little research examines variables which relate specifically to provision for special educational needs. Where variables such as incidence of behavioural problems have specifically been examined (e.g. Galloway, 1983) paradoxical findings have been made, with low levels of such problems correlating with low achievement.

Difficult-to-interpret findings such as these ought to have pointed to the danger of extrapolating from the complex generalisations of effectiveness research in order to make assumptions about what will be good for inclusion. Yet there has been an assumption that the findings of effectiveness research may be assimilated unproblematically into the debate about what characterises good curricular and social organisation for children who are experiencing difficulties at school.

As Hegarty (1993a) says, the school effectiveness research has ignored special educational needs, or has regarded them only in a peripheral way; it would thus be naïve, he says, to expect the findings to be directly applicable. Norwich (1993) makes similar points, asserting that 'improving schooling for all' is rhetoric, and not empirically based. What is good for the majority is not necessarily good for a minority. Reynolds (1995) concurs with this, saying that detailed interpretation of effectiveness research raises doubts about the use made of it within the special educational needs community. He goes on to say that 'change in schools to help one group of pupils may not necessarily improve the performance of other groups' (1995: 118).

Nor, despite the greater sensitivity brought recently by multilevel modelling to the analysis of the performance of specific cohorts of children, is this research able to offer useful analysis relating to the small numbers of children with serious difficulties in the classroom, or indeed the reciprocal effects which the integrated placement of these children and the organisational and managerial arrangements which accompany them introduce. There is a substantial literature which attests to the significance of these changes (e.g. Johnson *et al.*, 1983) and which shows that a good, well-organised classroom may not be so good for children with difficulties unless special steps are taken to include them.

Certain of the findings of the effectiveness research – for example the need for good leadership, good organisation and challenging teaching (see Levine and Lezotte, 1995, for a recent review) – would be uncontentious in any arena, and they can certainly be examined with some benefit by those seeking to promote inclusion. However, the major criticism of the appropriation of the findings of school effectiveness research to inclusive education must concern its insensitivity to particular processes introduced at school and classroom level to improve the inclusion of children with difficulties. It fails to examine (for this was never its remit) the effects of the specific organisational processes which may be associated with special provision in ordinary schools either for the 'special' children or for the majority (e.g. withdrawal versus support).

If, then, the conclusion to draw is that effectiveness research is too general and unfocused, and that arguments for inclusion cannot therefore rest upon it, what might be the hypothetical characteristics of schools and classrooms which promote inclusion? A number of experimental strategies and innovations to promote inclusion have been introduced recently, and the rest of this chapter will be devoted to exploring some of them, since many have implications for inclusion projects.

SPECIFIC INITIATIVES

Some of the particular strategies and adaptations made in schools in order to meet special educational needs have been examined in detail by West and Sammons (1996), and many of these are similar to those outlined in chapter 1. Putnam *et al.* (1995) asked a variety of interested groups (teachers, parents, academics, disability activists) what they considered were desirable trends towards future good inclusive practice. There was substantial agreement among respondents that co-operative learning in heterogeneous groups should be encouraged, but no expectation that this would be found in classrooms before the beginning of the twenty-first century.

Details are given by Fleming *et al.* (1990) of a specific initiative to promote the inclusion of children classified as having learning difficulties in mainstream mathematics. Whole-school management changes were made to ensure that there was a link teacher in each subject department who had responsibility for children with special needs, and the maths department was reorganised into mixed-ability classes, each with a team consisting of one classteacher and one extra for support, who could be used flexibly (e.g. for occasional withdrawal of groups or individuals). The head of department and link teacher each had roles as both class and support teachers, so that they were able to identify difficulties from both points of view. Initial staff concerns focused on three issues: how to ensure appropriate resources were available, what the role of the support teacher would be, and whether there would be problems due to variation in teaching styles and behaviour expectations. Various techniques were developed to encourage collaborative working, for example the use of computers in pairs consisting of one child with learning difficulties and one more able child. An evaluation of the first year's work suggested that pupils were already benefiting from the lack of labelling and encouragement of independent learning, but that staff still felt the need for 'expert' advice and help with pupil assessments. Despite this, the authors conclude: 'There is no doubt in our minds that all teachers can become successful teachers of children with special educational needs' (Fleming *et al.*, 1990: 184).

Moger and Coates (1992) report on successful inclusion in music and the arts. Links were made between a mainstream school and a special school catering for children classified as having multiple and complex special needs.

The goal was less that of improved academic progress for all, and more a greater involvement for special school pupils in their local community and a greater sensitivity in mainstream pupils towards the difficulties and abilities of their disabled peers, with the hope that these students' attitudes would eventually begin to influence those of others. The authors comment: 'Exam results and wealth creation are worth little if we neglect to live well with one another' (Moger and Coates, 1992: 10).

Ainscow (1995b) points out that the kinds of changes envisaged as necessary for greater inclusion are especially vulnerable to reductions in school budgets. These reductions may enforce a return to a 'bottom set' approach, clustering children with special needs in small groups again and withdrawing them from the general activity of the class. An emphasis on the way in which changes towards greater curriculum inclusion increase the effective education of children may 'supply ammunition with which to counteract financial challenges'. Clarke et al. (1995), describing research aimed at identifying good innovatory special needs practice in the mainstream, reported that the position of the SENCO in the school could be crucial in this context – for example in the leadership of team teaching which would improve curriculum delivery to all students.

A review of studies comparing the academic progress of matched able-bodied children in inclusive and non-inclusive classrooms (Staub and Peck, 1995) concluded that no able-bodied student was harmed by being in an inclusive classroom and that there was no loss of teaching time by the able-bodied as a result of the inclusion of disabled peers. However, the authors add caveats to their discussion: first, that most of the studies took place in early childhood environments, and second, that studies revealing positive advantages to the non-disabled from being in inclusive classrooms focus on social rather than academic benefits. (There are other cautions which need to be made about any research of this kind, as the discussion in chapter 1 revealed.)

Another area in which there is little research is the effects of disruption resulting from a perceived need for therapy. For such therapy children may be removed from the group. The effects of this withdrawal on curricular inclusion and on academic progress have not been specifically revealed in the research literature, although there is much research to indicate that supposedly expert 'remedial' help through withdrawal is less effective than simpler alternatives (e.g. Cashdan et al., 1971; Tizard et al., 1982; see also Thomas, 1995b).

HOW CAN DIFFERENTIATION BE USED TO PROMOTE CURRICULAR INCLUSION?

Pijl (1995), in an account of a comparative study of resources available to inclusive educators in five countries, states:

How far teachers differentiate between students in the use of methods and materials is . . . largely unknown. Research into differentiation with regard to the educational offering to students seems to be mainly a matter of concern in the Netherlands. . . . A tentative conclusion . . . is that teachers working in 'integrated' school systems do not differentiate more between the students in their classrooms than the Dutch teachers working in a clearly segregated system.

(Pijl, 1995: 59)

York and Tundidor (1995) reveal similar indifference – and even hostility by teachers to the possibilities of differentiation. Focus-group discussions disclosed feelings which mirror the views of some of the secondary school teachers who were interviewed for this study:

there was a strong assertion that inclusion of students with disabilities in general education classes was appropriate only when the respective curricular expectations, defined by course content, matched student abilities. For example, there were comments such as, 'He can be in class as long as he can meet the same expectations.' Related to this were comments such as 'No teacher can individualise education' and 'Teachers are already overloaded.'

(York and Tundidor, 1995: 38)

In a similar vein, Scruggs and Mastropieri (1996), in a synthesis of twenty-eight investigations into teacher perceptions of inclusion, conclude that two-thirds of teachers support the idea of inclusion. This acceptance, however, is predicated on the nature of the disabling condition, with more serious disabilities invoking more resistance. Moreover, the acceptance was theoretical rather than practical, since only one-third believed they had the time, expertise or resources necessary to make inclusion work.

These findings, taken with the interview data which will be detailed in chapter 9, remind us that there may be a long way to go on both sides of the Atlantic before the views of the majority of teachers regarding curriculum differentiation catch up with those of practitioners and researchers in the forefront of the inclusive movement.

Switching from the organisational/management perspective on curricular inclusion discussed above to a focus on differentiation involves a change of emphasis from planning for the school/class as a whole to looking more closely at the needs of individuals. The importance of the Individual Education Plan (IEP) in setting areas of specific individual need in the context of the classroom curriculum is emphasised by several commentators (e.g. Ford *et al.*, 1992). The need to look at all aspects of an individual's life, not just the most obvious, which may or may not be a disability, is also a crucial aspect of planning for curricular inclusion:

41

making certain aspects of the curriculum inclusive without attending to the child's whole identity or whole life is . . . inadequate. For example, adapting a Christmas craft activity so that [a child] is able to make decorations with the other children does not address the fact that the project may be inappropriate or insensitive to his or other children's religious differences.

(Sapon-Shevin, 1992: 20)

Udvari-Solner and Thousand (1995) portrayed teachers' attempts at curricular adaptation in inclusive classrooms as a decision-making process in which a series of self-posed questions determine the nature of differentiation for any one student at any one time. The first of these questions relates to whether differentiation is needed at all: can the student participate in the general work of the class without adaptation, achieving the same basic outcome? Reasons for answering 'no' to this question would suggest other questions to be asked, relating to, for example:

- the format of the lesson;
- the arrangement of groups;
- changes in delivery of instruction;
- adapted goals ('differentiation by outcome');
- different materials;
- personal support;
- an alternative task ('differentiation by activity').

If one multiplies the number of tasks in a typical week by the number of children in an inclusive classroom who might need this kind of consideration, it is easy to appreciate why so many overworked classteachers are keen to claim that differentiation should be the responsibility of support staff (as revealed in chapter 2).

Fletcher (1995) describes some of the ways in which she managed differentiation dilemmas in practice, demonstrating how language learning can be differentiated through strategies applicable to the education of the whole class. These include readers' workshops, writers' workshops in which 'each step of progress for each child is valued and celebrated, whether the child has produced beginning representative letters, single words, phrases, sentences or a full story' (1995: 88), response journals and learning logs, and various kinds of book sharing, all of them varied forms of differentiation by outcome. She also gives examples of differentiation by activity, in which groups or individuals work on separate projects according to their abilities, linked to the rest of the class by the common theme to which each project will eventually contribute.

Specialist advice on differentiating for children with particular needs is available, as well as the more generalised models reported above: the RNIB (1995) suggests that advance preparation of suitable materials for visually impaired students may be crucial to their participation in the lesson, that handling items may be an important adjunct to verbal explanation or diagrams, that extra time may be needed to complete work, and that direct teaching of concepts that sighted children pick up incidentally should not be overlooked.

The use of IT is becoming increasingly important in enabling inclusion; Sheppo (1995) gives many examples of ways in which students have been helped to think and learn, such as interactive video, electronic encyclopaedias and the Internet.

ASSESSMENT

This issue is related both to the one just discussed and to the one that follows (the National Curriculum). The work on differentiation, in emphasising the variety of outcomes which can be expected, suggests that any comparison of such outcomes would be difficult and/or meaningless, and that assessment in the inclusive classroom should therefore concentrate on recording the achievement of individuals exclusively in terms of their own progress, unrelated to that of their peers. Mittler (1995) warns that alternative means of assessment should not be allowed to lead to a lowering of expectations:

> research on effective schooling specifically highlights high expectations as one of the characteristics of an effective school. . . . Annual reviews, individual education plans and the process of transition from school to community provide us with an opportunity to challenge under-expectation.
>
> (Mittler, 1995: 3)

Mortimer describes the 'Playladders' approach to assessing the development of children with or without disabilities at the early stage. It does not involve withdrawal from group activity and is flexible enough to 'tap where the child is "at" whatever activity is being organised within the group' (Mortimer, 1995: 168). Biklen *et al.* (1995) address the problem of assessing the progress of students with multiple and complex special needs through the accumulation of portfolios, characteristic features of which can be identified in order to confirm the veracity of the authorship of facilitated communication.[1] Teachers of students with less severe difficulties in the inclusive classroom may find that they are expected to enter their pupils for standard National Curriculum tests. This will be discussed in the next section.

Attempts at researching the academic progress of disabled children in inclusive classrooms have been beset by the problems of assessment discussed above and by the complexity of determining physical and intellectual matches between comparison groups in special and mainstream schools, as noted in chapter 1. Tentative conclusions (see, for example, Stukat, 1993) suggest that academic achievement correlates with cognitive ability irrespective of educational setting. Baker *et al.*, however, combining the results of several studies, noted 'a small-to-moderate beneficial effect of inclusive education on the academic and social outcomes of special needs children' (1995: 34). This conclusion was made by combining figures from different periods (pre-1980 until the present). The methodological difficulties already noted in such comparisons are legion and great caution has to accompany any generalised statements about academic progress.

INCLUSION AND THE NATIONAL CURRICULUM

There would seem to be a danger that the National Curriculum, which at its best gives all children access to a broad and balanced curriculum is, in some cases, having the opposite effect in that 'broad and balanced' is determined in relation to the 'ordinary' child and may be inappropriate and restrictive to the extra-ordinary child. Yet there seems to be a widespread reluctance to 'disapply', as though this is depriving children of their so-called 'entitlement'.

(Fletcher-Campbell, 1994)

This comment summarises one of the findings of an NFER (National Foundation for Educational Research) study of link schemes between special and mainstream schools which concluded that some such schemes were being squeezed out by the pressures of the National Curriculum – by crowded timetables and the need for good results. This was particularly so in secondary schools.

Two other accounts examine the effect of National Curriculum assessment methods on classroom inclusion. Lewis (1996b), writing about research on Key Stage 2 tasks and tests, concludes that new arrangements for modifying tests and increasing the teacher assessment element have demonstrated that they are flexible enough to be used with children from a wide ability range, thereby adding credibility to the practice of extending inclusion within the confines of the National Curriculum. However, Lewis adds that some children may still achieve in ways that cannot be assessed through the present arrangements: 'Consequently, more searching and fundamental questions about the appropriateness of curricular goals need to be asked' (1996b: 14).

Fletcher-Campbell (1996b) reports on the Key Stage 4 aspect of the Small Steps Survey, an NFER study of possible modes of assessment, recording and accreditation for students working up to Level 3 in any Key Stage. Teachers interviewed had reservations about the concept of GCSE as a universal examination: for some students with profound and multiple learning difficulties, for example, they found it impossibly inappropriate. There has been much recent publicity about less disabled students being excluded from entering

GCSE examinations because of the perception that they, and the school league position which works on percentages of those entered, would receive no credit if they did not achieve.

Apart from the difficulties of the final assessment, there was a feeling amongst those in the survey that parts of the course were inappropriate to student needs and too demanding:

> Although there might be units or modules that were achievable (for example, Science modules on Materials, practical coursework in Drama, or fieldwork in Geography) there would be others which would not be (for example, Science modules on a more abstract topic such as Electricity, or written coursework in Drama or Geography.)
>
> (Fletcher-Campbell, 1996b: 15)

A range of features was identified which would support an inclusive curriculum at Key Stage 4. These included: recognition of the value of a small steps approach, a broad understanding of progression which would value experience as well as attainment, a variety of means of assessment (e.g. photos) and a focus on the positive, to avoid the setting-up for failure inherent for these students in much of the GCSE course. Flexibility of content and approach in the curriculum was felt to be valuable, together with applicability to the whole ability range and to a variety of educational contexts (schools, colleges and day centres) to ensure continuity of progression. Various forms of accreditation are highlighted which exhibit some or all of these features, some externally designed and assessed, like the Welsh Board Certificate of Education, some designed by the school and assessed externally, like the Youth Award Scheme, and some based on school-devised certification. All these forms of accreditation can be incorporated into the student's National Record of Achievement, and the motivational aspects of both participation and certification in these alternative courses were much appreciated by teachers.

Many of these courses can take place in inclusive classrooms where most students are following a GCSE syllabus. There are, however, sometimes difficulties in instigating or maintaining these courses because of the demands on a shrinking school budget for extra resources and because of the need to involve most teaching staff in changes affecting the curriculum.

Combes (1995) illustrates the way in which the pursuit of alternatives to the National Curriculum can act against the creation of inclusive classrooms. He describes how, as a Head of English, he was prompted to abandon twenty years of mixed-ability teaching in the face of larger than usual numbers of children with special needs in one year and a reduction of the coursework element of the GCSE. He devised his own National Vocational Qualification (NVQ) syllabus, basing work on positive attainment, lots of trips into the 'real world' and an avoidance of authoritarianism, and used it with a group of the least able pupils, with the help of a support teacher. He found that his changed teaching style improved student attendance and quality of work, but it did not address the wider problems of social exclusion and labelling.

There are many imaginative curricular ventures and adaptations of this kind. Given that one of the tenets of inclusion is that all students should have the chance to study the same curriculum, the question may arise as to how much of the National Curriculum some children can study. Moore (1996) comes up with some useful ideas on this issue. Talking in the context of history in the National Curriculum, she develops the idea of a *minimum entitlement* for pupils who learn more slowly. She suggests that this entitlement should ensure that pupils can acquire essential skills and understanding of the subject whilst not being hampered by too much historical content.

History is, of course, an appropriate subject area for such a distinction between understanding and content to be drawn, for it is in this subject that there has been so much debate about whether children need to learn specific pieces of information such as dates, or whether it is better to equip them with the conceptual skills needed to think about, interpret and understand history. Moore suggests that teachers should be able to select content from earlier or later key stages and decide for themselves what the minimum entitlement should be for particular pupils or groups of pupils. She goes on to suggest that pupils' minimum entitlement will be assured if teachers examine the focus statement to be found at the beginning of each history study unit and select those materials from the list of historical content which will give pupils an adequate understanding of the focus statement. An example she gives is that at Key Stage 3 all pupils must study History Study Unit 1, 'Medieval Realms', where the focus statement says that 'pupils should be taught about some of the major features of Britain's medieval past'. She suggests that teachers will still be meeting the requirements of the focus statement if children with learning difficulties are given a minimum entitlement. For example, the content could be the Battle of Hastings in 1066.

Lewis (1996a), Cox (1996) and many others describe similarly imaginative and interesting ways of differentiating and adapting the curriculum to provide good inclusive education. Imaginative and interesting as they are, though, there is nothing very special about the strategies and methods they describe. They simply represent good teaching, and this sums up the inclusive approach to meeting special educational needs. There are no magic formulae or extra-special curricular devices which have to be used with children who experience difficulties. There is no need to assume that certain special teaching styles or strategies are accessible only to those who have had long training or experience. The main requirement is for creativity and imagination to make the curriculum come alive for all children; if such creativity and imagination are used, then all children will benefit, not simply those with lower achievement or 'special needs'.

4

SUPPORTIVE CLASSROOM ENVIRONMENTS FOR SOCIAL INCLUSION

Merely putting children into integrated settings and expecting them to get on with it is not enough. Indeed, moving special children to ordinary classrooms may have effects very different from those we hope for and expect. Johnson *et al.* (1983) have shown that 'special' pupils may be viewed in negative ways when they are introduced into mainstream classes. And Ferguson vividly describes the reaction of mainstream students to a group of 'included' autistic students; the teacher in charge of the project reported that 'I even had a couple of them [mainstream students] scream, "Eek, he touched me" ' (1992: 158). As Higgins (1992) makes clear, in order to effect inclusion many people must work hard to make it succeed. It does not happen on its own.

Physical proximity carries with it, then, the possibility of making things worse rather than better. The success of inclusion (as distinct from integration) depends crucially on how teaching is organised and how interaction among pupils is structured and helped.

In order to establish what aspects of classroom and school ethos, organisation and social environment might need to be addressed to foster a climate favourable to inclusion, we now examine and discuss the development of social skills, relationships and self-esteem among students with disabilities in a variety of educational settings.

INTERACTION AND COMMUNICATION

Guralnick *et al.* (1995) report an unusual experiment comparing children's interactions in three sorts of playgroup set up specifically for their study. 'Typically developing' children and developmentally delayed children interacted generally more in the inclusive group, organised on a similar basis to the British 'opportunity' playgroups, than did their peers in segregated groups. The researchers attribute this to the availability for typically developing children of a greater diversity of children wanting to be directed in play, and to the stimulus of models and organisers for the developmentally delayed children. The news for inclusion was not all good, however, since the

developmentally delayed children were not as well accepted or well integrated socially as the typically developing children, nor did they receive as
many peer nominations. This points to the need for staff to consider ways of
structuring and helping along relationships, as happens in 'circles of friends'
(see below).

Moore *et al.* (1987) described the stages that slightly older children,
involved in a special/first school link scheme, went through before they
arrived at the point where interaction could take place. The mainstream
children had first to get used to a number of new adults in the classroom,
then to size up the new children on their own (which they did through
activities such as staring). They then initiated interaction through gestures,
which led at last to both groups trying to communicate verbally. The writers
point to the importance of three things in this establishment of relationships:

- carefully structured joint activities;
- opportunities for co-operation; and
- freedom from a continually hovering adult presence.

Special school staff observed that interactive behaviour learnt at the first
school was used by the disabled children in their segregated setting, emphasising the importance of peer models for social skills.

The making of friendships in inclusive classrooms has been the subject of
several investigations, most of which draw conclusions from various kinds of
sociometric ratings of popularity. Farrell and Scales (1995) explored a situation in which a small number of non-disabled infants had been introduced
into a nursery with a majority of children who had severe learning difficulties. There are some suggestions in the literature that this approach to
inclusion is more beneficial to the social development of the disabled children than an environment where non-disabled children predominate. The
disabled children, when asked to choose whom to sit next to or play with,
chose equally from non-disabled and disabled peers, whereas non-disabled
children chose more frequently from amongst themselves. This appears to be
a common finding which occurs irrespective of type of disability and educational setting. Markides (1989), for example, found that a low percentage of
hearing children in mainstream secondary schools in Britain chose a hearing-
impaired child as a 'best friend' and that, furthermore, hearing-impaired
children usually chose another hearing-impaired child, adding support to
the argument for the right of deaf people to develop their own culture.
Inclusive classrooms hoping to encourage more mixed friendships have to
address this issue.

Hall (1994) was able to draw more optimistic conclusions about the
promotion of social inclusion following a study of established integrated
classrooms in Australia and Belgium which found friendships between
disabled and non-disabled youngsters in every class, identified through

observations of proximity, peer nominations and pupil interviews aimed at elucidating the bases for friendship. She suggests:

> There may be benefits in supporting and enhancing these relationships before arranging teacher or researcher selected peers for structured social skills programs. In addition, if social support programs include children who like each other, there may be more generalisation of social interaction skills to various activities.
>
> (Hall, 1994: 312)

Hendrickson *et al.* (1996) make findings supportive of Hall's in a survey of over one thousand middle and high school students in the USA. Students felt that they should try to make friends with peers with severe disabilities. It was discovered that friendships were more likely to develop when students with disabilities were educated in general education classes and that friendships were promoted by having learning situations in which:

* students of different abilities worked together;
* teachers presented information on disabilities; and
* teachers and parents arranged social events for all students.

On the first of these points – enabling students of different abilities to work together – Aaronson and Bridgeman (1979) provide the useful idea of 'jigsaw groups'. In these groups each member possesses an element necessary for the completion of a task, and co-operation between group members is thus encouraged. Other similar ideas on co-operative work are provided by Johnson *et al.* (1986) and Johnson and Johnson (1994).

Crucial to the success of such programmes in encouraging communication and sharing of world-views is some understanding of how non-disabled mainstream children can be helped to develop sensitivity to their disabled peers. Maras and Brown (1992) devised a study to test the theory, developed from the field of ethnic inclusion, that sensitivity and understanding of others is increased by acknowledging and valuing difference rather than by ignoring it. Their results, while complex, appear to suggest that this may be true in educational contexts for characteristics that are easy to observe, such as the ability to run, but that appreciation of more abstract qualities is not necessarily enhanced by situations where disabled students are clearly identified as such. Lewis (1995b) confirms that a non-disabled pupil may sometimes make a wrong assumption about a disabled peer which affects attempts to communicate or work co-operatively; for example, the non-disabled child may assume that a child who does not speak is deaf. She characterises the speech of the non-disabled children involved in the 'Link 7' scheme as generally 'bossy', with the following features: 'Comments are repeated frequently and there are many instructions to do, or desist from, something. These instructions are phrased in a very direct way. There are few explanations and few genuine questions' (Lewis, 1995b: 80).

Communication practice through games and the teaching of sign languages such as Makaton can, she suggests, help to make this kind of interaction less one-sided, as non-disabled students become more aware of their disabled peers' personalities as individuals. Better communication also developed in activities where disabled pupils saw a need to assert themselves and, in the struggle to make their feelings clear, were pushed to adopt more complex language and more intelligible speech than they normally employed.

Other writers suggest that qualitative research methods such as careful observation have a contribution to make to the assessment of the 'situationally inappropriate initiations or responses known to contribute to low peer acceptance' (Frederickson and Woolfson, 1987: 47), which could be followed by helpful intervention programmes and changes in the classroom environment. This is borne out by some of the observations undertaken as part of the Inclusion Project research (reported in detail in Part II), an example of which is worth noting here since it bears on several of the points already made. The observations relate to Daniel, a boy in Y1 who has joined the class as part of the Inclusion Project. He is playing in the sand tray, when a little girl joins him; they play in parallel for a minute or so, then:

> Daniel says 'will you help me' to the girl (Jo) three times. She says something and does go to help him. She pushes him out of way, gently, and makes a tunnel under his construction. After slow start they are now talking quite frequently about their construction – she telling him what to do and he responding. Daniel stereotyped in his language. Jo making lots of imaginative comments, suggestions and directing the work in the sand. Actually gets hold of Daniel's hand [to help] at one point. When finished, she says 'Let's show Mrs X' [teacher] and he calls her. The two explain it to her. Another little girl joins the two of them. She's looking on, standing by Jo, and then moves in on construction. The three now work together. Jo still talks to Daniel and looks for response from him. Teacher tells new girl to move away – 'Only two in the sand'. Jo has taken over the construction quite substantially now and Daniel begins to look on – albeit quite happily. Jo chattering away. Both now move away from the sand and go over to the computer.

Evident here are both the easy willingness of children to engage in social intercourse with disabled peers and the 'bossiness' noted by Lewis. However, the bossiness was by no means over-assertiveness, but rather represented a seemingly natural desire to help and guide. Both children gained from the experience and both shared in the report which they ultimately gave to the teacher. The teacher was able skilfully to guide the report so that Daniel had his say, as indeed she had guided the sand play by unobtrusively monitoring the number of children at the tray and preventing Daniel's being 'swamped' by two other children.

SELF-ESTEEM

Lewis also discusses the possible contribution of the kind of link scheme she describes to the improvement in self-esteem of disabled children, emphasising that joint activities must be carefully chosen to avoid the unwitting creation of situations in which disabled pupils end up being tutored by non-disabled peers, with consequent lowering of social status in their own eyes, if not in those of others as well. Chiu (1990) tried to investigate the relationship between the respect students receive socially and their own ratings of self-esteem, introducing an element of comparison by assessing North American children who were only partially included (gifted or with mild learning difficulties) alongside those who were in full-time mainstream education, on the hypothesis that ratings would be affected by the availability of peers of a certain sort for children to measure themselves against. Teachers' assessments of self-esteem were also used. Those with mild learning difficulties were found to have significantly lower self-esteem than either of the other groups, on both their own and their teachers' ratings. It was found, furthermore, that teachers *over*-estimated the level of self-esteem of the gifted students. Chiu concludes: 'It is imperative that educators design effective curriculum materials and strategies to be utilised for developing and enhancing the feelings of self-worth for the mentally retarded' (1990: 267).

Another study using social comparison theory to explain its findings investigated self-ratings of behaviour, as well as of academic achievement and 'global self-worth' among children with learning difficulties in integrated classrooms in the USA. The results led the writers to a different conclusion from Chiu's, but one which is just as uncompromising:

> it would seem that integrated classrooms are unlikely to enhance the self-perceptions of scholastic competence, as well as related perceptions of overall self-worth, among children with learning disabilities unless such classrooms stagnate the growth of NH [non-handicapped] children – allowing children with learning disabilities to compare themselves favourably to their NH peers – or unless children with learning disabilities are taught not to compare themselves to their more academically proficient and socially adjusted classmates.
>
> (Bear *et al.*, 1991: 424)

The stress here is unnecessarily negative. The emphasis must surely be on the positive action which needs to be taken by the teacher to help deflect any feelings which arise out of comparison by the disabled child with non-disabled peers. And the 'up side' for the non-disabled children is surely in the rich social experience of helping others. It would be difficult to imagine how such experiences could 'stagnate the growth' of anyone, and there was certainly no evidence for such 'stagnation' during any observations of the Somerset Inclusion Project. Rather, the converse was the case.

The findings of a British study (Lalkhen and Norwich, 1990), which separated physical self-concept from other measures of self-esteem, also seem to contradict the results of Bear *et al.*. In this research, it was found that students in inclusive classrooms had higher self-esteem than their peers in either partially integrated or entirely segregated settings, although their physical self-concept was the lowest of the three groups, which would seem to provide evidence for the soundness of social comparison theory. However, the authors suggest that if 'self-esteem can be seen to be based on satisfaction for those personal characteristics and activities which are most valued personally' (Lalkhen and Norwich, 1990: 9), as opposed to being merely a reflection of respect accorded by others, more of this satisfaction is perhaps being achieved in inclusive contexts, in which case physical self-concept, no matter how poorly rated, becomes *comparatively* unimportant.

Further support for the inclusive classroom as a potentially beneficial social environment for disabled students comes from a longitudinal study carried out in the USA. In comparisons of the progress in developmental and social skills made by groups of segregated versus integrated young people with learning difficulties, it was found that there was no *educational* advantage to either setting. However, the social skills of the segregated group generally regressed over a two-year period:

> children from integrated sites generally improved in their ability to manage their own behaviour in social situations, provide negative feedback to others, accept assistance from others, indicate personal preference to others, cope with negative social circumstances, and terminate social contact.
>
> (Cole and Meyer, 1991: 348)

HOW CAN CLASSROOM ENVIRONMENTS BE DESIGNED TO PROMOTE INCLUSION?

Classroom changes in favour of inclusion may come about as a result of a whole-school initiative. (This is discussed further in chapter 5.) Spalding and Florek (1988) enumerate the elements of an inclusive school ethos on which practice at Connahs Quay was based. There was an emphasis on individuality and equality, a flexible approach to the curriculum, an avoidance of labelling, and a willingness to experiment with learning groups defined by characteristics other than the usual age or ability. Roaf (1992) sets the development of such an ethos in an equal opportunities framework, discussing the importance of a careful use of language in the establishment of a school environment and inclusive curriculum designed to allow students from all sorts of minority groups to feel comfortable and flourish educationally.

Jacklin and Lacey (1993) switch the emphasis to the preparation necessary for particular individuals from special education to join a mainstream school.

While they seem to write from an 'integration' rather than an 'inclusion' perspective, they have important points to make about the transition process, and in particular the way in which mainstream staff can help to support children who are unable to make the close friendships they may have enjoyed in the special sector.

There is an important role for the special school to play in initiating inclusion by developing co-operative practice with local mainstream schools, and this can often be a precursor to more developed inclusive practice, as Wilson (1990) describes. However, this has to be carefully planned to ensure success, particularly where children's disabilities are serious. Walter (1997) describes some activities which he undertook with his class of children with severe learning difficulties when children from local mainstream schools have visited. He makes the point that each session should have a shared activity and a practical result. Walter describes here what his sessions have included:

- Communication methods, e.g. signing, rebus, speech machines.
- Discussion of physical abilities, with an explanation of cerebral palsy and its effects on movement, feeding, epilepsy, talking (and how cerebral palsy is not catching).
- How to push a wheelchair and how to help visually impaired pupils to move around.
- A demonstration of how our pupils make choices and how to interpret their communication.
- Physical role playing: feeling what it is like to be pushed around in a wheelchair or not being able to speak. Feeling what it is like to be blindfolded. Getting them to help feed each other yoghurt when one is sightless is instructive.
- Each subsequent session is usually started in the same manner (in the primary age group) by using hand creams. When they come in, the mainstream pupils offer the special school pupils a choice of two different hand creams and rub their hands with their choice. This is an activity that they can start at once (no sitting around looking embarrassed), and it shows how the special school pupils make choices in an obvious way (reaching out, eye pointing or simply responding to stimuli). It makes physical contact between the two groups and it makes the room smell nice.
- Then we have a practical activity, and I usually try to ensure that they have something to take away at the end of each session: cooking (we have burnt some wonderful biscuits during these sessions) and making milk shakes etc.; art (the messier the better, clay, painting, collage etc.); story making with a rebus print-out from the computer; showing the visitors around the school; light room and sensory play areas; horses and stables (always a favourite); swimming pool; the 'Learning Curve' adventure playground.

One of the findings of the research reported in Part II of this book is that a major obstacle to new inclusive practice is fear of the unknown, and activities such as these will contribute greatly to the confidence of all in the mainstream – children and their teachers – of their capability to include children with disabilities.

Circles of friends

Establishing a circle of friends in the inclusive classroom can be one way of addressing this difficulty. Such a circle functions ideally not only as a means of mutual support but as a way of promoting challenge and self-advocacy. It may also be used for 'making action plans' – that is, enabling teacher, class, family and student to plan the individual's curriculum jointly (see O'Brien and Forest, 1989). The initiation of such a circle should take place before the child's arrival in school, and can involve support for parents from a network in the community, and the planning of a welcome for the child in the first few days of attendance.

Tamaren (1992) develops the idea of the class working as a team on behalf of one of its students, but relates it to the resolution of specific difficulties rather than to ongoing planning. The designed absence of the child herself during relevant class discussions makes the process seem patronising, but the author claims it 'has proven useful in building cooperation and understanding on the part of the class for the child whose behaviours may provoke conflict, confusion or concern' (Tamaren, 1992: 61).

Kishi and Meyer (1994) describe their research into the long-term effects of a circle of friends-type intervention in Hawaii, stating that short-term results have been found to be largely positive in promoting social inclusion in the classroom. They compared children with severe learning difficulties and non-disabled primary pupils directly paired in contrived 'special friends' relationships with similar pairs of students who either had had no contact with each other or had been educated alongside each other without special joint activities. After six years, few of the 'special friends' relationships had been maintained. However, the authors surmise that this was not because of the failure of the circles initiative, but because the disabled children had been sent to schools other than their local ones at secondary level. There are two important lessons here. The first is that neighbourhood schooling has distinct advantages over resourced schooling;[1] the second is that the simple solution to inclusion – the one that offers home-grown friendships and low-tech adaptations – is more effective than the more complex one which may offer more generous resourcing.

Newton et al. (1996) give some useful suggestions on the use of circles of friends when helping the assimilation of children whose behaviour has been found difficult. Making the interesting point that using this approach is very different from a behavioural approach which would centre on ignoring difficult behaviour, they outline some features of using circles with these children. These include:

- there is an initial meeting with a session leader and the focus child's class (without the child present), stressing confidentiality to the class;
- comments are invited about the focus child;
- there is a more general discussion about relationships with the child;
- children are encouraged to think about friendships and relationships in general;
- circles are drawn showing different kinds of friendship: perhaps family, close friends and acquaintances;
- children are encouraged to reflect on friendships and what the lack of them means;
- reflections are encouraged on what no friendships means for the focus child;
- ideas are sought for helping the focus child;
- volunteers are sought on who can become a circle for the focus child;
- the first meeting of the circle with the focus child is arranged.

Salisbury *et al.* (1995), investigated the strategies used by classteachers (as distinct from specialists) to promote social inclusion in classrooms. These included:

- the setting up of opportunities for interaction through organisation of activities;
- being open to learning from other students' perceptions of the disabled child, and to letting these students have some responsibility with regard to her;
- acting as a model of accepting and welcoming behaviour.

The authors point out that because they were looking for examples of good, rather than representative, practice they had focused on exceptionally skilled teachers employing strategies recognised elsewhere as being central to the education of *all* children.

Other work has aimed at establishing the types of task that best promote interaction which transfers easily into informal social situations. Eichinger (1990) reported that co-operative ventures were, unsurprisingly, more successful at this than individual ones. She concluded that opportunities for natural, unstructured, interaction during the day should be maximised, and that educational activities to encourage social inclusion should attempt to involve elements of choice for the participants so that students had a chance to experience the possibilities and limitations of normal social intercourse.

CLASSROOM ORGANISATION AND INCLUSION

The way a class is physically organised can have important implications for inclusion. Lucas (in Lucas and Thomas, 1990) describes her own classroom in which she fundamentally changed the 'geography'. Although she changed the classroom mainly to benefit general class management, special benefits accrued for children who had previously experienced difficulties. Implications can clearly be seen for children who are wheelchair-users, given the extra space which is liberated by the change in geography:

> Before I took the class, my predecessor had the organisation based on the familiar groups-of-tables approach. The tables were cluttered with the children's trays (containing books, pencils, apples etc.) because there was not enough space with the room organised in this way for the children to move about and reach distantly placed tray-racks. The teacher complained that the children were disorganised, lost pieces of work, and didn't seem to care about their work. . . . When I took over this class I decided to change the layout. . . . The children's tables (all two-seaters) were moved out to the walls so that they formed a 'ring' around the perimeter of the room, with their chairs facing outwards [to the walls]. I moved the carpet to the centre and positioned four units (one bookcase, two display units and a woodwork bench) at angles on the carpet corners. This was the basic structure of the room. It was very simple and very spacious.
>
> (Lucas and Thomas, 1990: 32–33)

She goes on to describe the benefits which arose from this organisation. One of the findings of the Inclusion Project research (see Part II of this book) concerns the difficulties that are raised when one or more large wheelchairs are introduced into a crowded classroom; the changes that Lucas introduced here could perhaps be replicated in classrooms where space is short. The near-ubiquitous groups-of-tables method of organising the British primary classroom has, in any case, been criticised for inadequately addressing the different needs of children as they pass from task to task (see Bennett and Blundell, 1983; Wheldall, 1988; and also Weinstein, 1979, for an American perspective) and new solutions to classroom planning seem overdue when these criticisms are taken also in the light of expectations for inclusion.

Important also for the social and academic organisation of the classroom where inclusion is concerned is the evidence (Delefes and Jackson, 1972) that an 'action zone' exists in many classrooms. Most of the teacher's interactions occur with children at the front and in the middle of the class (this is even in classrooms which in theory have no front). Research shows (Saur *et al.*, 1984) that if an action zone exists, then hearing-impaired children who happen to be sitting at the periphery of the class are doubly disadvantaged.

Not only children with sensory disabilities will be handicapped by the action zone: withdrawn children, or those who find difficulty concentrating, might also be doubly disadvantaged by the existence of such a zone. There is clearly scope here for thinking about the geography of the classroom, the movement of the teacher around the classroom and the placement of certain children within the class if those children's needs are to be met appropriately.

The discussion in this chapter once again illustrates the benefits which arise from organising the classroom for all. By looking to organisation which will benefit the social needs of children who may have a disability, provision for all children is enhanced. Positive action taken for children who may face particular challenges will benefit all children by encouraging and promoting more responsive and inclusive pastoral, curricular and organisational systems.

5

INCLUSION AND THE PHYSICAL ENVIRONMENT OF THE SCHOOL

LOCATION AND USE OF BUILDINGS

It has been argued that full physical inclusion in the classroom, while not a guarantee of total social and curricular involvement, is at least a necessary precondition for it (O'Brien and Forest, 1989). But the rhetoric of full physical inclusion is somewhat different from the reality, as indicated by Sebba and Ainscow (1995) in juxtaposing comments from different members of staff at John Smeaton Community High School:

> the school has continued to develop as a community school taking pupils from the community regardless of disability.

compared with:

> . . . no lifts. So, at the moment, [it's] not possible to take pupils in wheelchairs.

> (Sebba and Ainscow, 1995: 5)

Internationally, North America has been in the vanguard of attempts by local communities to promote the full physical inclusion in education of all their pupils (see Houston 1995; Udvari-Solner and Thousand, 1995; Ware, 1995). Lipsky and Gartner (1996) make the point, though, that there is a contrast between what has been stressed by American legislators on the one hand and teachers and parents on the other in promoting inclusion. The legislators (in law PL 94-142, the Education for All Handicapped Children Act) have emphasised adaptations to the physical environment of a school to enable inclusion, while parents and teachers have emphasised the need for services and other supports. This contrast captures the kernel of the debate about the physical environment of the school and adaptations to it. While it is easy for administrators and 'street level bureaucrats' (Weatherley and Lipsky, 1977) to home-in on the need for physical adaptations, in practice these adaptations seem to be less important than the attitude of receiving staff. In most of the literature (e.g. Jupp, 1992) findings about the success of inclusion stress the importance of factors *other* than physical constraints and school architecture.

58

Nevertheless, the physical parameters within which inclusion is framed are clearly important and reflect the attitude being taken to the subject. If, for example, 'inclusion' is provided by a physically separate unit within a mainstream school this betrays a particular outlook and philosophy to the incorporation of children with disabilities or other difficulties. Such a philosophy would be far different from one revealed by the provision of inclusion within the classroom. The broad physical provision within which the process happens can thus make the difference between segregation, integration and full inclusion.

And there is indeed a very wide diversity in these physical arrangements to support inclusion. Changes may take place from the inside, perhaps in the form of relocating an existing 'special needs' department to a universally accessible resource centre (often accompanied by a change of departmental title to 'learning support'), as at St Wilfrid's High School (see Sebba and Ainscow, 1995). This sends a message to all staff and pupils that learning support is available to, and may be required by, any pupils at some time in their school careers, rather than being the prerogative of a separate, and separately accommodated, caste.

In some cases, however, the term 'resource base' appears to be used as a euphemism for just such a separate form of accommodation for those with needs perceived as somehow more special than other students' needs, implying rather strangely that 'resources' (such as the books, tapes, cuttings and CD-ROMS kept in the resource centres that have replaced the old school libraries) are needed only by them. The closure of Etton Pasture Special School, and the dispersal of its pupils to six local schools, each with different ways of physically accommodating the new students, presented an opportunity to examine parents' and pupils' views of these differences. The researchers found that 'for the pupils who transferred to a more protective resource-based teaching system of integration, both parents and children were more satisfied than for those who transferred to a less protective, mainly mainstream class-based setting' (Kidd and Hornby, 1993: 19). They did not conclude that this was an argument in favour of separate bases as a permanent feature, suggesting that the length of time the pupils had been in segregated provision was a factor in these findings: separate bases might well not be necessary in situations where children had been in the mainstream all along.

A similar dispersal of pupils from Bishopswood Special School (now a school in name, finance and twice-termly meetings only) to local nursery, primary and secondary schools also resulted in the setting up of separate bases for the pupils involved, with limited opportunities for physical involvement in the wider environment of the school: 'Each Bishopswood class has its own room with a teacher and assistant. This provides a secure base from which pupils move for shared educational and social experiences in the mainstream, as appropriate for each individual' (CSIE, 1992: 3).

There is no indication that this separation is seen by the authors as a temporary state of affairs, since they have started to admit children who have never been in special education directly into these classes and they record their concern that Bishopswood School should continue to retain its identity as a discrete institution. Another special school for students with all kinds of disabilities has been relocated to Eastlea Community School and is now known, perhaps inevitably, as the school's 'Resource Area'. However, this relocation has enabled eleven of the ex-special school pupils to move straight into mainstream, by-passing the separate base altogether (see Sebba and Ainscow, 1995). This kind of rationalisation of physical resources is recommended by the Audit Commission/HMI in their management handbook *Getting the Act Together*:

> Releasing staffing resources is only one of a number of issues in the special school sector. Teaching the full range of subjects under the National Curriculum is a problem for small special schools with limited numbers of staff. These factors, combined with the opportunity to make better use of surplus accommodation and with changing patterns in the location of pupils in the authority, make a powerful argument for LEAs to review their special schools.
>
> (Audit Commission/HMI, 1992b: 3)

The pupils from Etton Pasture and Bishopswood were all classified as having some degree of learning difficulty. Another reason for the establishment of wholly or partly separate accommodation of children on a mainstream site may concern the physical unsuitability of the main school building, or, as at the school described by Doble (1986), the perception that physically disabled children require a unique kind of support. This support would be defined by their physical disability rather than by characteristics they might share with able-bodied peers – a 'medical model' as opposed to an 'inclusion' approach. Doble analysed the work of his own unit for physically disabled children, attached to a large comprehensive school most of which was fully accessible to wheelchair users. The unit had the services of a physiotherapist, doctor and school nurse but no specialist educational equipment, since virtually all teaching was done in mainstream. Although Doble doubts whether the students who were the focus of his case studies would have coped psychologically in school without the 'PH unit', his concluding remarks suggest that he had begun to feel that the unit needed to become more flexible, if only in the direction of becoming a 'resource area' for all the special needs children in the school. A report by Moss (1987) of improvements in the social acceptance by their hearing peers of hearing-impaired students who were moved out of an isolated and self-sufficient unit into form groups indicates the likely negative effects on social inclusion of the existence of such units.

The effect of *ad hoc* action, rather than long-term planning for physical inclusion at a particular location, also deserves a mention, since it was this kind of stimulus which initiated the Somerset Inclusion Project. Booth (1992) describes the varied events and situations which contributed to greater inclusion at the Grove Primary School in Cambridgeshire. These were: the ending of separate education for visually impaired children in the county, the school's physical and geographical suitability as a centre for these students, and then a fire, which enabled it to be rebuilt with facilities for the physically disabled students whose local special school had just closed. It is interesting to note that this school, like the Somerset secondary school with whom the Princess Margaret School staff worked, conformed to the common British model of physical concentration of students with a particular disability from a wide area on one site, rather than to inclusive ideals which emphasise attendance at the student's neighbourhood school: that is, the 'resourced school' model versus the neighbourhood school model. Staff involved with the Bishopswood initiative commented that 'the integrated education experience at Sonning Common is most effective when children live locally' (CSIE, 1992: 5).

In the classroom itself, imagination in the way the classroom is organised can pay dividends for inclusion. If space is at a premium, the changes described by Lucas and Thomas (1990) to classroom layout can provide benefits not only for children with disabilities but for all children. (These are discussed more fully in chapter 4.) The moves described by Lucas and Thomas involved minimum disruption for the liberation of a great deal of space – simply reorganising most of the groups-of-tables so that they faced the walls of the classroom instead of operating as tables in the centre. Curricular and social benefits accrued as well as physical ones.

PHYSICAL SUPPORTS FOR INCLUSION

Given the severe resource constraints on schools, it seems extremely doubtful that parental choice for non-segregated provision for pupils with SENs can in fact be ensured through a system of funding pupils which is intended to reflect parental choice.

(Wedell, 1994: 42)

The neglect of equal rights implicitly criticised in this ironic statement applies as much to the provision of physical supports for inclusion as to human resources such as staffing. What help is the literature in suggesting which areas should have priority in a climate of increasing financial constraint?

The CSIE *Checklist for Inclusion* (CSIE, 1995) points out that inaccessibility gets in the way of inclusion in many schools and is a factor that may need long-term planning and investment, but that

when considering physical access to school buildings and facilities it is worth remembering that disabled pupils are not the only people to be served by provisions such as lifts and ramps. Disabled teachers and disabled parents as well as other members of the community will benefit.

(CSIE, 1995: 3)

CSIE suggests that less expensive changes can still make a difference to possibilities for inclusion. Jones *et al.* (1983), for example, show how something as simple as a tray on the arm of a wheelchair can be made useful for laboratory experiments. The authors emphasise that the standard safety precautions observed by everybody (tying back long hair, wearing goggles and lab coats) are the most important guarantees of the disabled pupil's well-being in the lab. Field (1988) has a helpful list of ideas which may promote greater physical involvement in other 'hands-on' subjects, such as the use of food processors where pupils have little strength for chopping and mixing, and worktop-level microwave ovens for students without the balance to bend and retrieve a hot dish.

Donkersloot (1991), writing about the role of the Humberside service for disabled students, reminds readers that physiotherapists and occupational therapists are a useful source of help and might need to be consulted many times in a student's school career as her physical abilities, interests and needs change. He emphasises the value of simplicity (with its frequent corollary of cheapness): 'In all cases we are attempting to identify the simplest practical solution. A low-tech answer is often better than an expensive hi-tech answer and often more reliable' (Donkersloot, 1991: 7).

It is worth noting that it may be important for students to have access to all kinds of professionals at a single location: failures of transfer from Patcham House Special School to local mainstream schools were found to be partly due to the sudden lack of a network of professionals in one readily accessible centre (Jacklin and Lacey, 1991). It is significant, therefore, that initial anxieties of some parents over the changes proposed in the Somerset Inclusion Project concerned the feared loss of this 'one-stop' facility. Provision for physio on school premises, and swimming with the rest of the class rather than as part of a specialist hydro session, are possible ways of continuing to provide 'one-stop' support and simultaneously minimising disruption to timetables due to appointments and treatments.

The RNIB (1995) provides advice on improving the physical environment with inclusion in mind and suggests that forethought, rather than heavy spending, is the key to greater educational involvement for students with visual impairment. Low-tech solutions, as on Humberside, find the greatest favour. It does not go into detail about the many low vision aids, large print and Braille resources available, referring teachers to the LEA visual impairment service for individually orientated advice.

Low-tech aids available to enhance inclusion of children with hearing impairments tend to be human-based rather than physical, such as advice not to stand with one's back to the light and to enunciate clearly, for the benefit of lip-readers. Most teachers nowadays are becoming familiar with the uses of radio microphones and induction loops in classrooms including students with hearing impairment.

A tough educational and personal challenge for teachers trying to bring about a greater degree of inclusion is the attempt to establish useful two-way communication with students who have communication difficulties, and to help these students to express themselves in a variety of curricular and social contexts. This is an area where high-tech aids can be extremely valuable, as anyone who has listened to Steven Hawking will be aware. Pickering discusses the need for informed and careful selection: 'The most important thing to remember is that the equipment must match the level of ability and the needs of the user. The ultimate aim of any communication system must be to ensure that the user's potential for communication is maximised' (1996: 28).

It is apparent from this review of the literature that most commentators regard lack of money for physical resources as an inadequate excuse for post-poning moves towards inclusion. Ingenuity, knowledge of pupils' needs, professional advice and staff goodwill appear more than adequately to compensate for deficiencies in physical provision.

6

SELF-ADVOCACY AND INCLUSION

As we noted in chapter 1, the principle of self-advocacy is one against which the activities of any inclusive project must be judged. Consistent with the notion of inclusion is the principle that children and young people should be allowed and enabled to determine their own future, and that they should have a say in the way that their schooling proceeds. The alternative to self-advocacy, as Mittler (1996) points out, is a continuation of a situation in which professionals dominate decision-making about people with disabilities. In such a situation, children's abilities are often underestimated and they are put in situations which are inappropriate and in which they are open to indignity and injustice.

Mittler (1996: 280) quotes from the FEU (1990) the core components of self-advocacy, namely

- being able to express thoughts and feelings with assertiveness, if necessary;
- being able to make choices and decisions;
- having clear knowledge and information about rights;
- being able to make changes.

Mason and Rieser (1995) emphasise that the needs of disabled students as individuals cannot be met unless they are encouraged to have the confidence to explain the personal implications of their disablement and discuss the sort of support they feel they need. A school policy addressing the aspects of self-advocacy outlined below would, they suggest, help to nurture this kind of confidence:

> Do the disabled children have control over the help they are given? Do they attend the reviews of their statement (if they have one)? Are they consulted about facilities or equipment? How do they describe themselves? Are they allowed to complain about (evaluate) their treatment by staff or pupils in the school? Did disabled people help to write the policy? What words or phrases do the disabled members of the school find offensive? How would they like this to be dealt with?
>
> (Mason and Rieser, 1995: 43)

While the emphasis here is on ways of enabling self-advocacy for children with disabilities, the ethic of self-advocacy applies with equal force to all children in an inclusive school. Indeed, it is only through equality of approach that children with special needs will not be identified through the singular use of a procedure especially for them.

The entitlement to self-advocacy – or rather the lack of entitlement – afforded to children and young people in the UK is brought into focus if the legislative framework here is compared with that operating in Massachusetts in the USA. There, the particular version of PL 94-142 (the Education for All Handicapped Children Act) is known as Chapter 766 and it contains the following provisions for students who are over fourteen (taken from Vaughan and Shearer, 1986):

- the right to a pre-evaluation meeting;
- the right to be present at team meetings and to help write their own IEP;
- the right to have language used at the team meeting which is the same as that used at home;
- the right to see all records that the school has on file;
- the right to progress reports twice a year if the student requests them.

These rights are in stark contrast to the meagre offerings of the 1981 Education Act in the UK, although the 1993 Education Act with its Code of Practice (DfE, 1994) imposes more obligations on schools by way of integrative practice. In particular, schools must publish in their policies on special educational needs their procedures for ensuring integration and for discussion and partnership with parents. However, it is a source of regret that many schools failed to include these matters in their school policies (see Tarr and Thomas, 1997; OFSTED 1996b).

WAYS OF FINDING OUT WHAT CHILDREN WANT

If one wants to know what children want, the simple solution is surely to ask them. However, schools have for so long worked under principles of benevolent paternalism that the practice of asking children what they like or dislike about their schooling does not come easily. Lip service is sometimes paid to the children's 'voice' through the use of a school council, which in many schools has little real impact on practice (see Garner and Sandow, 1995). Indeed, so entrenched are the hierarchical principles under which many schools operate, that one could not be sure of an honest (as distinct from compliant) response from many children if they are asked for an opinion.

How, then, can children be *enabled* to give their views, opinions and ideas? Armstrong *et al.* (1993) review some of the existing work, noting that there has been an increased interest in children's accounts recently, with an increased validity being attached to these accounts, particularly in relation to education in the mainstream.

65

Another question which has to be posed with children who have disabilities is how to give voice to the feelings and concerns of children who have serious communication difficulties associated with their disabilities. Those difficulties may be due to problems of physical articulation or to learning difficulties. One of the central concerns of researchers lies in developing more effective ways of enabling children and young people with serious learning difficulties to articulate their wishes and needs effectively. Booth and Booth (1996) discuss some of the strategies they have developed in response to this challenge, which they characterise as entailing four possible problems for the interviewer: inarticulacy, unresponsiveness, lack of a concrete frame of reference and difficulties with the idea of time.

In the same context, the techniques of facilitated communication (FC) (see Biklen, 1990) have been proffered as a means of helping people with severe communication problems (especially people with autism) to articulate their views. Aside from the use of alphabet boards and electronic communicators, this technique embodies the following advice for facilitators. They should:

- be unpatronising, self-effacing and not use labels;
- believe in the person's competence;
- provide physical support (e.g. wrist support) in the use of equipment;
- be positive with the person;
- watch for other signs of communication (e.g. by eye pointing);
- provide opportunity for practice;
- avoid a test-like situation.

Most of this seems like useful advice. However, such remarkable claims have been made for the success of FC that questions have been raised as to its true value (see Hastings, 1996, and also chapter 7 below). The optimism of the proponents of FC is seen in sharp relief when set against the continuing reluctance of teachers (remarked on by Wade and Moore, 1993) to recognise the value of disabled students' views.

Techniques of communication are indeed important for self-advocacy in schools. However, perhaps more fundamental to the development of practice which articulates the feelings and desires of the student involved are core changes to the way that the learning process at school is conceived. A key development in enabling self-advocacy, therefore, comes from recent reconceptualisations of curriculum and pedagogy in schools for children with severe learning difficulties. Here, the widely used behavioural curriculum placed decisions about what happened in classrooms firmly in the hands of professionals. Recent thought on pedagogy for these children stresses, by contrast, the centrality of the student in determining the shape and direction of activity. As Nind and Hewett put it, 'what happens will depend very much on the student, following his/her interests and lead' (1994: 14).

WHAT HAVE SPECIAL SCHOOL STUDENTS SAID?

Attempts to enable the feelings, needs and opinions of disabled children to be recognised by the educational community were made by Thomas (1982) and Anderson and Clarke (1982). Thomas revealed that the limited research which actually asked children what they wanted established a preference for mainstream schooling. Resentment was felt at being continually 'done to', often without adequate explanation. The study of Anderson and Clarke, which interviewed young people of fifteen to eighteen, also found a preference for mainstream schooling. One of its most important outcomes lay in the pinpointing of specific respects in which students felt a lack of control over their own lives:

- ignorance about their disabling condition;
- powerlessness regarding plans for transition between schools or to adult life; and
- inadequate preparation for independence, choice and responsibility in daily living.

Shelling (1996) drew similar conclusions following interviews with young adults who had recently left special schools, including some who had experienced mainstream schooling. The concerns of the interviewees proved to centre around low expectations (on the part of professionals), and a need for more choice, autonomy and equality for pupils. But since the feelings of these interviewees were by no means unanimously in favour of integrated education, Shelling concludes that discussion about appropriate schooling should be conducted in terms of the broader schemata of choice, autonomy and equality rather than the cruder notions of segregation or inclusion, which may mask the fine-grain detail of people's concerns.

Wade and Moore (1993) investigated the reactions of students with learning difficulties to questions on nine school-related topics. Students from all types of school along a continuum from complete segregation to complete inclusion were represented. A section of data on 'feeling different' indicated that although academic inferiority was sometimes a worry, inclusive settings were less likely to induce a poor self-image than segregated ones. Moreover, counselling and efforts aimed at increasing sensitivity of both teachers and able-bodied students could help to abate feelings of difference that did exist. This research, like the earlier accounts, emphasises the stated preference of children for education in a non-segregated setting, particularly for leisure pursuits (although many students expressed a dislike of breaktime because of cold and isolation).

The title of a chapter by Walsh (1993), 'How disabling any handicap is depends on the attitudes and actions of others', makes clear the importance of being able to speak up for oneself enough to influence those attitudes and actions. The author, a disabled ex-student, describes how her parents encouraged *all* their children to think hard about their own needs and interests and to communicate about these needs and interests to other people. She was able, perhaps unusually, to carry this process into school life and, with her family's backing, to challenge staff decisions made for her, for example that she couldn't do sport or learn Japanese. Involvement in discussions about subject choice is a crucial area for self-advocacy policies in schools.

The value of accounts such as Walsh's in enabling teachers to understand the perspectives of their students is discussed by Potts (1992), who emphasises that this is one way to try to even up the unequal power relationships which have no place in inclusive schooling. The work she introduces – four accounts of the effects of disablement in childhood – serves to illustrate the uniqueness of everyone's experience and, following from this, the futility and injustice of treating all disabled students the same. Given this uniqueness, Potts stresses the importance of a comprehensive knowledge of the needs, views and abilities of the individual in an inclusive setting. Research by Beveridge (1996) on what pupils classified as having severe learning difficulties felt about their participation in a link with a mainstream school has a similar point to make about the diversity of individual response and the need to take this variation into account when planning the development of the scheme.

Lewis (1995a) points out that there are many surveys of mainstream students' views of schooling which can shed light on the feelings and educational careers of lower attaining pupils. She quotes, for example, a study which indicated that children with special needs were more likely both to bully and be bullied, and that they were 'more likely than other children to record negative feelings, such as loneliness and unhappiness, about school' (1995a: 58). Her own research, which concentrated on special school students (many of whom had transferred from mainstream), discovered a high degree of satisfaction with special, as opposed to mainstream, schooling, which contrasted with the results of studies of *parental* satisfaction, such as those recorded by the Audit Commission (1992a).

Ways of resolving, or at least acknowledging, conflict between the views of parents and their disabled children have to be built into any system which attempts to empower both parties to express needs and concerns. For parents do not necessarily express their children's views (although they undeniably express their sincere views as to what is best for their children). This dilemma of how far to accept the parent as advocate is partly addressed by Chinapah (1989) in discussing counselling for physically disabled students, but features little in the literature on parental involvement in advocacy.

Overwhelmingly here the focus is on the relationship between parents and professionals, as distinct from parents and children. Orlowska (1995), reviewing the literature on parent-to-professional communication, points to some of the obstacles in the way of closer involvement and better communication. She identifies lack of time on the part of both parents and professionals, differing visions of a child's future, reluctance of professionals to recognise the validity of non-politically correct views or a questioning attitude from parents, and the need for the effects of decisions on the rest of the child's family to be considered. Parents whose commitments prevent them from joining high-profile parents' groups should not be assumed to be bad parents who don't want to act as advocates, she says, but should be approached on a different, individual basis. Madden (1995) summarises these points in his comment that parents should be seen as part of the solution rather than as part of the problem. The contribution of such professional/parent groups towards the development of inclusive classrooms in New Zealand is discussed by Ballard (1995), who recommends the carrying out of action-research by parents and disabled people as a way of illuminating the world-views underlying school policies for exclusion and inclusion. He further suggests that 'family networks' be created whose members act as supports and advocates for inclusive practice.

Broomhead and Darley (1992) report on a group which evolved from a research project which aimed to increase active parental participation in procedures such as assessment and statementing, as well as guiding parents in the provision of advice and support to others. Its advocacy role was emphasised when budget cuts threatened services. A project described by Mapp (1995) goes a step further, in attempting to include people with learning difficulties themselves, as well as their parents, in the monitoring and review of services in South Wales. Training packs have been provided to increase parental confidence and funding is available to reimburse participants for expenses and loss of earnings. However, few parents of younger children become involved:

> You have to persuade them that their views matter and that they are an important part of the monitoring process and are going to make a difference to the way services are provided and delivered. Parents who have got all this caring to do think 'What good would I do?'
>
> (Mapp, 1995: 17)

It is noticeable that most of these initiatives are community-based rather than school-based and that the professionals involved are not, in the main, from education. This is presumably due to the small numbers of disabled students currently in mainstream schooling and the perception that influencing schools in favour of inclusion therefore has to be orchestrated from the outside, as one of the ingredients in Wolfensberger's 'advocacy salad' (quoted by Hall, 1992: 21).

SELF-ADVOCACY AND THE SCHOOL

There are few illustrations in the literature of the direction in which school-based advocacy projects might go. Garner and Sandow (1995) make some helpful suggestions on the way that self-advocacy can be developed in schools, highlighting the importance of promoting *effective* school councils (as opposed to *notional* ones), and communication systems with parents and children.

Greenwood pursues a train of thought suggested by the 1994 Code of Practice recommendations on eliciting, recording and acting upon pupils' perceptions of themselves as learners. She argues that unless the views of *all* pupils are sought, there is a danger that a focus on disabled individuals will lead away from inclusion towards a greater emphasis on difference:

> Pupils need to feel that they belong to school and classroom communities in which all members contribute to a continuous dialogue about learning and in so doing develop a shared language for talking about and reflecting upon learning. If they are to be empowered as learners, pupils need to feel that they belong to communities which invite and respond to all pupils' perspectives on schooling as well as their shared and individual perceptions of themselves as learners in school settings.
>
> (Greenwood, 1995: 178)

Tamaren (1992) points out that:

> Children are often relieved to learn that every individual learns differently and has particular areas of strength and weakness. With this insight, students can reflect on their own manner of learning as well as develop an understanding and sensitivity regarding the learning challenges of other students.
>
> (Tamaren, 1992: 26)

Her introduction to the self-advocacy curriculum guide *I Make a Difference!*, based on a programme initiated in Massachusetts, highlights the aims of such a programme in contributing to an atmosphere supporting real dialogue in inclusive classrooms: building the self-esteem of all pupils, providing models of interaction through teacher example, celebrating co-operation, encouraging peer support and sensitivity, and establishing ground-rules for expectations of good behaviour.

Part II

FROM SPECIAL SCHOOLS TO INCLUSION SERVICES

In this second part of the book we give a detailed case study of one special school's confrontation with the facts and logic of inclusion and its journey, along with its partner schools, in transforming itself from a special school to an inclusion service. It is the story of a group of schools in which teachers, assistants and children have striven to make inclusion happen. The findings of an eighteen-month study evaluating the success of the inclusion project are given in detail in the chapters that follow.

Chapter 7 describes the framework for the research and the way in which we decided to go about undertaking an in-depth case study. To set the scene in which the project was undertaken, we then give a description of the inception of the Somerset Inclusion Project, including a narrative of the change from the headteacher. The remaining chapters each describe an aspect of the research – into the process of changing from a school to a service, into the social and curricular inclusion of the children and young people concerned, and into their academic progress. The division of inclusive experience in this way – into curricular, social and academic – is perhaps a little artificial. Although it provides a convenient way of dividing the analysis, it gives the impression that inclusive experiences are divisible and compartmentalised. In fact, one of the clearest findings emerging from the research is that inclusion is about a whole experience; it is, as much as anything, about an attitude on the part of receiving staff. There are no curricular levers to be pulled or social buttons to be pressed which will effect inclusion. On the contrary, children may be fully included even if they are exempted from the official curriculum, as long as the experiences which they are receiving are ones which promote their involvement and acceptance in the classroom.

Throughout, we have put the findings into the context of the discussion in the first part of the book and made recommendations which we hope will be of interest to others who are considering similar ventures.

7

RESEARCHING INCLUSION, AND METHODS USED IN THIS RESEARCH

BACKGROUND AND PRINCIPLES

Hegarty *et al.* (1981) set the scene for research on integration and inclusion with great clarity. They say that it is not for the researcher to answer the big questions, such as, 'Include or segregate?' As we have noted earlier, answers to these questions – even if they were clearly defined questions in themselves (which they are not) – are more for society than for researchers to answer, since answers rest on the ethical stance taken by the society answering. The researchers' contribution, say Hegarty and his colleagues, is an ancillary one, providing evidence and helping to frame the terms of reference. In providing such evidence, the researcher will look at the effects of inclusion on the students and the school. It is then for others to make judgements on the basis of the evidence. In the final analysis, judgements will be made on a mix of empirical evidence and the values held by society.

The research into the Somerset Inclusion Project has the advantage of standing on a superstructure of research which has been undertaken in the fifteen years that have intervened since the seminal study of Hegarty and his colleagues, and in that time there has also been significant public debate about the merits or otherwise of integration and inclusion. While the results of comparative and other research have shown difficult-to-interpret results, as we have noted continually in the preceding chapters, it is interesting that it is Hegarty's own conclusion now that

> the absence of a clear-cut balance of advantage [in the research evidence] supports integration. There has to be a presumption in favour of integration and, in the absence of decisive countervailing evidence, it must be regarded as a central principle governing provision.
> (Hegarty, 1993b: 198)

Hegarty's conclusions reflect those of society, which appear to be crystallising in favour of inclusion, as we noted in chapter 1. The Inclusion Project evaluation therefore rests on a knowledge-base different from that which guided early studies of integration, and it also adopts a different stance.

Other influences have also played their part on the nature of research in education, especially where research questions address the experiences of disabled children and young people. There has been a reaction against research 'on' disabled people, and there is now rightly more emphasis on the involvement of the people who were often formerly thought of as 'subjects'. Not only this, but there has been an increasing realisation that children can and should be directly involved in the formulation of research questions, share in the findings and discuss the conclusions. All 'stakeholders' should be involved.

There is also an increasing realisation now of the role of the observer not only in interpreting the results of the research but also in setting its agenda. This agenda-setting goes beyond the framing of the questions for the research or even assisting in disentangling the threads which go to make up the weave of empirical and ethical issues that we have just referred to. It extends to an examination of how researchers – by their language, their assumptions, their jargon, even their demeanour and dress – go (in sociological jargon) to 'construct' the research situation, as Clough (1995) notes. Oliver (1992) has taken this reasoning one step further in insisting that research is a political process and that it should not collude – merely by its construction – in what some have called the oppression of disabled people. Rather, it should be 'emancipatory'.

While one can follow this logic, it is not a logic with which researchers need necessarily align themselves. The newer qualitative approaches have deep roots in various traditions – from Kierkegaard's insistence on the legitimacy of the subjective view, to Gadamer's hermeneutics – and their recent appropriation by 'anti-theorists' (see Skinner, 1985) such as Foucault does not give legitimacy to the deliberate use or construction of research as a political instrument, as Oliver and others suggest. Indeed, such a stance would be antithetical to all that Foucault stood for. He talked about dismantling and discarding one's own theoretical framework and political starting point (with all the epistemological baggage that these entail) in order to develop a 'polyhedron of intelligibility' with regard to a particular situation.

This is not merely academic banter.[1] The point of discussing it here is to establish the legitimacy of non-aligned, or non-partisan, research in a political context (that of inclusion) in which there are forceful demands for research to take a particular position in effecting change. The pioneers of hermeneutics have enabled researchers to acknowledge and take advantage of the situatedness of their view. Their arguments about the richness of data which comes from observing as a participant (not pretending that one is a fly on the wall, having no effect) have been accepted and used in this research. As Gadamer (quoted in Outhwaite, 1985) makes clear, we should not presume to research as though there were some virgin territory of facts, but rather should accept and accommodate our own prejudices.

This does not, however, extend to a licence to change the shape of research and engineer its results with a particular view in mind. As Hegarty pointed out (see p. 73 above), researchers must have a certain humility, since their findings will surely lack credibility and the power to change if they read like a manifesto. The stance taken in the undertaking of this research is therefore that the researchers recognise and acknowledge the principled decision which has led to a move to inclusion, and likewise acknowledge the already existing knowledge-base upon which such a decision is taken. These set the frame for the research. However, they do not constrain its findings. If, for instance, parents say, 'We don't agree with inclusion' (which one or two have) this must be reported, though it is necessary also to interpret what they have said, and to attempt to understand such a comment in the light of the experiences they relate.

WHAT THIS RESEARCH IS NOT

It is important also to say what the research reported here cannot do. Much commentary surrounds the relative efficacy of qualitative and quantitative approaches to evaluation; the general arguments against an over-reliance upon supposedly objective designs and quantitative methods were summarised well by Parlett and Hamilton (1987) and have been rehearsed ever since (see, for instance, Oakley, 1996). The arguments between what Cronbach (1982, 1987) calls the 'scientistic ideal' and the 'humanistic ideal' are long-standing and need not be rehearsed here, though it is worth noting that a more rational and pragmatic tone has recently entered the debate (see Hammersley, 1992). Suffice it to say that the particular characteristics of inclusion and inclusion projects make them especially difficult to evaluate by controlled experimentation (or indeed by the oft-preferred alternative of the field researcher, quasi-experimentation[2]). In addition, this evaluation of the Inclusion Project contains particular features:

- Because the research started at the beginning of the Inclusion Project, there are no reliable or consistent 'before' measures of children's progress, and it cannot therefore compare progress 'before and after'.
- Because it studies a limited set of institutions (four), and a few children (nine), it cannot claim to be representative of a larger population; it is a study of the working of a particular project, from which inferences may be drawn for other projects. Generalisations, however, are not possible.[3]
- As with all other studies of integrative practice, the heterogeneity of the children and their complex disabling conditions means that accurate assignment of children to experimental and control groups is impossible. Nor can there be a genuine control group in a situation in which the group being studied is self-selecting (for parents will always have a legal right to select schools).

These, then, are some of the boundary-lines within which this research is set.

CHARACTERISTICS AND AIMS OF THE RESEARCH

This research is a case study. For Hammersley, a 'case' is a

> phenomenon about which data are collected and/or analysed . . . that corresponds to the type of phenomena to which the main claims of a study relate. . . . It [a case study] involves the investigation of a *relatively small* number of *naturally occurring* (rather than researcher-created) cases.
>
> (Hammersley, 1992: 184–185)

This particular case study incorporates a number of methodological considerations. It examines the experiences of a limited number of children and young people as they have moved from a special school to mainstream schools. It examines this experience by observing them in class, by asking questions of them, of their parents and their teachers, headteachers and support assistants. Given that the project is an ongoing one, the thrust of the research is not merely retrospective and summative, but it is also developmental. In other words, its aim is to reflect on the information given and collated to suggest how this and other projects may develop in the future.

With the limits enumerated above in mind, the goals of the research become clearer:

- The research is of a particular situation which it seeks to understand in depth.
- It seeks to understand the process of change in the Inclusion Project and the academic and social experiences of the children as they have passed through its first year.
- It contains elements of action research, in that it is designed with the prospect of research informing practice. The insights gained will also help to inform practice in other similar situations.

Given these limits and goals, the research examines in detail the progress of the Inclusion Project using a variety of methods. It uses interview data with all the principal participants in the project, including students, parents, staff in partner schools and Inclusion Project staff. It employs observation, with the researchers making classroom observations and taking field notes of their impressions, discussions and observations. It uses documentary analysis and techniques such as sociometry to help build a picture of students' social relationships.

These methods are now well recognised, understood and described (see, for example, Burgess, 1984), and there is no need to explicate them in further detail here. The validity of the data obtained from them and the analysis resulting from them rests in part on assumptions about the truth of the accounts and observations which participants and observers bring to a situation. Ferguson *et al.* (1992) discuss interestingly the use of interpretive research in understanding the experiences of disabled people.

One of the corollaries of the position we took in undertaking this research is that there is no clear research question which can be set with any validity at the outset, since the themes must emerge from the process of research as it proceeds. An assumption of such a position is that it is not for the researcher to set the issues with pre-formed ideas. Nevertheless, it is possible to frame the research by restating one of its goals, which is *to understand the process of change in the Inclusion Project and the academic and social experiences of the children as they have passed through its first year.*

SAMPLE

The notion of what Glaser and Strauss (1967) call 'statistical sample' is anti-thetical to qualitative research. There is no *a priori* assumption that the sample is representative of a wider population. Glaser and Strauss draw the distinction between 'theoretical sampling' and 'statistical sampling'. The purpose of the former, they say, is to discover categories and their properties and 'to suggest the interrelationships into a theory' (1967: 62). The adequate theoretical sample is judged on how well it enables a 'saturating' of categories, or in other words, whether it amasses sufficient data to ensure that a full set of categories is obtained.

In the sense that this is a theoretical sample, the number of students and institutions is immaterial. It is important, however, for the reader to have some knowledge of the backgrounds of the students. These are as in Table 7.1, with all information anonymised. Anonymity is always used in the analysis which follows this chapter, with varying degrees of anonymity used depending on the sensitivity of the information being disclosed. Sometimes pseudonyms are used, but given the small number of institutions, children and young people involved, these are often too transparent to be of any value. Where this is the case, and where the sensitivity of any disclosure demands it, identity is revealed only by general identifiers such as '[Inclusion Project student]' or '[Teacher, primary]'; in other cases even these identifiers are withheld.

The children involved were the nine children whom the Inclusion Project was supporting in mainstream from September 1995: six in Somerset primary schools and three in the secondary sector. Four of the primary children were already in mainstream, and two of these had been there for more than two years. All three secondary students transferred from Princess Margaret School in September 1995. Most of the students were wheelchair-users, with a range of physical, communication and learning difficulties. More details of the Inclusion Project students, their histories and progress, can be found in chapter 8.

Parents and young people were all involved in the process of the research, which included detailed interviews with them. All prospective participants received a letter introducing the research, its purpose and the researchers, and requesting consent. Questions were invited via 'phone,

Table 7.1 The schools and the students (pseudonyms)

School (pseudonym)	Inclusion Project student (pseudonym)	School year-group
Primary School A: Heather Grove	Caroline	Y2
Primary School B: Oakwood	Luke	Y5
Primary School C: West Hill	Joe	Y4/5 ('Class 3')
	James, Tom	Y4/5 ('Class 4')
	Daniel	Y1 ('Class 1')
Secondary School: Meadow Hill	Jerry	Y11
	Greg, Mike	Y10
Princess Margaret School (own name)		

letter or intermediary, but none was received. No one who was approached refused to participate, and further discussion about the purpose and conduct of the research often took place as a preliminary to interview sessions. Where school records were examined, parents and students were asked for their consent beforehand.

The schools which the students attended are described in more detail in chapter 8. Summary information is given in Table 7.2.

Overall, seventy-three informants – staff, parents and students from the schools and the Inclusion Project – contributed to the data analysed. The status of these informants is usually clear in the analysis, though specific identities are protected through pseudonyms or by complete anonymity. Teachers have been referred to as 'classteacher', 'headteacher', 'subject teacher' etc. where relevant. The designation LSA (Learning Support Assistant) has been used for both school and Inclusion Project support assistants.

PROCEDURE

Instruments

Burgess (1982) claims that interviewing is the most commonly used instrument in qualitative research, and it was the most important instrument used by Hegarty *et al.* (1981) in their research into integration. The main procedures used in this research comprised interviews and informal observation, with documentary analysis and sociometry also being used where appropriate.

Interviews were semi-structured, with the aim always being to allow interviewees to shift the agenda and contribute their own line of thought whenever they wished. The aim was to obtain accurate uninhibited accounts from informants that were based in their personal experience and knowledge.

Table 7.2 The participating schools

School	Brief description
Princess Margaret School (PMS)	all-age school for physically disabled children which has re-modelled itself to the Somerset Inclusion Project
Primary School A: Heather Grove	village primary school in new buildings some distance from PMS
Primary School B: Oakwood	large urban primary school some distance from PMS
Primary School C: West Hill	new, purpose-built, medium-sized primary school in same town as PMS
Secondary School: Meadow Hill	new, purpose-built comprehensive in same town as PMS

Classroom observations, general observations and field notes were made throughout the research. While all students were happy to be interviewed and observed, the secondary students were not willing to participate in the planned diary scheme. Greg and Jerry made one or two sporadic entries, via computer or scribe, in the first term, but then found the work too onerous on top of all the demands of the curriculum. Mike did not want to take part at all, since he felt included at Meadow Hill and did not want to dwell on things which made him different.

Classteachers in the primary schools were asked to carry out a sociogram – an exercise in which every student names peers whom they would like to play with and/or work with.

Pupils' school records were available, with students' and parents' consent, for data on National Curriculum (NC) levels, comparisons of special and mainstream timetables, and teachers' comments on progress of all kinds, lending a longitudinal aspect to the discussion of some issues. School SEN policies illuminated aspects of the context of inclusion.

The research was guided as it proceeded not only by the findings as they appeared but also by the comments and observations of a termly advisory group which comprised members – one of whom was disabled – from academic, voluntary and professional backgrounds.

Analysis

All data were analysed using a constant-comparative method. This involves examination and re-examination of the data to discover the inherent themes. Themes which appear to emerge from a first reading are refined and developed as more data emerges and as data from new sources is triangulated with already analysed data and with insights which have emerged from a review of the literature. McCracken (1988) develops the constant-comparative method and an adaptation of his methodology for data-analysis was used here.

It is worth noting that efforts have been made to include the 'voice' of the student in this research. Recognition of the fact that children have a voice which must be heard should not thereby imply a denial that there will be questions raised concerning access to data, and concerning validity in the analysis and interpretation of data obtained – as there will be in any research. In addition, when considering children with disabilities (who may not be conventionally articulate), there are questions to be considered in the interpretation of what is being said, sometimes tersely, sometimes seemingly over-compliantly. The aim must be to avoid re-interpreting, over-interpreting or misinterpreting. Much discussion and controversy surrounds this issue (cf. Biklen, 1990; Cummins and Prior, 1992; Biklen, 1993; and Hastings, 1996). The aim was to gather views and feelings as naturalistically as feasible, acknowledging and taking into account at all times the concerns just expressed. However, the difficulty of interviewing Luke, the student with severely limited communication, was extreme, even with the help of a speech therapist, and it would be unwise to regard the interpretation of his answers as definitive, since they depend on facial gestures, and often arm movements when using the 'talking book' and the 'Total Communication' system. (Booth and Booth, 1996, discuss interviewing techniques which may be useful in similar circumstances.)

RELIABILITY

The establishment of validity in qualitative research rests on assumptions about – and acceptance of – the knowledge and insights of informants, and the issue of reliability is complex. Some claim that the notion of reliability in qualitative research is a misnomer, misappropriating a concept from the normative paradigm. For there is no expectation that qualitative data will be reliable in the sense meant in quantitative research; the assumption is that in a small, local situation knowledge is specific and findings are not necessarily replicable. However, it may be that there are 'different sides to the story', and in this sense data and analysis from only one source may indeed constitute a distorted picture.

For this reason qualitative research usually contains elements of triangulation. Cohen and Manion define triangulation as 'the use of two or more methods of data collection in the study of some aspect of human behaviour' (1985: 254), while Elliot and Adelman define it as 'gathering accounts of a teaching situation from three quite different points of view; namely those of the teacher, pupils and a participant observer' (1976: 76). Burgess (1984) resolves the differences in these definitions by clarifying that the term refers not only to the combining of methods of investigation but also a number of data sources or a number of accounts of events.

Cronbach (1987) has noted that data developed from different kinds of studies should be viewed as interactive; data from different kinds of study ought to be able to feed each other in order to identify further questions or areas for revision.

All these elements of triangulation are used in this study: different methods are used to illuminate the situation and different informants' accounts are employed. All are reviewed in the light of other research and commentary.

ORGANISATION OF THE FINDINGS

Three foci were used to organise the findings:

- the process of change;
- curricular and academic experiences; and
- social experiences.

The researchers' presence in the schools of the study and in children's homes was undertaken in the spirit of an ethnography. Observation was continuous and field notes were made continually. While there were specific foci to the interviews, observations were wide-ranging and mixed. It was in subsequent analysis that the totality of data in the field notes, observations and transcripts was organised around the three bulleted sub-headings above and themes then drawn, using the constant-comparative procedure outlined.

THE PLACE AND THE PEOPLE

This case study is of a particular special school and a particular group of partner schools in which we have examined in depth the process of developing inclusion. While we cannot generalise from the experiences of the staff and students in these schools, we can draw inferences from those experiences, as long as we are aware of their context. That context is given in this chapter.

It is worth noting here that although the school at the centre of the Inclusion Project was a school for physically disabled children, the experiences gained from its closure and the setting up of the Inclusion Project are relevant for all schools. The principles behind inclusion are not bounded by the old categories of 'handicap', nor indeed by the notion of learning difficulties. The principles embodied in inclusion are concerned with a philosophy of acceptance and providing a framework within which all children – regardless of ability, gender, language or cultural origin – can be valued equally, treated with respect and provided with equal opportunities at school. In other words, inclusion is not simply about including disabled pupils or those presumed to have learning difficulties, but about providing an environment in which all will thrive.

It is in this spirit that the analysis in the chapters which follow is offered. The history and background of the project are given in the rest of this chapter. We start with an interview with Dave Walker, the school's headteacher, as a dynamic narrative of the changes as they happened. In the second part of the chapter we give a factual account of the changes which took place in the special school prior to its transformation to a service. In the third part, we give biographies of the partner schools and the children and young people in the project.

INTERVIEW WITH THE HEADTEACHER

In this first part of the chapter we give an edited transcript of Julie Webb's interview with Dave Walker, who at the time of the interview was the principal of PMS and in charge of the Inclusion Project. We intended in this interview to find out about the process which had led Walker and his staff to bring about the closure of the institution which employed them.

What in fact emerged from the interview was a remarkable personal account of the changes in thinking which led Walker and his colleagues to embrace inclusion. This was not simply a technical description of change but a narrative about the way it happened – from the seed of an idea to the difficult and sometimes painful process of turning that idea into actuality. This included confronting the reality that a school which had been a second home to many children and a secure place of employment for staff would have to close.

What is striking in this is that detailed plans arose not from some grand strategy and business plan. Instead, they grew out of the congruent personal philosophies of key staff, the chemistry of personal relationships and the happenstance of having local headteachers – and in particular one especially energetic and sympathetic head from a nearby primary school – who agreed with Walker and his colleagues and were prepared to take risks. It required a particular confluence of personalities and principles to make the project happen. In particular, it needed the courage to see those principles through to their logical conclusion. Rather than destroy the quality and flavour of that narrative, the interview is given in full.

A host of matters is covered here: the initial idea; the developing of a mission; the setting of working groups; the employment of consultants; the fears of staff; the anxieties of parents; the key role of Barnardos as an institution which exists to promote children's interests; the role of the LEA and negotiations with them; the issue of choice for disabled people; the future.

JW   *Could you tell me about how the inclusion initiative came about originally?*

DW   Yes. It's quite a long story really, I think, because there's two things that happened. If you like, there's the outer events and for me personally there were some inner things that were going on as well. In 1991, I'd been [headteacher] at the school three years, and in that time we increased the occupancy, we built the school up from a position where it had been in some difficulties, and it was doing well. So we agreed that at that point we would just look around and see what was on the horizon in special educational needs. And we looked at a lot of things, not just at inclusion. We looked at things like conductive education, special therapies, all sorts of stuff. One of the things that *I* went to, and Steve Connor[1] went to, was the first Inclusion Conference, which was held in Cardiff . . . they invited the Canadians over, George Flynn, Marsha Forest, John O'Brien and Judith Snow. And Barnardos committed resources to staff going, so there were quite a lot of Barnardos staff there. There were something like ten Barnardos staff there.

Some of the things that George Flynn was saying about the

83

outcomes for people who'd been in special education: joblessness, alcoholism, potential for crime, vulnerability . . . all those things hit me very powerfully at a time when I was personally feeling quite vulnerable. And also I think that the sense of – there was an alternative to the special school. And it affected me a lot.

And I think the other important element was that Steve Connor had gone as well. So I wasn't going to something and then coming away on my own – I actually had somebody I could talk things through with. Steve and I *did* talk it through, an awful lot. I think Steve is extraordinarily good at thinking strategically. You know, he can get hold of something and he can have a sense of how you could move towards it. He's better at that than I am. But where I think I can help is that I can operationalise that. Kind of, 'OK, if that's the direction we're going down, this is what we need to do.' And so between us I think we actually formed a very good alliance. And it was quickly apparent – it was shortly after that that Vivian[2] was appointed as deputy and we had a clear ally in Vivian. And Peggy had taken over as administrator around that time and Peggy was also an ally. So as the senior management team we were quite strong.

JW   *So would you say that those issues, of outcomes for segregated schooling, were something that you hadn't really devoted much time to before? Was there not much research available in this country or . . . ?*

DW   My own background before being at PMS was children who have emotional and behavioural difficulties. And I suppose at some level I'd always been concerned with *those* children that there was very little follow-up after school as to what happened to them. I think perhaps, I don't know, I was busy *doing* the job, and, in a way, not knowing about what happens afterwards is kind of – useful. You don't have to think about it. And once it had been articulated for me by George Flynn, I think there were two things: one was it felt right when he said, you know, 'These are the outcomes.' I thought, yes, at some level I knew this, and I think the second thing was, once you know something, once *I* know something I can't ignore it, can't leave it alone . . .

So I think at that point it was clear for me – it sort of emerged over the discussions I had with Steve – in effect I was being faced with two choices: one was to leave and go and do something else somewhere else, or two was to take this school through the process – either I was going to leave the school or the school was going to leave me. And I suppose I began to – it wasn't an immediate thing – if you put something far enough in the future it doesn't feel like it's too desperate here and now, does it – so notions about including children and so on were talked about at that point about five years down the line and we were quite clear in our own minds it would take about five years to do this. And we held to that in fact. But by doing that we gave ourselves time, I think, to say, 'Well, OK, so are there some small things that we can do now?' And I think that was actually, well for me it was quite important.

JW   *So you're saying you held to that view that it would take about five years but it's taken a lot less than that hasn't it?*

DW   No, I think it's taken – I mean '91 was when the idea first came up – and '96 [the closure of PMS]. If you look at what's happened in that time there have been a number of steps, I think. The first step, following that conference, was that we fairly quickly got into the partnership with Somerset, around Val Lane – the joint appointment of an advisory teacher.

JW   *So that was a direct result of your going to this conference and seeing the need for links with the mainstream?*

DW   We'd talked about it before but it certainly gave added impetus, and it clarified for me a route for the children back into mainstream.

JW   *Yes. So that was seen as her main role?*

DW   Yes, that's right. Whereas before, the discussion had been about her acting as a support to the teachers here rather than being a route out. I think that was one point. And the second was that as a management team we began to develop the school purpose, you know, that statement.

JW   *The 'Mission'?*

DW   Yes. And I don't know about other schools, but perhaps unusually, we actually saw that as a working document, the thing that we were working to. And so I think that what followed from that document was the need for us to involve other staff with the discussion and the debate and so on. And originally it was called the 'Futures Group'.

JW   *Oh yes.*

DW   And then we had the 'Primary Group' and the 'Secondary Group'. But I actually think that the primary and secondary group were a group too many. That was part of the aspect of us still being too inward-looking, I think. But we did. The other thing was we took on the first consultant that we had – we took on Angie Ash. And Angie did, I think, some important stuff around, in particular, helping us as a management team to get our heads clear as to where we needed to be concentrating our efforts, and a basic round-up of research. So the value for us as managers was that that round-up of research almost became – well for me it almost became a mantra: inclusion would work if it was resourced properly, if there was commitment, and if it was planned properly. And having a simple message about the research becomes very valuable because if you're talking to sceptical parents or whatever, getting into the 'perhapses' and 'maybes' is not going to help you.

JW   *They need a clear message to take away and talk about?*

DW   That's right. So having it presented in that way, although in some ways it was an oversimplification . . . it was actually really useful. And I think there was a number of things that happened as a result of Val Lane's appointment. There were voices within the school who were sceptical about the possibility of any child being able to manage in mainstream – that kind of ethos: they're here therefore they must need to be here and they could never possibly manage outside. So one of the things that happened was Paul – was the first child that went into mainstream and that voice changed: 'Well, maybe *some* . . . '. And I think that the next thing that happened was we had a whole-school training day, which gave people, the whole staff, a chance to talk about what they thought was best for the children and what their hopes and fears were and so on. And it was interesting – what for me was powerful about that was that I did have some complaints from some members of staff afterwards that they had felt afraid of putting forward a view that said that segregation was best. And I think what was powerful for me in that was a sense that actually that's the power of the message – that actually we've got enough people here saying inclusion's best that the people who are promoting segregation are on the defensive. That's not what I'd expected at all. It was quite the opposite.

JW   *I suppose you have to allow for one being seen as politically correct?*

DW   Of course. That's right. But it did say to me that those people who'd promoted segregation are actually on the defensive. And that told me we could be bolder. So the next thing, I think, that happened was in a way as a management team we'd got to a point of: we knew we had to make a big step forward. And looking back it's quite obvious that what we had to do was set a date for closing the school. And I think we did everything but that – we just avoided that, for all sorts of purely internal reasons. . . . And in a way, firstly, we were rescued a bit, I think, by two things. One was we had projected that the numbers at FE were going to go right down . . . so suddenly we had a window of opportunity to actually close the FE painlessly. And the second was that Carol Bannister[3] came to us and said, 'I want to take the class to West Hill.'[4] So in a way that was both positive – we were still moving in the right direction – I also think it enabled us to, enabled *me*, I think, particularly, to avoid the big decision about 'When does this close?' So on the positive side I do think that with Carol's initiative particularly I saw West Hill as developing a bridgehead – you know, actually we'll have some children there, we're going to have some staff working there: that's a very powerful message. And I was very clear in my own mind that both kids – only two kids went – if that required five teachers and twenty-seven assistants I didn't care what it cost – at that point. It was vital that we got in – it was going to succeed.

JW *The implication of that is that once those kids are out there's nobody coming into the PMS secondary {department}?*

DW That's right. And so it begins to have that impact.

JW *At no point was Barnardos providing the impetus for any of that? That was purely . . . ?*

DW No – and it is unusual for Barnardos but I think it's fair to say that we were pushing Barnardos. There was a process with Barnardos where we were writing papers, in effect saying 'This is what we're doing.' And gaining permission. In fact with West Hill, Carol came and saw me, we saw the parents, we had a ding-dong with some of them and others were *quietly* supportive – I wish they'd – well anyway . . .

But it was actually just before the Easter that we met with them, and at that point we had nothing on paper, we didn't have a proposal on paper, so I actually sat down and wrote: this is what we're proposing to do, etc. etc. Got it agreed with Paul,[5] showed it to the parents. I said, 'This is it, this is what it looks like,' and then only after doing that took the decision that we were going to have to go ahead with West Hill. We'd talked about it on the basis of 'What do you think of this as an idea?' And it was only when it was quite clear, with implacable opposition from two parents, that our job was to *do* something and get something on paper.

So Barnardos wasn't involved at all at that level. And equally, really and truly, neither were the LEA. You know, we just did it and *then* involved them afterwards. And I'm actually really pleased now that that's how we did it because I think if we'd once got ourselves tangled up with the bureaucracy we'd still be faffing about.

So what that then did was – well, West Hill worked well, there's no question about that, so we had to do two things I think. One was to develop a proposal for what has in effect become the 16+ project, so that took up quite a lot of energy and time, developing the business plan for that. The second was, we couldn't avoid any longer the decision about how long is it to close the rest of the school. And we had a day on it, with Steve. And eventually we got to that question and Steve basically said, 'OK When? How many years?' And at that point I think I said something like, 'Well, there's still about four years', and we kind of looked at kids actually going through, about four, and somebody else said 'Five', and so on. And Steve said, 'Well, I was thinking more of one year.'

JW   *Oh!*

DW   Yes! Well, that's exactly the reaction we had: 'Oh my God!' and it was . . . I think he was absolutely spot-on. And it galvanised us – we were faced with: we can't drag this out over another five years, sometime, maybe never. And I think we then – again, one of the things that we didn't do was we really didn't look at: how could you do it? In the detail, for every kid. And so, thinking about it at that point, we actually had to look at that very carefully. And it was clear to us that actually it couldn't be achieved in one year. And so two was where we got to. And there was a further couple of weeks or so and we had a further meeting with Steve, and I think as the impact of that hit me I really began to feel very vulnerable. And I was actually in tears at that point around, you know: 'I don't know if I'm the person who can actually do this.'

And it was very – we were *all* in quite a state really. But I think that was also the point at which we realised, as a group, that we *could* do it, so long as we stuck together and supported one another. Which we've done.

JW   *There was still no partnership with the LEA at this stage?*

DW   There were talks with the LEA but they were fairly aimless. They weren't going anywhere. I think from the LEA's point of view we were not a high priority, that they were having all sorts of problems with EBD [emotional and behavioural difficulties], and one thing and another, and something that might happen three, four, five years down the line –

JW   *Concerning quite a small –*

DW   A small number of kids. Not very interested, basically this is small stuff. So we got agreement that we would involve the stakeholders . . . and two things followed from that: one, we had to tell the staff; two, we had to tell the parents.

JW   *And at that stage did you envisage all the children going into mainstream?*

DW   Yes. That's what we were saying, that we would close the school and we would work to make it possible for all the children to be in mainstream. I think we did realise that there would be some parents would take their children away. Of course we got into all sorts of time-wasting, stupid, games trying to second-guess what parents would do. A few we even got right!

But it's the thing about, you know, relinquishing control. We found that hard, all of us. . . . So we met with parents and told them as a group, and we had a range of views from them in response. It is fair to say that from quite a number of the parents, clearly, as soon as that was announced, had made up their mind what they were going to do. They were going to remove their children from the school. That was particularly true, I think, for parents of children who were boarding, from Dorset. And that was related to the fact that there was an alternative readily available. So most of the Dorset kids transferred to Victoria School.

JW   *So the parents that wanted to keep their children in special education – that didn't necessarily relate to the severity of the children's disabilities?*

DW   Oh absolutely not, no. It was purely their parental wishes. Kids' needs didn't come into it.

JW   *But I just wondered whether the parental wishes related to the kids' needs – whether the parents of children who were more severely disabled would choose special education as opposed to mainstream?*

DW   I think there's some correlation there – but if you think that, for example, one boy is going to go to Meadow Hill [comprehensive] – I think, you know, that it's hard to think of anybody having a greater range of disabilities than he faces. And yet he's going to be going to the mainstream. I would have liked there to have been more parents who could have had the faith. I suppose my conception about that is: what were we asking the parents? We were asking them, one, to trust us – in effect we'd just said, 'Well, whatever we were doing in the past is actually not good enough,' so, you know, that's not the best basis for trust! We had very little to show them – we had something in West Hill [primary school] but nothing in secondary. We ourselves were not able to say to them, 'We have a signed, sealed, delivered agreement with the LEA' – we've got an office space, for example. A couple of parents were *very* concerned: 'Well where are *you* going to be, Dave?', and those kinds of things.

JW   *It's a point of contact.*

DW   Yes. It's the location, you know. What physically is this going to look like? So we were asking parents, I think, to take a great leap of faith, and clearly some parents felt able to do that and others didn't. I think in addition to that the Dorset parents clearly had – when they turned to their LEA, the LEA was giving them very clear messages about 'Integration in our schools is not actually an option for disabled children – Victoria School will be the alternative.' So they clearly were not giving a supportive message. Certainly in the early days the Somerset LEA *were*.

JW   *Yes. So are you saying that Dorset wouldn't have provided funding for them to attend mainstream education here?*

DW   Well, ultimately what we did was to put a proposal to Dorset, a formal proposal which we wrote up. It would actually have cost them less: there would have been more Barnardos money for the children, and they still said 'No'.

JW   *Just a question of philosophy?*

DW   I think so. I think there's probably a couple of things. One was the philosophy, two, in fairness to the LEA, there was the unitary authority business looming on the horizon, and Dorset in particular has been affected by that: they've lost Bournemouth, they've lost Poole or somewhere or other, which meant that their financial situation would be very uncertain. So I think a combination of factors really. . . . But Devon was a bit less clear. I had quite a lot of talks with East Devon in particular, which was where most of our Devon children came from, and there was a lot of interest. At the end of the day I think there were two concerns. One was that it was actually a small number of children and two was the concern about the differential in treatment being very visible. And they, reluctantly I think, withdrew.

JW   *But in fact they are funding individual children aren't they, like Greg?*

DW   Yes that's right, they're still funding Greg. And in fairness, I mean, Dorset have funded Maxine, and June is working with her. And would have funded another youngster in mainstream but – the classic thing – with that particular girl we'd actually organised for her to be in mainstream and got it all settled, June was going to provide the support, and at the last minute the girl thought about all her friends being at the special school and decided to go, literally the last day of the summer holidays. It was heart-breaking. Anyway, to go back to the parents after we'd announced our plan . . . we then set up the parents' consultative group, to represent *all* the views of the parents. They certainly represented *some* views very well but not all of them! They didn't represent those parents who were in favour of what we were doing.

JW   *Why was that?*

DW   Because the group, the parents' representative group, in the main was composed of parents who were opposed to what we were going to do.

JW   *But why didn't the others join and put their point of view forward?*

DW   Because – we had information back from those parents – in effect what happened was if they tried to put a positive stamp, they just got drowned by the anxieties and worries of those people who were nominally in charge of the parents' representative group.

JW   *So was that a group set up by you or by the parents?*

DW   It was set up by us. We wanted to have – I'd always seen it as a big weakness of the school that we hadn't got parent governors and there had been long-standing difficulties with Barnardos' charitable status. I know that other charities have managed to resolve those problems but Barnardos has not. So we'd not had a history of liaison and working closely with parents. So after we'd announced that we were going to close, we invited parents to join our parents' consultative group, to do it on the basis of: there would be representatives of primary, secondary and FE. Well, the FE parent dropped out pretty rapidly and it was therefore the primary and secondary parents that were most involved, and that actually ultimately came down to three, maybe four, sets of parents . . . and Joe's parents. Joe's parents were in a very interesting position. They wanted to support everything we were doing at West Hill but they also wanted to fight on behalf of other parents who wanted segregated education! And I could understand that – they'd want to stand shoulder to shoulder with other parents. But that group clearly formed itself into a 'We are going to fight the closure' group. That was their point of view. I think they also had an agenda of perhaps, perhaps I'm being unfair, but there was a sense of 'If we can't stop the school closing we'll do everything we can to oppose any alternative.'

JW   *Oh! Really?*

DW   There was a sense of that. . . . But we had those meetings and we also had set up another group that would meet with every parent to run through what they wanted for their child. Which was a massive undertaking, really, meeting with sixty parents. All this was going on between October and March, and the workload was just phenomenal. And trying to hold on to all the things that parents were saying and wanting. But we did actually achieve that. And we were able, at the end of the consultation period, which was the end of March, April . . . able to say quite clearly, well, everybody's had a chance to put their view, the parents were able to put their view to Barnardos and to the LEA, and it was agreed and ratified by both organisations that we would go ahead: it would close in '95/'96. What was interesting, I think, with the parents was that there was a strategy available to them that they didn't use, and that strategy was to delay things. They put all their energy into *stopping* the closure, but we had put forward, in terms of a proposal about how the school might close, an alternative scenario which would have taken a further year. And they didn't want to look at that at all. And I've often thought I didn't understand quite why they didn't want to do that – Barnardos would have gone for it, I'm sure . . .

JW   *Well, I suppose they felt that if the decision's got to be made, better make it sooner rather than later. I mean, from the point of view of individual children, that obviously makes sense, doesn't it?*

DW   Well, for some of the individual children of the parents who were most opposed a further year would have taken their children to the end of their schooling, so I did think . . . so we had that battle going on. The LEA were now much more heavily involved. . . . The parents did set off one hare which we had to follow, which was an idea for a unit attached to a school, primary to start with. And again, looking back, it's interesting how far we were prepared to run with that without actually doing any checking ourselves. Because when we actually *did* check, the school that they'd spoken to had had a completely different notion of what was being talked about from what the parents had. And had no intention of wanting a unit at all. They *had* said, 'If we take these children we will need some extra space' – to provide physio etc. But a *unit*, you know, a *unit* was not in it. But we, again, we were so embroiled in the process we allowed that notion for quite a while before we really dealt with it. And the LEA got themselves wound up about that as well. I suppose overall, I think, looking back, that the relationship we had with parents was invariably correct and polite, even with those who clearly *loathed* everything we were saying, and I think it's a testament to everybody concerned, the parents and professionals alike, that we were able to discuss the issues – highly emotive issues, and difficult things, but by and large there was never any really personal nastiness. . . . The other thing that struck me, looking back, is actually the disparity of power between the professionals and the parents was very disempowering. You know, Barnardos proposes –

JW   *And you put up with it!*

DW   Yes. There was a sense in which we went through this consultation process – we did try to listen to what parents had to say, and we did modify aspects of what we were proposing – but the bottom line was that it was a consultation exercise and at the end of that . . .

JW   *. . . the school would close anyway?*

DW   That's right. So on the really principled issue, on the substantive issue we weren't going to change.

JW   *No. Were you prepared to give them help with finding alternatives if they did go for special education? Was that part of your role?*

DW   Yes. That was the intention behind the individual meetings. But once we'd got a sense from those individual meetings of what the parents wanted then we did set it up in a way so that there was clearly somebody here who could help them achieve that, and that was Martin,[6] so Martin then had a very clear role, to be there for parents, to get them the things that they wanted. And I think, you know, we could have been much harder about that, we could have been more hard-nosed in terms of, 'Well, we will support those parents who want inclusion but not other parents: they'll have to go and make their own arrangements.' We didn't do that but there was quite a lot of support for it. But the other element I was thinking about, before that: we'd taken on, I can't remember exactly when, we'd taken on Sue Rickell as consultant, and I think Sue had a number of important roles, really. One was, in the meetings with parents I think she was a very powerful influence: some things became not sayable because Sue was there – about disabled people. And two, she was able to challenge some of the assumptions that parents had about children not being able to cope in mainstream school. And Sue's own experience had been that she had transferred to a mainstream school in her last year at school and it had been the most important year of her life. So that was a very powerful message.

JW *She wished she'd done it earlier, did she?*

DW Yes. But doing it then transformed her life – I mean, she literally was able to – she was able to make new friends, all the things that we know, *and* go on to university. You know, it really did have a very powerful effect. And I think that was not just important for parents, it was also important for us who were agonising about poor Jerry, you know –

JW *Yes!*

DW Transferring in his last year, and suddenly we had somebody who could rephrase that and say, 'Well, actually it might be the best year he ever has.' And we hadn't allowed ourselves to think that. And we couldn't know. We actually had to acknowledge: we couldn't know. It might be awful for him – equally, it could be the most wonderful thing that's ever happened to him. Just to simply *assume* that it's going to be the worst isn't, is not, fair. It's denying somebody an opportunity. So I think Sue was very powerful in that way.

There is a sense in which parents, LEA, Barnardos, all have demanded levels of proof that it works, of inclusion, that they've never demanded of the [special] school. And that, I think, is very difficult to take sometimes. I know it's always the case with something new, but nobody ever said to me, 'Well, what difference academically does segregated education make?' So to be faced with that kind of stuff feels like there's a bigger burden of proof imposed on inclusion, and I think it's basically unfair. And that is true in all sorts of areas; it's not just the research. Somehow –

JW *It's the unknown, isn't it? You can see how your child is doing in special education and you know where you are with that, but this is something totally untried.*

DW Yes, I can see that, but there is also this – that suddenly the future is going to be required to demonstrate things which nobody seems to have cared about in the past.

JW *They didn't?*

DW No. The classic would be – bullying. They'd say, 'Our child is totally safe here.' Well I know bullying went on here but it becomes, in the mainstream school: 'We must ensure that no bullying ever takes place, ever', whatever. Well, it's not realistic. And it's not realistic to make a comparison with here. So it's those sorts of things that are difficult.

JW *Yes.*

DW So we'd informed parents, we'd involved them in a process, we'd informed the LEA and involved *them* in the process. We'd informed staff . . . I think we took a fortnight telling staff, because I actually went round every member of staff, in small groups, so the kitchen staff, whatever – because this was about redundancies, and I felt it was really important to meet with them all. And that was an interesting experience because I got all kinds of reactions, almost none of them the ones I expected! The kitchen staff, for example – there'd been lots of anxiety and worry in the senior management team about, you know, they'd been here a long time: what were they going to do? and so forth. So when I met with them, I'd geared myself up, you know: 'This is going to be a group who are really upset.' And they said, 'Well actually we thought that was about it – we'd worked it out anyway ourselves,' and when we sat down to talk about: 'Well what do you think this'll mean for you?' one of them had already made up their mind that this was the only job they'd ever had, they didn't want another one, and there wasn't going to be a problem for her financially, and that they'd actually only come in really for the, um . . .

JW *The social bit?*

DW Yes, the social bit. And somebody else had seen, 'Oh, does this mean I could get some re-training? I used to be a secretary actually.' I mean it was just interesting: suddenly people were into their plans rather than . . . So again, one of my assumptions had to be re-thought: this wasn't a disaster for everyone. For some people it was, clearly, but nothing like the numbers I think that I'd assumed. And some of that team were up for early retirement or whatever . . . so there's all those kind of different things coming out. I think that was a real learning point for me. I don't know quite how to put it. It's a sense of 'We've finally got ourselves clear. This is what we're going to do.' And the value of that was that then other people could begin to plan and react to it. So the staff suddenly – all this stuff had been talked about and talked about – when was it going to happen? Suddenly, then, there was a very clear time-scale. And they could then begin to make plans – what was going to be best for *them*.

JW *Presumably there was still some uncertainty in that you didn't know how many staff you'd be able to re-deploy in the new service?*

DW There was certainly that. But there were clearly some staff who wouldn't have wanted to go to the new set-up and some staff for whom it wouldn't have been possible, the kitchen staff for example. So from that point of view there was greater clarity for many staff but not for everyone. Equally, the LEA now began to work rather harder than they had done. We'd clearly moved up their priorities list. Barnardos began to pull in people like Personnel and Training

94

and so forth, in a way that they hadn't done before. And of course we were now talking to *actual* schools, about *actual* children. So I think achieving our own clarity was perhaps the single biggest step forward that we took. Whether people were for us or against us, they actually knew where we were. Now those people who were against us, I think, the parents who were upset with what we were doing and so on, we were able to say to them at least: we can be fair about what we're not going to do. There *are* some uncertainties about the future . . . and in a way, it's hard, it's like a bereavement or a separation or something like that: suddenly the partner is very clear that they're going to be somewhere else but at least it *is* clear. And I think that was quite powerful. And of course some of the parents took their kids off and went.

JW *Did you have any sort of official agreement with the LEA by then?*

DW Well, we had the agreement, yes, because in effect what we'd had was – it had gone through committee in the June, and Barnardos council at the same time, and both parties had agreed that over the next two years they would work in partnership to get an agreement and to work that up into a contract.

JW *Yes. So the financial aspect hadn't been decided at that point?*

DW Hadn't been decided, but what *had* been decided was that we would have the discussion and get agreement. Certainly we talked in terms of the same sum of money being available as had always been, historically, so between 550 and 600 thousand [pounds]. So that was the kind of sum that we had in our minds. You're pushing for the upper limit, obviously, but were prepared to negotiate on it. That would have been quite realistic.

So the first year we actually implemented it: the plan then took place. More kids actually arrived at West Hill. We began working with Oakwood Primary and the whole thing began to develop. I suppose the big issue then was how to separate out staff. In effect what we were trying to do was run two services with no additional increase in staffing, and some people would be facing redundancy at the end of that first year: all of that stuff had to be dealt with. It was a complicated process, really. And inevitably a bit messy, I think.

I think the other thing that then happened really was last summer when to all intents and purposes Barnardos dropped a bombshell on us. We thought we had an absolute agreement about the money that would be available to make the change happen and suddenly found that that had been pulled back. And in itself I think that that was fair enough – the organisation found it was harder up than it thought it was . . .

JW *What about the future of the project?*

DW There's a number of thoughts really. But firstly, last week I was at the National Inclusion Conference – again. And I was running some workshops there on what we'd done. I talked with a lot of parents and they, from all over the country, found it hard to believe that there was anywhere where this was happening, because they were struggling so hard with their individual authorities to get into mainstream . . . heart-rending stories. So to hear that there was actually a special school that was prepared to *do* this, to shut itself and *do* this, was – you could see it in their faces, you know: Is this real? So that was powerful, I think. For me, I think we've achieved quite a lot. I think we've actually stopped doing something that we believed to be wrong. Well, I won't draw any lessons from that but I just think that's the fact. I do think that we have influenced Barnardos in terms of its policy and so forth – it ain't there yet but we have shoved it on at least.

JW *Do they have other special schools for physically disabled children?*

DW No. We were the last. But EBD schools, and others: my perception is that those schools are increasingly on the defensive. They'll have to address the issues sooner or later. Barnardos has signed up to CSIE's Inclusion Charter, so that's a step – it is beginning to move. It hasn't developed its own policy and statement about inclusion yet but it has had its conference. But there are steps, you know, so I feel pleased really that we've had a part to play in that. We've moved the organisation rather than the other way round. We have overall, I think the figure is somewhere between thirty and forty youngsters are now in mainstream as a result of what we've done – that's either mainstream college or school . . . which is quite a lot. We have had a part in the wider debate. . . . Our staff have had an impact in the schools that we're working with, and that won't go away. The LEA is going to have to respond at some level, even if it's not fully – so I think, for one small special school in the middle of nowhere, really – Somerset being as near to nowhere as it's possible to get! – I think we've achieved quite a lot. We *haven't* achieved all that we wanted to, but then maybe you never do. I think the biggest disappointment was that we have not been able to impact significantly on Somerset's special needs policy.

I suppose there's always the wish that we could have done more, that we could have persuaded the LEA to take that leap, make that change, and I haven't totally lost the notion that they might still do it. . . . As I say, I'm just glad, really. I wouldn't have missed *any* of this. Sue Rickell said – I can't remember what I said but we were talking about how difficult this process feels and so on – what she said was: 'You are moving from being an oppressor to an ally, and that is always a painful process.'

JW   *A bit of an extreme way of putting it, isn't it? You wouldn't have seen yourself as an oppressor?*

DW   No, but I did think then – clearly my head's gone into quotation mode – in *Hamlet*, isn't it: 'That a man may smile and smile and be a villain.' And I do think that the more I've been with disabled people – articulate, thoughtful, disabled people – the more I've had to recognise that the whole segregation process is a form of oppression. It is what able-bodied people do to disabled people. And they do it with the absolute best of intentions – but that doesn't make it right.

JW   *But are you implying that they shouldn't have the choice? In which case you're still oppressing them?*

DW   But they don't have a *choice*: that's the issue.

JW   *But you're removing a choice by closing the school?*

DW   But it's not a *real* choice. If the power imbalance is such that for disabled people there isn't a *real* choice between mainstream and segregated, and actually they don't want that choice, increasingly: a lot of the parents are saying, 'I don't *want* that choice. All I want is the same choice as any other parent.' So actually, if you shut all the special schools you, on one level maybe, are reducing choices but on another, you'd actually be funding to provide the resources to make it possible for the parent of a disabled child to have the same choices as any others do – and actually that is the *key* choice: you know, the choice to go to one of the three primary schools in the area.

JW   *Rather than the only one that's accessible, yes.*

DW   Yes, that is the *real* choice. But we're a long way from that. . . . And the present system, it seems to me, is incredibly wasteful. You have two systems, both of which have to be managed, both of which have to be resourced. It just doesn't make economic sense, and increasingly it doesn't make *educational* sense. And some kind of mechanism, I think, will need to be created at some point to make it possible for special schools to be absorbed into mainstream.

HOW THE SPECIAL SCHOOL CHANGED

In the second section of this chapter we give a factual account of the changes which took place in the special school prior to its transformation to a service.

The history

Princess Margaret School was a Barnardos special school for children and young people with physical disabilities. Opened in 1966, the school educated more than fifty day pupils and forty boarders. The day pupils were bussed in from all over Somerset; the boarders, in the main, came from the Dorset and Devon and occasionally from Cornwall, Avon or Wiltshire.

Following the 1981 Education Act, Somerset LEA developed a policy of integration 'where possible' and this began to affect the numbers of children and young people attending the school. In order to offset this decline in numbers, and meet a demand, the school's second principal, Kit Hartley, established a further education unit for students aged 16+ which aimed to offer work skills training and experience. However, by 1987 the school's occupancy continued to be low and serious consideration was given to closing it as it had become a considerable financial drain on Barnardos' resources.

A new principal was appointed in early 1988 with a clear mandate either to increase the occupancy of the school and bring its financial affairs into order or to develop and implement a closure plan. In the event the principal did both. Between 1988 and 1992 the school's occupancy was increased from fifty-six pupils and students to seventy-three; the boarding accommodation was completely refurbished; a primary reception class was established and increased to two classes; exam results were improved; the school's fees were re-negotiated; the further education service developed links with the local further education college; and the population of the school changed with a greater proportion of pupils/students having significant learning difficulties.

Thus when managers at PMS began to consider inclusion as an option for future development, they did so within a context of considerable achievement and success as a special school. In 1992 the school was financially secure, occupancy was good, morale was high and the quality of service on offer was excellent. It was these factors that enabled the school's managers to decide to review what the school was doing and begin a process of developing a vision and strategy for the future. Although the quality of service offered by PMS was seen by managers as a strength, it also could operate as a barrier to change. We were to hear, many times, variations on the theme of 'If it ain't broke, don't fix it', from staff, parents and other professional groups.

With more than ninety staff and forty-five volunteers, managers at this time recognised that any change process would be complex and would take considerable time and resources to achieve. The complexity of any change process was a function of several factors which included the variety and range of professional groups within the school – such as teachers, managers, physiotherapists, speech and language therapists, nurses, residential social workers, administration staff and ancillary staff – as well as the financial structure of the school which charged a substantial fee to the LEA for each child/young person referred. Additional income was generated from Barnardos' voluntary allocation. In simple terms, increasing numbers attending the school meant increased resources, while decreasing numbers had the opposite effect.

Therefore, a planned change process was vital if there was not to be a cata-strophic collapse in the school's financial wellbeing (see chapter 1 for a discussion of the financing of inclusion).

Scanning the horizon

Before making any decisions about the future of the school it was agreed with Barnardos' managers that the school's management team would look at examples of 'best practice' elsewhere. This meant visiting a range of schools and projects and attending the first international workshop on inclusion. At this early stage inclusion was simply one among a range of options being considered. Other options explored included conductive education; devel-oping the school as a resource centre; and developing a pre-school intensive therapy centre.

In the event, the decision by the school's managers to pursue inclusion was heavily influenced by an inclusion conference held in June 1991. It was part of a series of inclusion workshops led by the Canadians, George Flynn, Jack Pearpoint and Marsha Forest and Judith Snow. What immediately captured those who attended was the insistence on *values* as the necessary precondition to action. The conference featured speakers from the Waterloo School Board in Canada who had, in 1986, shut all their special units and embarked on a programme to include all children in 'regular classes'. By 1991 the process was embedded in practice at Waterloo board schools. A number of important concepts which became fundamental to the thinking of Managers at PMS were first encountered here. These concepts were encap-sulated in brief and memorable aphorisms:

- One road not two;
- Everyone belongs; and
- Values into action.

These concepts challenged the whole basis of PMS as a separating and segregating special school and formed the basis of the planning which managers began to undertake. There is a very real sense in which many of the ideas and practices described in this book are simply elaborations or footnotes to the pioneering work undertaken in Waterloo Board and shared with British colleagues in 1991. The impact of the concepts was strength-ened by what PMS managers saw happening in the schools they visited, particularly Impington Village College, Cambridge, where Eileen Webber and her team had created a service which integrated disabled children into the mainstream school. During that visit, and in subsequent meetings, it was clear also that explicitly articulated values had played a significant role in the development of Impington Village College and that the whole school had benefited from the inclusion of disabled children.

First steps

After looking at the range of possibilities for the school, the managers undertook in 1992 to spend three days considering and debating its future direction. This was a difficult process for the five managers concerned. It was difficult because the group recognised that it would be taking decisions that would affect the future of the school and everyone in it. The whole group was highly committed to the school and had worked hard to develop it. Eventually the group produced a vision for the school, which was called the school's 'purpose' (see Table 8.1). This 'purpose' committed the managers to action in three areas: empowering pupils; developing the school's services; and influencing the wider environment. The purpose particularly in relation to the second and third areas was a major shift of direction for the school.

The practical manifestations of this change were two-fold. First, a joint-appointment advisory teacher (physical disability) was made and funded jointly by Barnardos and the LEA. Second, LEA and PMS managers began a process of involving other members of staff and other groups within Barnardos in developing inclusion.

The post of joint-appointment advisory teacher was developed jointly between Somerset LEA and Barnardos during 1991–1992. Half of this person's time was to be given to supporting those mainstream schools which already offered places to disabled pupils (i.e. a 0.5 post to support *all* the schools in Somerset). The other 50 per cent would be working at PMS supporting staff and developing an integration process whereby children and young people would be able to transfer from PMS to mainstream schools. The first child's transfer soon took place and others began to follow. The process was deliberately called an *integration* procedure. The aim was to make it possible for the children and young people to fit into the schools they were attending. There was no intention at that time to work with the schools over a longer period of time in order to assist them to become more generally inclusive.

In the first three years, twelve children and young people were returned to their local schools. Although highly successful in its own terms, it became apparent to PMS managers that its very success was, in fact, storing up problems for the school. The children and young people who were re-integrating were the most academically able of the PMS population.

During this same period the school's managers established what became known as the futures group. The group was composed of staff representing each department in the school with an interest in developing the future. It was, quite deliberately, a non-hierarchical group. The futures group met regularly over a period of two terms.

The aims of the group were to develop Princess Margaret School thinking about inclusion and to spread this thinking into the staff team overall. It also assisted with strategic planning by generating the material which

Table 8.1 The school's 'purpose'

To enable all children and young people to share their uniqueness and to be fully included in their communities, by:	
1	*Empowering Individuals*
1.1	Maximising each young person's potential
1.2	Enabling young people to achieve personal autonomy
1.3	Enabling young people to be their own advocates
1.4	Valuing the work of individuals
1.5	Involving families, children and young people in the process of change
2	*Developing Schools and Services*
2.1	Providing a high quality set of services and resources to children and young people with disabilities, their families and carers, and the community
2.2	Evaluating and adapting services as circumstances or needs change
2.3	Actively promoting equal shares to facilities and resources in the community
2.4	Promoting our values through our organisation and structure
2.5	Creating opportunities for individual and group development, ensuring staff feel valued by involving them in opportunities for staff creatively to respond to the issues and demands of change
3	*Influencing a Wider Environment*
3.1	Being advocates for young people's right to be included
3.2	Being actively involved in the debate regarding inclusion in the wider community
3.3	Influencing and encouraging change in other organisations' existing attitudes and services

enabled managers to submit a paper to Barnardos seeking agreement to begin a process of consultation with stakeholders.

It is difficult now to recapture the excitement and the quality of debate which was such a feature of the futures group meetings. It is not too far-fetched to suggest that it was an empowering process for the staff who were involved, as many of them became highly involved in the next stage – making inclusion happen.

In at the deep end

In 1993/94 the major area of development for the school was in the FE department. Managers had chosen to develop this area of PMS's services first because it already had strong links with mainstream colleges. The building in which it was based was leased and the lease was ending and unlikely to be renewed. Staff were experienced in inclusion and numbers in the department were falling (as a result of efforts to integrate more young people in their local colleges). These changes were, in the main, welcomed by everyone. Managers had no plans for developments elsewhere in the school during this year.

However, a more surprising and radical development was then to take place: the teacher in charge of the Year 4/5 group in the primary department put forward a proposal that her class transfer to a local mainstream primary school. Over the previous term her class had had a weekly afternoon session based at West Hill Primary which had been deemed by both schools to be successful and beneficial for all who had taken part. By September 1994 there were to be five children in the class and the proposal was that she, the classroom assistants and the services of PMS physio and speech and language therapists would transfer to West Hill Primary.

Parental views were sought, and it became apparent that there was a split in views among parents. Two parents did not want inclusion for their children and found it hard to accept the changes proposed as they were happy with the service their children were receiving from PMS as it was. Two parents were enthusiastic and positive about the proposal, and one set of parents decided they wished to pursue a different option for their child.

After consulting with parents, West Hill Primary School and the PMS staff who would be most closely involved, the decision was taken to pursue the link for four reasons:

- Without the link, the curriculum opportunities for this particular group would be limited as a result of small class size, different ages and abilities, and a variety of communication difficulties (only one child in the class used verbal speech and there was a gender imbalance with only one girl in the class).
- PMS managers felt that West Hill Primary staff and governors shared the commitment to inclusion and would be committed to making it work.
- Children who had had some part-time experience at West Hill were enthusiastic.
- Most significantly, PMS staff were convinced that the children's educational and social opportunities would be significantly enhanced at West Hill Primary.

The managers of both schools therefore drafted a joint policy which established the aims of the partnership as being:

- to give pupils from PMS as full an experience of mainstream education as possible;
- to ensure that PMS pupils are fully included in all aspects of life at West Hill;
- to enhance West Hill children's understanding of equal opportunities and the needs of those with disabilities; and
- to evaluate the value for all pupils and staff of this particular mode of inclusion.

In the event, only two of the five children actually transferred. One child remained at PMS and the other two children were placed by their parents in their local mainstream schools supported by Somerset LEA. So, of the original five, four children transferred to mainstream but only two transferred to West Hill Primary.

PMS managers pursued a deliberate policy of generously staffing these two children. As well as the normal primary school staff offered by West Hill, PMS offered a full-time teacher and a two full-time equivalent classroom assistants, plus speech and language therapy input and physiotherapy. This very high staff/pupil ratio was justified at the time by PMS managers on the grounds that the partnership with West Hill was unknown territory in terms of the demands it would make on staff; and it was essential that inclusion at West Hill was successful (and seen to be so).

As part of the preparation and planning for inclusion, Barnardos had commissioned a review of research relating to segregated and integrated education. Although brief, the report concluded that:

- Overall, if integration is properly planned and resourced and there is commitment to it, the outcomes for children and schools are positive.
- There is no body of evidence to suggest that segregated special education has significantly greater benefits for pupils compared to ordinary school placements with support.
- A range of 'facilitating factors' which bear positively on the success of integration can be identified.

The report was valuable to hard-pressed managers in that it offered a simple response to critics of inclusion. When asked if inclusion could really work in the real world, they were able to respond with some confidence that inclusion 'works' if it is resourced properly, if there is good planning and if there is commitment to it.

Partnership

By making the shift from educating children and young people at PMS to developing a partnership with West Hill Primary, the managers, perhaps without quite realising it, were 'moving from a focus on structures to a focus on processes' (Dyson and Gains, 1993). In other words, it was a recognition that PMS need no longer be the structure or organisation that offered the children education. Rather, it could, through collaboration at school and class level, develop processes which would enhance the ability of mainstream schools to deliver a curriculum which would include a much greater diversity of pupils.

THE SCHOOLS AND THE CHILDREN

In this final part of this chapter we give a brief account of the personnel involved in the Inclusion Project, its partner schools and the children and young people who were part of the project. Each of the schools and each of the individuals is referred to in the chapters which follow and these details are therefore given to enable the reader to contextualise those references.

The Inclusion Project personnel

Table 8.2 sketches the way that the special school became transformed into an inclusion service. It gives an impression of the significant organisational and personnel changes which had to take place. Details of the new role of the teacher-co-ordinator are given in chapters 9 and 10, where the changing role of the LSAs is also discussed.

The partner schools

Meadow Hill Community Comprehensive

Meadow Hill is a new purpose-built comprehensive school. It has about 800 boys and girls on roll, aged eleven to sixteen. It was designed with the new access regulations for public buildings in mind — there are two lifts, for example, and wheelchair-accessible toilets.

Two boys, Greg and Mike, joined Year 10 from PMS in September 1995, and one, Jerry, joined Year 11, also from PMS, at the same time. Before the partnership with Barnardos began, there were already two physically disabled students at the school, as well as those attending the county unit for hearing-impaired children which is sited there.

A full-time teacher-co-ordinator was appointed from the Inclusion Project, managed by both the Meadow Hill SENCO and SIP: she also taught some French and was co-tutor, with the Head of English, for the registration class

Table 8.2 From a special school to an inclusion service

Princess Margaret School (73 children, 40 boarding)	Somerset Inclusion Project (18 children, none boarding)
1 principal	1 project leader
1 deputy principal (education)	
1 deputy principal (care/social work)	
1 administrator	1 project administrator
14.5 teachers	5 teacher co-ordinators (fte) (inclusion co-ordinators)
12 classroom assistants (LSAs) (fte – in fact 25 part-timers)	20 classroom assistants (LSAs) (fte)
25 residential social workers	
2 nurses	
4 physiotherapists	2 physiotherapists
1.5 speech and language therapists	1.5 speech and language therapists
1 volunteer co-ordinator (40+ volunteers)	1 volunteer co-ordinator (20 volunteers)
1.5 family social workers	1 family social worker
5 kitchen staff	
7 ancillary staff (cleaners, drivers, etc.)	
2 technicians	
4 administrative staff	1 project secretary

Note: fte means 'full-time equivalent'

Greg and Mike were in, taking part in some PSE (personal and social education) lessons. A team of six part-time LSAs was appointed from PMS.

Heather Grove Primary

Heather Grove is a modern all-age primary school in a rural Somerset village. The new, fully wheelchair-accessible buildings replace older ones in the same village. Some of the classrooms, Caroline's for instance, are quite cramped, and there has been a problem with accommodating the large amount of equipment that she needs to keep at school (the standing frame and two sorts of chair as a minimum).

Caroline joined the reception class from PMS when Heather Grove moved into its new buildings. SIP serviced the school with a part-time co-ordinator and two part-time LSAs, both of whom were already working with Caroline at Heather Grove.

Oakwood Primary

Oakwood is a very large primary school, comprising two separate establishments, Infants and Juniors, with their own heads, on neighbouring sites in the industrial area of a large Somerset town.

Luke had never attended PMS and support for him was eventually made available at the request of the school through SIP. This resulted in the appointment of a part-time teacher-co-ordinator from PMS, who was responsible for liaison and the delivery of parts of the IEP, and a team of two, later three, part-time LSAs.

West Hill Primary

West Hill is a community primary school in new buildings in the same town as PMS. The buildings are attractive and fully wheelchair-accessible. West Hill was a pioneer in the project, starting the primary phase on the initiative of one of the teachers from PMS, who is now the teacher-co-ordinator based at West Hill and sits on the school's senior management team. At the time of the research, West Hill had four children from the project: Daniel, Joe, Tom and James.

The children

Caroline (Heather Grove Primary)

At the time of the study, Caroline was seven years old and in Year 2 (a year below her chronological age) at Heather Grove, her local village school. Her older brother is also a pupil there. Caroline is a wheelchair-user and gets around independently. She has good spoken language and a friendly outgoing personality. She needs some help with personal care and has difficulty with literacy and numeracy.

When she was two, Caroline tried an opportunity playgroup in a nearby large town but her parents felt the emphasis of this group, with a majority of ambulant children who had learning difficulties, was wrong for her, so she started to attend the village playgroup with her neighbours. She stayed there until she was nearly four, at which point a decision about her primary education faced her parents. Although they would have liked to send her to the village school (Heather Grove) with her brother, the school was at that time on an inaccessible site and suitable adaptations would be unforthcoming because it was scheduled to move to a new building within the next couple of years. Her parents were initially reluctant to see her in special education but visited Princess Margaret's, liked it and were attracted by the facilities for physiotherapy. She went to PMS for two years, as a day pupil.

At this point, the new, more accessible, school at Heather Grove opened and both her parents and the PMS staff felt Caroline should try it. Caroline's transfer took place before the initiation of the Somerset Inclusion Project.

The following year Caroline's parents, aware that the Heather Grove staff were finding their first experience of inclusion hard-going, wrote to Princess Margaret School asking for her to be supported by the new project, so that more advice and co-ordination could be made available. This resulted in her being one of the first children to be involved when the project began, in September 1995.

At the end of the 1995/96 year Caroline was found to have made little academic progress, as measured by NC levels and the seven-year-old SATs, but progress towards other goals, such as taking more personal responsibility for the use of time, and becoming more aware of, and able to assert, her own feelings, was considerable.

Luke (Oakwood Primary)

Luke was nine when the study began, and in Year 5 at Oakwood Primary. Luke is a wheelchair-user, but not independent as yet, needs help with personal care, including eating and drinking, and has severe communication difficulties which make it hard for teachers to assess his level of under-standing and academic progress. He is able to indicate 'yes' and 'no' when he wants to, and has a talking-book which can be helpful if used with someone who understands its functioning and limitations. He has a very good friend, Ollie, who has been in the same class as Luke since they started school together when Luke was just under five.

Before attending the Infants at Oakwood, Luke had been to an opportu-nity playgroup. His first three years at the school were part-time only, with two days a week at a special school in a large city. This arrangement was dropped when it became apparent that Luke did not enjoy the experience of special education. His parents had chosen Oakwood, although it was at the other end of town from their home, because it had good wheelchair access. Luke became involved in the SIP in September 1995 after a year of full-time mainstream education, on the initiative of the joint LEA/SIP specialist teacher who, through discussion with Luke's parents and the school, became aware that both his classteacher and the assistants would welcome extra physical and logistic forms of support, and advice on educational issues.

A tension developed during the first SIP year between the wish to include him in class as much as possible and the need for him to work individually on literacy and numeracy and communication, in order for the educational disparity between himself and his classmates not to widen further. It seemed that he was becoming increasingly isolated, so steps were taken, in planning for the following year (1996/97), to ensure a much higher level of inclusion in class activities.

Tom (West Hill Primary)

Tom was nine years old when the study began. His home is several miles from the school and he is brought by transport to the school daily. Tom is severely physically disabled, is a wheelchair-user and needs a great deal of help with personal care – washing, feeding and toileting.

When he was three he attended a local opportunity playgroup of mixed disabled and non-disabled children three days a week before moving on to attend the Princess Margaret School, first on a phased basis, then full-time when he was five.

He moved on to West Hill when the inclusion project began in September 1994 and during the period of the research was in the same class as another SIP student, James. His mother reports good progress since he started. She says that he is now more independent, with better language than when he attended PMS. He made friends quickly and soon established a close relationship with one of the boys (Wayne) in his class. After a couple of months his friend had even stayed a night at his house.

He takes place in all curricular activities, including swimming, with the other children in his class. He is at Level 1 in reading and almost at Level 2 in maths. This places him at the lower end of the mixed-year 3/4 class in which he was placed.

James (West Hill Primary)

James was ten when the project began, having moved with his mother from Poland to join her husband in England. In Poland he had not attended any school or playschool; his parents report that this was because – as they had been told – he would 'frighten the other children'. James needs complete care for all personal needs and the parents receive no help at all with this at home. He is now of a size and weight which makes this very difficult for them to manage.

James started at West Hill at Easter 1995 with no English. Nor had he had any significant school experience, having attended only for a short period at PMS. During the period of the research he was placed in the same class as Tom. He is currently working towards Level 1 in all areas of the curriculum and is therefore not working at the same level as the rest of the class. Although he has picked up English well, he has suffered also because of his lack of school experience before coming to England. Although he relates well with the other children in his class, he has not made any special friends, as Tom has.

James's parents are pleased with his progress in the SIP, and particularly the opportunity it has afforded for him to be with other children. They report that he loves school and hates the holidays, saying that he was inward and introverted before the project, but is now a different child. Their main concern, though, is with the continuity of physical and medical support since the inclusion project began: physiotherapy has reduced from twice to once per week and hydrotherapy, which used to be daily, will stop entirely. James gets stiff easily and the reduction of regular therapy gives them cause for anxiety since they are unable on their own to provide the intensity of therapy which James requires.

Daniel (West Hill Primary)

Daniel was five when he entered West Hill in Year 1. He lives with his family in a village a few miles from the school. Daniel's disability means that he is able to move around completely independently and is able to cope with most personal care, though he needs help with buttons and zips.

He previously attended the local playgroup for disabled and non-disabled children and began to attend PMS, first part-time and then full-time at five. Transfer to West Hill came when he was nearly six at the beginning of the SIP.

His stepmother (who has looked after Daniel since he was eighteen months old) feels that he has done well at West Hill. He has progressed academically and is, she feels, treated less leniently at West Hill than he was at PMS.

Daniel's teacher reports that Daniel thinks as quickly as the other children, though his co-ordination difficulties mean that writing and recording in general is a problem. He is at a level commensurate with that of the other children in the curriculum generally. He has had some problems mixing with the others in the class, though these have now largely been resolved.

Joe (West Hill Primary)

Joe was eleven at the time of the project. He is profoundly disabled and has transferred schools several times. His parents used to live in a town in the north of Somerset before moving to their current address. From this town Joe first attended an opportunity playgroup, which they describe as 'brilliant'. On reaching school age, he was sent to a school for physically disabled pupils in a city some miles distant. However, the journey took up to one and a half hours in each direction and the parents report that Joe would return from school with lumps and bites on his body. While he attended this school, Joe was sent to Hungary for conductive education.

Because of their dissatisfaction with that school, Joe was moved when he was six years old to a more local school – this time one for children with severe learning difficulties. Although not happy about Joe's placement with children who had such difficulties, Joe's parents were pleased with his progress at this school, where he established a sight vocabulary and began to communicate through signing.

On moving to their current address, Joe moved to PMS. He was then nine years old. His parents were happy with his progress there and mistrustful of the motives – as they saw them – behind the inclusion project. Although they are pleased with West Hill as a school, they feel that he has not maintained the progress that he had made earlier in his school career. They are also highly critical of the fact that the Inclusion Project did not give Joe the chance to attend his neighbourhood school in his local village.

In class, Joe needs constant help and is working towards Level 1 in all areas of the curriculum. He uses a wheelchair and a 'talking-book'. He is well accepted and liked by the other pupils, as shown by the sociogram (fig. 11.00).

Joe will stay at West Hill for his Year 7, making him a year older than his peers there. The plan is for him to transfer to Meadow Hill in Year 8, though his parents are adamant that this should not happen, since Meadow Hill is not his neighbourhood comprehensive.

Jerry (Meadow Hill Community Comprehensive)

Jerry was already sixteen when he joined Year 11 at Meadow Hill in September 1995, so he was a year older than most of his classmates. He is the third child in a large family and has siblings and step-siblings. He enjoys the company of his peers and being part of a mainstream environment, expressing this particularly strongly perhaps from his vantage point as someone who began his education as a non-disabled person.

Jerry went to a mainstream playgroup in his home village, and then on to the local primary school when he was nearly five. The following year he was diagnosed as having a degenerative muscular disorder. The family moved house, and Jerry again attended the local primary school. At ten he moved on to the middle school, where a lift was installed for him since he had now begun to use a wheelchair. The year he was due to leave the middle school, at thirteen, he spent some weeks in hospital recovering from a spinal operation, following which he attended the middle school part-time because inadequate facilities and training meant that staff there found it hard to cope with his changing needs. Realising that he was missing out educationally because of this, Jerry decided, with reluctance, to opt for Princess Margaret's.

He was at PMS for two years, as a day pupil with a week's respite care once a month. Despite his initial reservations, he settled down well there, and he and his family were happy with their choice.

He started at Meadow Hill in September 1995. He had finished one GCSE already and was half-way through others in which he had followed a different syllabus. However, he managed to finish the courses, with scribing help from LSAs, and took the exams, receiving the results with mixed feelings. Socially, he had a rather difficult transition, being naturally somewhat shy and unwilling to make the first move towards friendship. He was befriended by a girl who hoped to work with disabled people and they kept in touch by 'phone in the summer holidays, but it was felt by staff that his wheelchair and the more or less continuous assistance of an adult, combined with his lack of outgoingness, presented considerable obstacles to the establishment of relationships. He also had to try to come to terms with the realisation, apparently new to him, that his life expectancy was more limited than that of his peers.

Mike (Meadow Hill Community Comprehensive)

Mike, aged fourteen, joined Year 10 in September 1995 with another pupil from PMS, Greg. Mike is a quiet, friendly boy with a dazzling grin, an enquiring mind and a burning desire to be as independent of adult help as possible. He is a wheelchair-user but gets about the school entirely on his own (including the use of lifts) and needs help only with personal care and some CDT tasks.

Mike's spinal disorder was diagnosed when he was three, after which he went to a local opportunity playgroup. Mike went to the local village infants' school and then on to the junior school. His parents were unhappy with Mike's final year there. They had the impression that overworked staff found it too much effort to arrange things so that children with limited mobility could take part.

Problems of size and access at the local comprehensive schools led the family to consider Princess Margaret School as an option for Mike's secondary years, although they were not happy that he would have to be a weekly boarder. With hindsight they feel that Mike gained a great deal of confidence from his time at PMS and benefited from all the activities arranged for pupils in the evenings.

Once at Meadow Hill he threw himself into the work and extra-curricular activities with equal gusto, making many genuine friends, including one 'best' friend who has visited in the evenings at PMS to play billiards and to stay with him at home over half-term. (Access problems prevent reciprocal visits.)

Mike made good progress in most subjects, but found sociology less interesting than he expected. He became involved in stage management and the running of the stationery shop and has been appointed a prefect for the 1996/97 year. He also took part in the Kielder Challenge.

111

Greg (Meadow Hill Community Comprehensive)

Greg joined Year 10 at Meadow Hill from PMS at the same time as Mike (see above). He is a sociable, talkative fourteen year-old with a wide vocabulary for his age (not always used appropriately). He has no problems with mobility but finds some other sorts of co-ordination, both gross and fine motor, difficult. This affects his handwriting and his ability to carry out some sporting and technology activities. He also has some difficulties with literacy and numeracy.

Greg went to an opportunity playgroup during his pre-school years, and also to the local village playgroup two mornings a week, from where he moved on to the local primary school with his peers. Around the age of nine and a half he appeared to be falling behind both academically and socially, despite the help of an LSA employed by the school, and was obviously no longer happy there – his mother described him as 'irritable, aggressive and unintentionally disruptive' at this time. The very large size of local comprehensives pointed Greg's parents in the direction of Princess Margaret's at the secondary stage.

After starting at PMS, Greg quickly gained confidence and became a much happier person. His parents found it a 'bitter blow' when the school's closure was announced: both they and Greg's educational psychologist had hoped he would stay there until he finished his GCSE courses at sixteen. As they were reluctant to send Greg anywhere as a boarder (because they didn't want him to become institutionalised and knew that continuous contact with his family, extended as well as close, was very important to him) his parents decided he should go to Meadow Hill, starting in September 1995 rather than 1996. There would thus be no disruption to his exam courses.

Greg followed a slightly modified curriculum, studying two technology subjects instead of one and one of the humanities. He had individual LSA help in virtually all lessons to begin with and still needs this in most subjects. He works extremely hard, often appears very enthusiastic and is, according to his mother, being exposed to a much wider range of knowledge. He has difficulty motivating himself to do homework, a problem which has been tackled by the provision of an LSA twice a week to help him get it done at school after the school day has finished.

Greg's greatest difficulty during the year has been the social side of school life. Desperate to make friends but unable to interact on an equal footing because of his immaturity and social naïveté, he got into a certain amount of trouble centring on the theft of money to buy cigarettes. He was also over-keen to show his appreciation of the opposite sex in his first days at Meadow Hill.

Both Greg and his mother have very mixed feelings about this first year at Meadow Hill. He spends a lot of time wishing he were back at PMS, and his mother feels he's lost most of the personal confidence and self-esteem he developed there and is again showing the irritability and aggression that were evident in his last years at primary school.

9

THE PROCESS OF CHANGE

INTRODUCTION

In the previous chapter we examined the changes in thinking which had given rise to the establishment of the Inclusion Project. In the current chapter we move on to look at the changes which occurred as the project started and ran through its first eighteen months. Perhaps inevitably, given the stress associated with change, it is a story of mixed emotions, and of frustration as well as success.

A variety of data sources have been used to undertake the analysis, as outlined in chapter 7. Briefly, these include:

- direct observations in classrooms, playgrounds and at home;
- field notes from informal discussions or observations taken in any of these situations;
- interviews with support assistants, teachers, students, and parents.

Following the process outlined in chapter 7, categories have been drawn from the data and these categories describe facets of the change process identified during the research. These have been grouped with two main goals in mind. First, it has been important to retain the integrity of the story which the research and its participants have told. However, where possible the categories have been grouped in such a way that the developmental consequences for inclusion projects are made clearer. Thus, the second main goal has been to provide an analysis which will guide practice.

With these goals in mind, a number of broad categories began to emerge from the data regarding the process of change. These comprised:

1 features of partner schools which appear to have helped promote transition to inclusion:
   - attitude of staff;
   - school policy;
   - quality of management;
   - physical suitability.

2 features of partner schools which appear to have hindered transition to inclusion:
- lack of communication;
- unsuitable buildings;
- host staff attitude;
- lack of resources.

3 features of Inclusion Project teams which have helped promote successful change:
- flexibility;
- organisation of service;
- professional expertise.

4 features of Inclusion Project teams which have impeded or delayed successful change:
- organisation of service;
- comparability of pay scales;
- co-ordination of roles;
- existence of 'separatist' attitudes.

5 the sharing of expertise and developing of trust between Inclusion Project and partner schools:
- benefits of learning by example from Inclusion Project staff and students;
- positive training experiences;
- lack of confidence in the continuing support of LEA.

6 the changing attitudes of partner schools:
- reflection on expected problems which did not materialise;
- perception of benefit to school;
- continuing perception of problems.

7 the changing roles of staff, and

8 the continuity of services.

These themes will be considered one by one, with illustrative quotations taken from transcripts of interviews or field notes as appropriate. Before doing that, it seems necessary first to give some idea of the weight attached to the various sub-areas within these main headings, since some were mentioned and/or observed with far greater frequency than others.[1]

On the first theme of the features of partner schools which appear to have helped promote transition to inclusion, there were numerous expressions as to the benefits accruing from the generally accepting attitude of staff, as shown in Figure 9.1. A smaller proportion of comments and observations relate to the quality of management in host schools, together with the strength of the school policy and/or the quality of school buildings.

On the other hand, institutional features hindering inclusion were associated primarily with a perceived lack of communication and information within the organisation, as Figure 9.2 shows. Although the lack of commu-

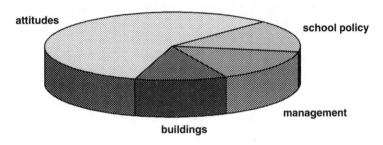

Figure 9.1 Promoting transition in partner schools

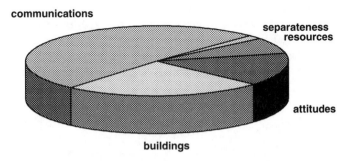

Figure 9.2 Institutional features hindering transition in partner schools

nication was primarily noted between staff within the host school, the boundaries of communication difficulties were often blurred and extended to school–Inclusion Project contacts also; these are examined in detail in the section below. Buildings, staff attitudes and lack of resources arose commonly as impediments to the successful development of the Inclusion Project. These too, though, are complex issues and will be examined in detail in the relevant section below.

The fact that a theme such as the quality of buildings should appear as both facilitator and inhibitor of inclusion might at first sight appear to relate to the nature of the situations in which the study was undertaken: two of the schools are new and built with accessibility in mind, whereas the other two are older. However, closer examination of the data shows that these were not necessarily related to the nature of the host environment. Even where facilities were notionally good, problems were still experienced. The culture of the school appeared to be more important than the fabric in facilitating inclusion. The interconnectedness of these issues is disentangled below.

Certain features of Inclusion Project teams were repeatedly mentioned or observed to be promoting inclusive practice, as indicated in Figure 9.3. Interestingly, the features of Inclusion Project teams which appear to have most effect on inclusive practice are flexibility of working practice and method of organisation; special expertise was not mentioned or observed to be important nearly as frequently (significantly, in the light of Skrtic's (1991) analysis discussed in chapter 1).

Four themes dominate the features of Inclusion Project teams which are perceived to have delayed or impeded successful change, as shown in Figure 9.4. These centre around the linked themes of the organisation of the service and the co-ordination of roles. Also figuring significantly are the questions of comparability of pay scales and 'separatism', or the carrying-over of special school practice or attitude to the new situation.

In the remaining themes, there was both strongly supportive commentary and areas in which the commentary indicates the inhibition of smooth progress. Figure 9.5 shows that there are clear benefits which have emerged from the strong professional relationships which have been developed between Inclusion Project staff and staff of the partner schools. However, the

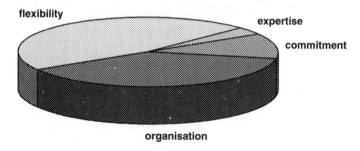

Figure 9.3 Features of Inclusion Project promoting transition to inclusion in partner schools

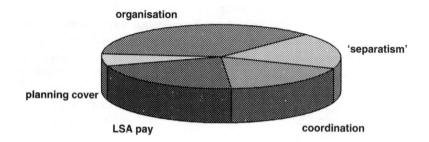

Figure 9.4 Features of Inclusion Project delaying transition to inclusion in partner schools

116

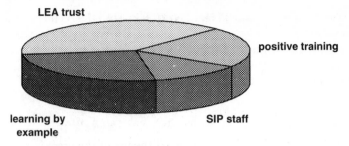

Figure 9.5 The sharing of expertise and development of trust

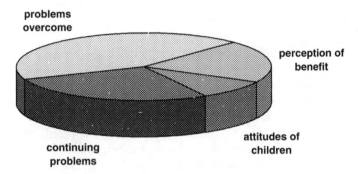

Figure 9.6 The changing attitudes of staff

changed position of the LEA during the first year of the project, with many perceiving as reneging on promises, has contributed to a loss of confidence.

Figure 9.6 shows that there were also positive and negative facets of staff attitude to inclusion in general and the project in particular in partner schools. These were broadly as follows:

- *Anticipated problems overcome.* In most cases, staff were positive about the Inclusion Project and commented that – often contrary to expectation – the experience of including these young people had been wholly beneficial, for the ex-special school students, for the partner school students and for the staff.
- *Attitudes and behaviour of children.* Many positive staff attitudes related to the manifestly inclusive behaviour of the host children.
- *Perception of benefit.* Many comments and observations related to the benefits perceived to accrue to the school from the Inclusion Project.
- *Continuing problems.* However, despite the goodwill which this experience had engendered, there were still perceived to be hurdles to overcome.

THE FINDINGS IN DETAIL

Features of partner schools which appear to have helped promote transition to inclusion

Policy

Although partner schools' policies make commitments to inclusion, staff were often unclear as to the contents of their own schools' policies. This, however, conforms to the national picture on policy awareness by staff (see OFSTED, 1996b; Tarr and Thomas, 1997). What is more significant than specific knowledge of the written policy is the understanding by staff of the commitment which is made by the school management to a policy of inclusion and to the implicit understanding that this commitment is embodied in the policy.

In one of the primary schools involved in the project, for instance, the teacher-co-ordinator from the Inclusion Project is a member of the senior management team of eight people, which is the core planning team for the school. This provides unmistakable evidence of the importance attached by the headteacher and governors to inclusion and to the project. The head of this school makes it a central objective to keep the profile of inclusion high and to ensure its regular discussion at meetings of staff and governors. The policy on inclusion is clear and this clarity is demonstrated in the expressed attitudes of staff and the behaviour of the children.

Staff – more often those in secondary schools – gave as their notion of the school's policy a hybrid of their own views and the perceived consensus of the staff. A secondary school teacher, for instance, said, 'I *think* that is the school's policy . . . that the children are included if they would have been included if they were able-bodied.'

This is clearly not consistent with an inclusive attitude, implying that children only from certain kinds of special schools would be welcome in the school. The view was repeatedly expressed, especially by the secondary teachers. There were also imagined to exist certain policy limits on the numbers of children who could be accommodated. The expression of a consensual view as though it were policy points to the need for continual review of schools' policies, with such a review process involving senior management, governors and representatives from the Inclusion Project. There is perhaps a role here for senior Inclusion Project staff in initiating the annual review of the schools' special educational needs (SEN) policies and in facilitating the continuing discussion of the policy with staff.

Official SEN policies, which schools are obliged to write under the 1993 Education Act, are not the only articulation of policy. The school's policy is expressed in a variety of ways and through a range of documents. In one partner school, the inclusive ethos was expressed in the production of a document on the role of the support assistant produced collectively by Inclusion Project and mainstream staff. The notion of collective responsibility for the mechanisms behind inclusion is clearly an important one.

Physical suitability

Few comments were made about the benefits of access-in-mind buildings. Even where buildings are new, there are constraints on the ability of the school to take children with disabilities, and these have caused tensions where there have existed differing expectations as to the capacity of the school to accommodate students with special physical needs. In other words, even where buildings are acknowledged to be relatively 'friendly' with regard to access, constraints are still felt to exist.

Attitude of staff and parents

Positive staff attitude appears to have been an important factor in promoting successful transition. In all the schools, there was a great deal of goodwill expressed both towards the children and the project in general. Comments expressing a positive attitude in schools outweighed negative comments by about two to one. The 'positivity' of comments appeared to be linked with the ethos of the school as articulated by senior management: in the school in which inclusion had been most clearly developed at policy and practice levels, comments of all staff were uniformly positive. The following are some examples of the generality of comments among the partner schools:

This has helped our understanding of what society is about.
(Headteacher, secondary)

I mean there aren't so many children in wheelchairs, are there? So even if we took all those needing a school place, in the area, I wonder if there would be a problem really?
(Teacher, secondary)

There is nobody who has expressed any suggestion that we shouldn't have Luke in school – there's been no negative feedback.
(Headteacher, primary)

The attitudes pointed to here are supportive and pro-inclusion. Parents' comments were overwhelmingly positive, though there were some serious concerns expressed about continuity of health-related services and the need for community schooling as part of an inclusion project; these are covered in the section below on continuity of services (p. 138).

119

Management

Where communication was satisfactory, there was an apparent link with the quality and clarity of management structures. Given the complex management relationships introduced by the project there was an expressed need to know who was responsible for what. Where this clarity existed, attitudes were consistently positive.

A secondary LSA commented that she enjoyed being part of a learning support team in a larger environment rather than in the more 'oppressive' atmosphere of a special school. She commented that 'the managers at [the secondary school] are good, and it gives me confidence being part of the learning support team.'

Despite the strength of some internal procedures and the sometimes clear lines of management within the host school, the Inclusion Project had introduced some complex changes which it was proving difficult to deal with, as indicated in the following section.

Features of partner schools which appear to have hindered transition to inclusion

Communication

Comments about communication related not only to the everyday contacts with Inclusion Project staff (which were uniformly unproblematic) but also to two major issues:

• communication during the process of changing from one system to another; and
• the ongoing communication systems.

On the first of these, it was frequently felt that a major innovation had been introduced in a way which did not adequately address partner school staff concerns, particularly in the weeks and months which preceded the introduction of the children. (This was reported in most but not all schools.) Concerns were very soon dissipated once Inclusion Project staff had started work in partner schools, and once the young people were on the premises, but there were considerable strains felt *before* the project began. The strains were for a number of reasons. There was the feeling in the secondary school that the project had been initiated without sufficient consultation. There was also the feeling that the style of presentation to staff had not 'taken staff with the project', and was presented as a mission rather than a shared enterprise:

> We seemed that first term to assemble in the lecture theatre to be told about the cuts in the budget and how . . . we'd have to lose so many teachers. Then the next time we were assembled in the lecture theatre

was to be told we were going to take on this exciting challenge! I mean, it couldn't have been worse for the staff.

(Teacher, secondary)

It is worth noting that these concerns about preparation arose principally from staff in the secondary sector, where the potential for problems is magnified because of the larger number of staff involved. Inclusion Project staff acknowledge the shortcomings of their presentation to secondary school colleagues, but have pointed to the very limited amount of time that was available to them to make their case.

The second point concerns both communication between members of staff within one school and between Inclusion Project and school staff. One set of difficulties concerns those which arise from making time for meetings in full timetables, and the problems which arise when normal exigencies disrupt a full programme. Other problems concern a continuing attitude that because the Inclusion Project exists, then it exists separate from the mainstream systems of the school. Because of this, communication is inhibited − and inclusion is not realised. Take the following comments as examples:

I'm distressed that we are pretty much two teams, separate.

(SENCO)

There is definitely isolation from other members of staff − a 'them and us' feeling a bit. It's not deliberate, just happens because [the child] is not seen as the concern of the whole school as other pupils are − and we're seen as separate, as experts: but we're not.

(LSA, primary)

There are, then, 'them and us' concerns, together with concerns over clear lines of accountability.

Ongoing liaison between Inclusion Project staff and partner school staff reflects the same issues. Particularly in the secondary school, certain LSAs reported that contact with form tutors was less (in amount and effectiveness) than it might be. The roles of different tiers of staff within the Inclusion Project and their relationship with parallel staff in the host school are not always clearly understood.

Another facet of 'two cultures' − with a separate set of staff specifically and conspicuously dedicated for one set of students − is that contacts between parents and mainstream staff are more limited than they would be for the other children in the class. This is partly because the partner schools are not neighbourhood schools for many of the students, but also because mainstream staff rely on Inclusion Project staff to undertake the responsibility of parent liaison. This was noted as commonly in primary as in secondary schools.

Physical unsuitability

While the obstacles posed by physical constraints should not be insurmountable, it is clear that they present real hindrances to full inclusion if they are not adequately resolved prior to and during a child's attendance at a school. Staff seemed well able to cope with minor inconveniences, but many saw real problems to be overcome. Even in the access-in-mind new buildings, there were serious difficulties encountered.

The exigencies of everyday life, particularly in the larger secondary school environment, impose real constraints on the ability to be flexible, as this secondary school SENCO makes clear:

> You've got to have a cut-off somewhere along the line, given how many accessible loos have you got, how much is the school really, physically, able to take – given the fact that the lifts are so – I mean we've had one out of order for ages.

Other comments were made in the primary schools relating to the pressures imposed by lack of space and facilities, and these were linked to limits on the numbers of children these schools could be asked to take.

There do seem to be problems that remain to be resolved with regard to the physical fabric of the schools. The difficulties are significant and highlight the need to consider the relative merits of 'resourced schooling'[2] (seen as a compromise in Newham; see Jordan and Goodey, 1996) or truly inclusive schooling at neighbourhood schools. The limited experience here indicates that while the theoretical advantages of resourced schooling seem clear, in practice many crude but nevertheless difficult-to-resolve problems will remain even if schools are supposedly 'resourced'. And there will be additional problems arising from the designation (officially or unofficially) as a resourced school, if minor and unanticipated physical-fabric problems are exaggerated by the unexpected intake of additional pupils, which puts a school above its supposed 'quota'. With a designation as the resourced school for an area, an equilibrium could easily become unbalanced with such an unexpected intake of disabled students, and this was a real fear for many staff, as the next section shows.

Attitude of receiving staff

In contrast to the positive attitudes recorded earlier, some partner school staff were antagonistic to the introduction of an inclusion project. (It should be re-emphasised that these were in a minority.) Generally, these staff tended to express the opinion that only limited numbers of children were acceptable and/or that children with physical difficulties were acceptable, but that more disruptive children or larger numbers of children with disabilities would cause problems. For example:

> I am concerned for children with mental disabilities. It's very hard for them in places like this . . . they need so much help.
>
> (Teacher, secondary)

> I wouldn't be happy to see it open to people no matter what their disability. I think that could land us with all sorts of problems we've got no training to cope with.
>
> (Teacher, secondary)

While the most immediate consequences of such attitudes impinge upon planning for continuing professional development for staff, there are substantial concerns also for the project, given the distinction drawn earlier between 'resourced' schools and neighbourhood schools. The continually expressed fear of being 'swamped' has its roots in loose understanding about whether particular schools are 'designated' to take children with particular needs, and if so whether adequate resourcing will accompany such a designation. This perhaps has consequences for the future placing of children, with less stress on the necessity of specially provided physical resources – which provide in reality less than was expected and hoped for.

Where opposition to inclusion is analysed further it appears that there has been resentment over the first year of the project, especially about the perceived allocation of resources to the Inclusion Project children which is assumed to be out of proportion to their needs:

> There are so many problems and disabilities [amongst the other children] . . . which are not normally called that. Behaviour problems, for instance . . . I'm afraid the phrase 'dancing attendance' does seem to apply to these chosen few and . . . the bottom set for English have needs just as serious.
>
> (Teacher, secondary)

Such views may not reflect simply resistance to inclusion. It may be that the perception of an allocation of resources which is disproportionate to need is a real one, and it is one which is borne out in observational material on curriculum delivery (this is examined below). The more flexible use of the Inclusion Project resources in such a way that they can be delivered to more students is the possible implication.

Attitudes which arise from the perceived inappropriateness of recommendations about differentiation, however, would seem to have direct implications more for continuing professional development:

> [Learning Support told me that] everything should be blown up from A4 to A3 . . . and so on. Well, these sort of recommendations are basically cloud-cuckoo ones because no way can a teacher do a one-to-one

support like that when you've got the other twenty-eight in the class that you're aiming the lesson at.

(Teacher, secondary)

The recommendations which had been made to this teacher do not appear to have been too difficult to implement (especially with the provision of support) and her reluctance to consider them conflicts with a) the school's vision on equal opportunities, and b) far looser expectations concerning the differentiation of work for all children. In other words, she does not appear to have considered that these recommendations may have benefits for a wide range of children. An inclusive philosophy does not seem to have been assimilated and there are implications here for ongoing mainstream staff training by Inclusion Project staff.

Resources

Although shortage of resources was mentioned from time to time, and was observed occasionally, this by no means represented an insistent theme. If anything, the reverse is the case, as indicated above: mainstream staff would be more likely to comment on the generosity of resourcing (particularly of personnel) for the Inclusion Project children. Observations confirmed this: there was a marked contrast in the amount of assistance which children in the Inclusion Project received compared with those with other special needs. However, resourcing needs were mentioned and observed and these usually related to time for co-ordination. As one primary head commented, 'A huge amount of time is needed for meetings and discussion.' Because timetables are so full, meetings and discussion are usually squeezed into odd moments during the day.

Where resources did seem to present intractable problems for staff and students, this appeared to arise more due to the difficulties of co-ordinating several services than to shortage of funds. (For example, from a primary co-ordinator: 'The computer is still a problem [after a year]. . . . It was a disaster for [student] last year.') Other persistent low-level irritations (for example, ridges in floors, even of purpose-built schools), or more significant features of school life which would require some resource solution (for example, a child's inability to take part in activities involving large gym apparatus) occurred from time to time, and usually seemed to take longer than anticipated to resolve.

Features of Inclusion Project teams which have helped promote successful change

Flexibility

As noted in chapter 2, there is much current discussion nationally on the role of learning support assistants, with a consensus developing on the benefits which accrue from a flexible deployment of their expertise – that is, to enable and encourage LSAs to work with a wider range of children than those to whom they are specifically 'allocated'. There was much evidence that co-ordinators have encouraged such flexibility in the Inclusion Project, and where this was the case it was well received by staff in partner schools.

> The LSAs are very, very good at their job of adapting what's going on. [The co-ordinator's] trying to get them to withdraw a bit, so that Caroline develops more independence, so now they wander off and help other kids.
>
> (Teacher, primary)

> At first, I was only involved with one child (whereas I had been involved with several at Princess Margaret School) until [the child] found her niche and could be helped by the school LSAs – like if they were going round the class hearing everybody read – in which case I'm free to help others.
>
> (LSA, primary)

Not only this, but there was innovative use of a team approach in the deployment of LSAs, with their allocation changing depending on curriculum content, student needs and LSA skills. This is a new and important development in the use of assistants and was well received by staff:

> At first it was a bit odd because every time I looked around there was someone different, but now it's something you get used to and in actual fact it's much better because [the co-ordinator] will try and give me the assistants that she knows will know more about that subject.
>
> (Teacher, primary)

However, the development of flexible ways of working was idiosyncratic, and depended upon the initiative and creativity of individuals, despite the evident willingness of mainstream staff to sanction more flexibility.

On the other hand, flexibility on the part of LSAs was occasionally actually resisted by mainstream staff:

> some of them [LSAs] hardly sit with the people they're supposed to be with at all, you know, just sort of wander generally round the class.
>
> (Teacher, secondary)

125

It seemed from this that a policy development forum with project staff together with key staff from partner schools was necessary. This would enable those who have not yet developed flexible practice (because of an implicit assumption that dedicated attention to project students is the rule) to move in this direction. There are developments here which are important for inclusive practice, and it is necessary to give them official sanction.

The co-ordinators too had developed flexibility, and such flexibility marries with an inclusive philosophy here also:

> In the beginning I felt that this [the project group of children in a primary school] was my class of kids, albeit that they were in different [mainstream] classes and I felt that I almost had to justify my existence and I didn't want the class teachers to feel overloaded, so I was sort of in there saying, 'I can do this, I can do that,' whereas now I'm more confident at saying, 'I'm here to help you and do what you want me to do.' And you let them [classteachers] take a bit more control and therefore get more ownership – and then *they're* more included.
>
> (Teacher co-ordinator, primary)

While flexibility was not uniform across all Inclusion Project staff, there are clear moves in this direction.

Organisation of service

The day-to-day organisation of the service and the professionalism of its members were commented upon. One LSA comments on the changes she has noticed since one of the children moved to Inclusion Project responsibility: 'There are a lot of improvements . . . There's a huge amount of support now – and it's nice to have a teacher taking responsibility for his education.' Such comments, however, must be read alongside the observations and comments reported above concerning problems in communication and difficulties of organising staff within different professions, systems and institutions. (Those observations outweigh these.) Again, there is evidence of idiosyncratic practice: in some situations communication is unproblematic and lines of responsibility are clear, whereas in others there are frequent breakdowns and misunderstandings.

An important point about the organisation of service delivery is made by the Deputy Principal i/c Inclusion Project – and this is of relevance in the context of the history of service delivery for children with special needs. Commentators such as Weatherley and Lipsky (1977), with their concept of 'street level bureaucrats', and Wolfensberger (1990) note that the provision of a *service* often has concomitants which are not necessarily in the best interests of the supposed recipients. In short, it is easy for the service to become merely advisory, and progressively to avoid 'hands on' activity. The new service has successfully avoided this path:

Although we could be a sort of consultancy, or advocate for the children's rights, all sorts of good and worthwhile things, I feel that one of
the things that has shifted schools on this has been the actual practice
of us doing it, in classrooms, not having somebody coming round and
[offering advice]. . . . It's the difference between an advisory role and
[doing it]. . . . It's the actual *being there.*

(Deputy Principal i/c Inclusion Project)

The avoidance of merely advisory work, and the continued provision of
hands-on delivery, is significant given the pull towards professionalisation
and bureaucratisation which inheres in 'service' delivery. The Inclusion
Project's success here can be attributed at least in part to the characteristics
of the new service: its roots in a compact, established team, and its clear
sense of purpose with a set of children for whom there is responsibility.

Features of Inclusion Project teams which have impeded or delayed successful change

Organisation of service

Overlapping with the theme *communication* identified as part of institutional
resistances to inclusion, were observations concerning the structure and
organisation of the service itself. As with the communication theme, issues
here focused on lines of management and accountability in multi-professional,
multi-agency collaboration.

Co-ordinators offered some useful insights about the structure and organisation of the service and its success in encouraging inclusion. If inclusion is
to mean not merely re-placement, but rather the introduction of a range of
empowering and facilitating structures (as discussed in Part I of this book)
to the school, then those structures have to be put in place, and this
demands some fundamental rethinking of attitudes and reworking of practices from those which existed in the special school. One primary
co-ordinator points to the 'dependency culture' of the special school and the
danger of this being continued in any service based on the school:

I think special schools promote dependency culture. They're spoon fed
– we've even taken their children to the dentist! . . . and it's about
educating them and *not* looking after them . . . they're here to learn so
they should be as independent as they can be.

(Co-ordinator, primary)

Her feeling here was that the move to the mainstream in itself invoked this
change in part. This weighing of physical and educational priorities was also
of concern to some partner school staff. However, other comments and other
observations (including repeated references in discussing children's needs to

talk about their *physical and care* needs) indicates that there is still some considerable progress to be made here.

Having children attend their local, neighbourhood schools figured strongly in the earlier discussion as to what comprised 'inclusion'. Several of the children in the Inclusion Project did not attend their neighbourhood schools, and this was a cause for concern for certain (but not all) parents, and for some staff. One co-ordinator attributed the 'resourced schooling' to the 'the way it started' – in other words to the inception and organisational foundations of the project. Given that the Inclusion Project was an innovation in organisational practice, this was perhaps inevitable: the seeds of the project lay in the initiatives of particular individuals who had an interest in enabling inclusion in collaboration with a local primary school headteacher. However, the school of this headteacher was local to Princess Margaret School rather than necessarily local to the children's homes, and children were therefore not placed, following these first exploratory moves, in their neighbourhood schools. Subsequent firming-up of these early placements seemed an obvious way to proceed, rather than moving children yet again to neighbourhood schools. Likewise, links were made with a secondary school which appeared to offer significant advantages in terms of the fabric of its new building, and this again provided rationale for a 'resourced school' placement strategy.

While these early decisions were understandable and perhaps inevitable, given the organic nature of the growth of the Inclusion Project, future development of similar projects can perhaps learn from this of the probable benefits to be gained by the planned placement of ex-special school pupils at their neighbourhood schools.

One of the elements of inclusion identified by the Council for Exceptional Children, and identified in chapter 1, is the development of *systems for co-operation* within the school, such as peer tutoring, buddy systems, circles of friends, co-operative learning. The active development of these is a need for the future, as highlighted by this co-ordinator:

> SIP has to offer something else, other than what LEA can provide –
> like counselling, or circles of friends. But there's going to be confusion
> between what SIP can aim to do and what the LEA would be wanting.
> (Co-ordinator, primary)

The latter part of this comment refers to the need for consonance between the policy of the 'purchaser' (in this case the LEA) and the provider in the development of any truly inclusive service. If the purchaser sees – and articulates in written policy – a continuing need for significant levels of segregation in special schools, it will be unable to provide sufficient resources to provide the facilitatory elements of service delivery referred to above.

128

Comparability of pay scales

A surprising number of comments during interviews related to disparity of pay scales between LSAs, about which there appears to be resentment from LEA LSAs, who are paid less than Inclusion Project LSAs. The problem here would not seem to be the fault of the Inclusion Project; nor is it within its ambit to solve them. They stem from a lack of attention nationally to the growing profession of support assistants in schools and point to a need for rationalisation of pay scales and conditions of service.

Co-ordination of roles

This theme represents yet another facet of the plethora of roles, professions and agencies involved within the project and outside it. The general sub-themes discovered here are as follows:

- Isolation of Inclusion Project LSAs from other LSAs.
- Organising cover for absent staff. One co-ordinator, for instance, is unable always to manage cover for absent staff because of her part-time nature. Therefore the job reverts to the Inclusion Project manager, but only if the appropriate message is passed on by the school.
- Regular liaison. The geographical spread of the Inclusion Project, together with part-time work and the exigencies of timetables, means that person-to-person contacts of Inclusion Project staff are not always as regular as they need to be for good co-ordination.
- Parental contact. Because Inclusion Project staff exist, mainstream staff may withdraw from initiating contact, and conversely parents' automatic first point of contact is Inclusion Project personnel. One teacher commenting on lack of contact with parents of one of the project pupils comments: 'I suppose from her [mother's] point of view it must be quite difficult to know who to refer to because she's used to calling and talking to [Inclusion Project staff] but she's not as yet grown accustomed to talking to me [whereas] I see all the other parents on a daily basis.'
- Inter-agency contact and agreement. In one example, there was apparent agreement on the need to move to a different regime of physiotherapy, yet an inability to effect this change since the person who could make the decision was not available.

Existence of 'separatist' attitudes

There were evident in many of the expressed attitudes of staff and in class-room observations a retention of attitudes concerning pedagogy and needs which stressed the separateness of the Inclusion Project pupils. Inclusion Project students would often (but not most of the time) be doing different tasks on their own and away from other children. This is covered fully later in the section on the curriculum, but it is mentioned here insofar as it has implications for initial and continuing professional development of staff. Some illustrative comments are given here:

> [Inclusion Project student] doesn't interact a lot because of the helper. He sits on his own table using a lap-top because the other kids would use him as a distraction.
>
> (Teacher, secondary)

> She's [Inclusion Project student] started to say she doesn't like being withdrawn for individual work – but [co-ordinator] has told her that she has to do it.
>
> (LSA)

> I'm surprised at the amount of time [Inclusion Project student] is coming out of class, but [classteacher] is adamant that this is valuable.
>
> (Co-ordinator)

The attitudes and practices observed here are often those of individuals, and there is much heterogeneity in attitude and practice amongst individuals. The separatist attitudes concern the putative special needs of the Inclusion Project students. Usually, in considering these supposed needs, the benefits which arise from full inclusion are ignored or played down. In making these assumptions about need, there may be the retention of an attitude that special needs of Inclusion Project students can best be met by specialist staff, and that mainstream staff should be discouraged from 'dabbling'. Or there may be the view that given the presence of Inclusion Project staff, those staff should dedicate themselves to those most in need. Whichever is the case, the view is inconsistent with current views on the deployment of specialist staff and the implications are clearly for continuing professional development.

The sharing of expertise and developing of trust between the Inclusion Project and partner schools

Benefits of learning by example from Inclusion Project staff and students

Benefits accrued to mainstream staff and students from the Inclusion Project experience, and this was due to two main factors: first, the presence of new staff who had skills to share with mainstream staff which would be of benefit not only to the Inclusion Project students but also to many of the other children, and second the presence of the Inclusion Project students provided what was called by more than one mainstream teacher a 'humanising' presence for the whole school. The second point is illustrated by this teacher's comment:

> I think it's very good from both sides, from the normal able-bodied children being able to accept and relate to youngsters in wheelchairs,

as well as for [Inclusion Project student] having to deal with people who are all . . . doing the same activities as him.

(Teacher, secondary)

Positive training experiences

Most comments about training came from LSAs. In other words, it was LSAs rather than teaching staff who felt that they themselves had learning needs (e.g. 'We had in-house training at special school in lifting, but nothing educational as such other than lots of discussions with teachers: we need more non-contact time for this'). The observations already made in this chapter point to a wider set of training needs – not just for LSAs, but also for teaching staff at all levels. These do not relate to curricular knowledge, but rather to the ethos behind inclusion and the organisational practice which makes inclusion a reality.

LEA trust/liaison

Given the travails of the project over the year of the study, there were unsurprisingly many observations relating to the LEA, its motives in withdrawing from the original arrangements, and the negotiations with it. These have general as well as specific implications, and for that reason are discussed here.

Several staff pointed to the financial advantages for an LEA of agreeing to a programme of closure and then failing to maintain the ensuing inclusion project, and clearly the contractual basis of future arrangements with other LEAs in any future project must be secure against such contingencies.

Others (both Inclusion Project and LEA staff) pointed to the policy of the LEA needing to be unequivocal in its support of inclusion before a project could go ahead. The consequences of a less-than-clear endorsement of inclusion results in inadequate funds being freed up to support it, as has been the experience in the USA (discussed in chapter 1). In the US, though, Public Law 94-142 (the Education for All Handicapped Children Act) enables parents to challenge segregationist policies with more success than its less robust equivalents in the UK (the 1981 and 1993 Education Acts) and all states are now being instructed to implement inclusionary policy and associated funding mechanisms. Until LEAs are obliged to devise more radical policies, it seems likely that the pressures on them which the Audit Commission (1992a) highlighted will result in the status quo being maintained in most cases.

The changing attitudes of partner schools

Reflection on expected problems which did not materialise

One of the clearest themes which emerged concerning the process of change since the start of the project was its success as far as the partner school staff were concerned. In all schools, and especially in the secondary school, staff admitted to feelings varying from mild anxiety to 'panic' about the introduction of children with disabilities. However, equally clear is the change of attitude once pupils had started. As the headteacher of the secondary school commented, 'Once it started people relaxed.' Some quotations illustrate the power in the transformations in feeling:

> I was *very* apprehensive about teaching [Inclusion Project child] . . . about the physical organisation and its effect on the rest of the class, and about how to talk to her. Now I don't know what I was worried about: it's no problem. She's just lovely and fits in with what we do. My fear was fear of the unknown.
>
> (Teacher, primary)

> As a faculty we were all concerned about the fact that the labs are pretty small, and so we thought that there were going to be problems with safety as far as carrying out practical work was concerned. I mean in the end these fears have largely, I think, proved to be groundless.
>
> (Teacher, secondary)

> [I was worried] about how the child was going to integrate with the others and the fear of them being seen as an outsider and wondering how to try and get the group to break that problem down. I think that was the main worry about it, really. That's turned out to be completely groundless as far as [child's] concerned, which has been great.
>
> (Teacher, secondary)

> It's actually doing it that educates you. And I think my mind was closed anyhow, because I think I was so frantically busy.
>
> (Teacher, secondary)

> The odd thing is that the ones [in the staff] who were most vociferous, I would say are probably now the most positive.
>
> (SENCO)

There was complete unanimity in the direction of these comments, as regards initial fears not being realised. There were no comments at all saying that initial concerns had been borne out by practice, nor were there any comments expressing concerns about the children or about their influence on the class. In all respects, the Inclusion Project students appear to have been welcomed by partner school staff and students and their presence has been seen universally as beneficial.

Perception of benefit to school

Linked with the previous theme is a clear perception of benefit to the school of the presence both of the new children and of the service:

> They're nothing but an asset as far as I'm concerned.
>
> (Teacher, secondary)

> I feel that I'm doing something really worthwhile . . . that was one of the reasons I became a teacher: it wasn't to shout at kids and be a disciplinarian, it was to give the kids the best start in life that they could have. And teaching [two Inclusion Project students] makes me feel really good . . . it's good for your – your soul.
>
> (Teacher, secondary)

> It's positively affected their [the class's] tolerance and empathy and patience.
>
> (Teacher, primary)

In contrast with observations in a previous section about difficulties of communication, there were also comments about the organisational *benefits* which the project had brought with it:

> Things happen quicker now (for example, a special table will arrive much sooner than it would have before) and who pays for what is more straightforward (e.g. the provision of a calculator with big buttons). Barnardos' funding of [the specialist teacher] one and a half days has freed special needs teaching for others in school – also [the LSAs] work with rest of class, so there are benefits for the other children too.
>
> (Teacher, primary)

> Having the additional adult in the class has benefited other children at the same time because sometimes Luke has been working as part of a group and so the other children have benefited from having Luke's helper there as well.
>
> (Teacher, primary)

There are contrasts here with the comments quoted earlier both in the observations about organisation and in the flexibility in the use of LSAs and teaching staff. The fact that such different practice can exist in different elements of the project points both to the importance of the host culture in developing practice, but also perhaps to the effectiveness of individual personnel in effecting organisational change and in disseminating ideas about inclusion. Again, the implications appear to be for the preparation of partner schools and in-service education both for host school staff and project staff.

Continuing perception of problems

The 'continuing perception of problems' theme is one that was fairly consistently observed, yet in reality this was a perception of *hypothetical* problems introduced by new students who would pose some hypothetical hazard, organisational difficulty or pedagogical problem which would be insurmountable. These anxieties about hypothetical difficulties were harboured despite the positive experiences so far and the universal experience that initial worries about the existing Inclusion Project children had evaporated very quickly in practice.

> [Staff have been] deciding how much they could accept, how far they could go. They've said to themselves, 'I could have *that* disability in my class . . . but I couldn't go *that* far.'
>
> (SENCO, secondary)

> Q   *What sort of disabilities would worry you?*
>
> A   Well, speech; I don't know, perhaps cerebral palsy, children who are unpredictable in their behaviour.
>
> Q   *You don't have any of those already?*
>
> A   Well we do, course we do, yes. But on the other hand – and I'm sorry to use the word 'normal' but life is full of normals and averages, isn't it? – you deal with normal children in certain ways. You cannot deal with children who are disabled in the same ways.
>
> (Teacher, secondary)

It should be re-emphasised that these views were expressed about hypothetical situations, and staff usually made an explicit contrast with these hypothetical children and the actual children in the Inclusion Project, about whom they were positive. Nevertheless, the implication is for preparatory in-service education which gives examples of successful inclusion in other schools and pointers to effective practice.

The changing roles of staff

Teachers

There was little evidence from staff comments that staff had changed their teaching styles in response to the children. Classroom observations confirm that a more common response to the presence of the children is to 'pretend nothing's happened' – in other words to accept and welcome the new children but then largely to leave the job of teaching them to the specialist staff. The following comment is illustrative:

> I haven't allowed it [my style] to be changed. Whoever has been supporting him has had to do all the fetching and carrying . . . so what tiny bit of practical work he is capable of he's never had to move the wheelchair around the room [for], and I haven't altered my teaching style so far as he is concerned.
>
> (Teacher, secondary)

An LSA in the secondary school notes that teachers seemed inhibited by the presence of the LSA to go and work with the child, because, she felt, 'many [teachers] mistook the facilitating role of the LSA for one of teaching, and were perhaps reluctant to appear to be teaching another adult, or to look as though they were assuming the adult hadn't understood.' However, some teachers did note a change in their own style:

> I try to make them as much part of the group as I can without being obvious. I will change my teaching style and the materials that they need where it needs to be changed, but I want them to fit in. I want them to be part of the mainstream without it being obvious. And to treat them like any other classmate. If they need preferential treatment – no, not preferential but different – I try to make them feel like anyone else in this school.
>
> (Teacher, secondary)

This was confirmed by classroom observation: in one case an experienced primary teacher was noted skilfully to incorporate the Inclusion Project student in the work of a group of children without identifying him or marking him out for special comment. However, her questioning and language were sensitively adapted to his needs.

The degree of adaptation made by teachers in general seemed to be less to do with the specific learning needs of the children in question than with the experience of the teacher and to her/his view of how children with special needs should be taught.

LSAs

Many issues arise concerning the delivery of support and many of these in turn focus on an appropriate role for the LSA. Some of these issues have already been covered, centering on the issue of the dedication of an LSA to one child. An aspect of this is the influence of LSAs on classteachers – an influence which they have merely by their presence. There is the possibility here that that presence may inhibit the classteacher from becoming more involved in the work of the 'special' children. For instance, one LSA described how she enjoys the role of 'expert' in the larger environment of the secondary school; she recognised that while this adds to her status it does not promote the notion of a 'giving away' of special expertise, nor an empowering of mainstream staff.

If LSAs do enjoy this status it may inhibit more inclusionary practice – which may be incipient or tentative in the classteachers, ready to emerge if encouraged but failing to emerge if not sanctioned by 'the experts'. This teacher's comment attests to this:

> The PMS [Inclusion Project] staff are focused on one child. Because it's more intensive they're not available to work with the rest of the class and give them the benefits of their talents. PMS LSAs are fully occupied with [Inclusion Project child] so they're not able to do that – but maybe if he's in a group they could work with the group?
>
> (Teacher, primary)

The diversity of view among the LSAs on this issue, however, is shown by this comment by a primary LSA, which indicates a desire for a 'freeing up' of the role: 'I'm hoping to do more general work in classrooms – I'm trying to get "out of the cupboard".' Others desired and welcomed this freeing up also, and there were many observations of Inclusion Project LSAs attending to and helping other children. Indeed, where one particular Inclusion Project student conspicuously did not need continuous support (except in science and CDT practicals), the assigned LSA had taken the initiative and negotiated with classteachers to do other work, which included helping other children and leaving the classroom to prepare materials. This general help was seen as benefiting all children but also (in the preparation of materials for the computer) as benefiting the Inclusion Project students as part of the larger whole of which they were one element. Another LSA (primary) summed up the new, more flexible role as, 'On-the-spot differentiation'.

This extension of the role beyond that of merely one child's helper has developed over the year in a number of ways, from simple monitoring to more complex activities. The value of the former is exemplified here:

> There's never once been an occasion when I've wished, 'Oh Gosh, I wish they [LSAs] weren't there.' And they're not just an extra pair of hands – they're an extra pair of eyes, because you know they're looking around, and if I'm not looking that way they might be.
>
> (Teacher, primary)

Other comments related to the value of the LSA even being able to discipline the whole class, which was welcomed by some.

Parents were not consistent in their support for more flexible working by the LSAs. One student's parents acknowledged that their son needed support only for a minority of the time and suggested that it would not be in his interests to have dedicated support 100 per cent of the time. They therefore suggested the idea that a paging device be used by the LSA, so that she could be called whenever needed. This seems a creative and relatively inexpensive idea and one that could be adopted not only with this student but wherever appropriate. Another parent, however, felt that the LSA was there solely for her son, an expectation which will have arisen during the inception of the project. The Inclusion Project students themselves were unequivocal in their support of the ways that they were being helped by the LSAs.

The process of change from special school to Inclusion Project employment has been accompanied by several changes for the better as far as some LSAs are concerned:

> it has meant meetings with [co-ordinator] once a week, and there's now a specialist teacher supporting in class whereas before there either wasn't one or there was confusion about the roles of the classteacher and the specialist teacher.
>
> (LSA, primary)

The negative consequence of additional responsibility, however, lay in extra meetings (which were difficult to get to) and additional paperwork, though the value of and need for these were recognised.

All of the above areas point to preparatory and in-service training, and the need for it was explicitly articulated by some LSAs, such as this comment from a secondary LSA: 'Teachers are not sure how to approach LSAs, who need to explain what they're there for and how their role could relate to the school's development.'

Teacher-co-ordinators

The role of the teacher-co-ordinator has developed idiosyncratically in different situations depending on the needs of the children involved. In the secondary school, it is summarised as:

> to give information on each pupil's IEP and needs – and then they and the learning support team develop this liaison with subject staff together – [the SENCO] has planning meetings with faculty heads, in which [the co-ordinator] is involved, and there's also joint planning for differentiation. For the development of IEPs, there's more liaison between learning support and teachers needed, even if it's just at the end of lesson.
>
> (Co-ordinator, secondary)

A primary co-ordinator emphasises different aspects of the role:

> We wrote extra bits into the basic teacher job description ... the teacher bit is essential, partly because you're having to prepare and differentiate work and partly to have credibility with the other teachers. I have an oversight of each individual child's curriculum so I

talk to the classteachers about what they're doing with the other kids and whether things can be modified – in some cases they can and in other cases it's just not appropriate – and whether they'll do it at a different level. I keep records and talk to parents and liaise with them. It is very much a team. If the child needs physio . . . the three of us talk informally every week but on a formal basis once a half term.

(Co-ordinator, primary)

The co-ordinator's role comprises essentially:

- differentiation of work;
- organising record-keeping;
- co-ordination of staff;
- liaison with other agencies;
- liaison with parents whose children attend non-neighbourhood schools.

All parents and partner school staff were supportive of the contribution of the co-ordinators and the essential role that they fulfil. Note has been made above of the need to ensure that direct contact between parents and school staff is facilitated. In other words, parents may be inhibited in making direct contact because they know that the 'correct' line of communication is through the co-ordinator. There is perhaps an additional role here for the co-ordinator to facilitate such contact.

The continuity of services

Preliminary documentation about the inception of the project indicated that some parents had expressed concern at the outset over the continuation of the services which their children had received while they were at the special school. Would they continue when the children were in the mainstream? Several parents expressed their fears forcefully at meetings about the proposed project. It was thus felt necessary to discuss with them their perceptions as to the actual situation several months into the project. It must be remembered in the reporting of these findings that this group is self-selecting; in other words, those who were most hostile to the inclusion service will have moved their children to alternative special schools.

The perceptions of parents are different and sometimes contradictory, perhaps representative of different experiences of the several teams with which they now have contact, and the success of each of these in establishing successful liaison. Parents' different experiences and perceptions may also be governed by the nature of their children's disabilities. It may be that perception of reduction is associated most closely with those children with the most serious disabilities.

These perceptions are therefore presented in several themes. One concerns the generally positive reception of the Inclusion Project:

He was inward and introverted [at special school]. Here he is like a different child.

(Parent, primary)

She [daughter] never said she wanted to go back to Princess Margaret School – but now she always wants to go back to school at the end of the holidays.

(Parent, primary)

Educationally-wise he's being stretched more. Because there are children of higher abilities than him and a lot more, um, independent children I suppose. They're more street wise.

(Parent, secondary)

The standard is so much higher now, and the variety of work, of course, is also helping him with ideas. He is having to think more and work more, because of the competition. Not thinking, 'Oh well, yes, this is good' and 'I know it's going to be good enough.'

(Parent, secondary)

One of the students bears this out in interview:

STUDENT: Well. Life's sort of, it's more concentrated for me now.
INTERVIEWER: How do you mean?
STUDENT: You get a task and you're expected to do more.
INTERVIEWER: Work? Is it difficult in any other way? What about the sorts of people you're meeting now?
STUDENT: There's loads of different people. There's good teachers, bad teachers.
INTERVIEWER: Do you think it's worth the extra effort that you've put in to be here?
STUDENT: Yes, definitely. I think it's all paid off.
INTERVIEWER: In what way has it paid off?
STUDENT: I'm working harder than I've ever done in my life and I feel great about it.

The second theme, by contrast, represents a perceived contraction of facilities:

The facilities have been good, though not good enough. The physio only visits once a week as against twice a week before and swimming is now going to stop – he had it every day at Barnardos. We are really worried about the lack of physio: he's getting very stiff. [3]

(Parent, primary)

She has half an hour [of physio] a week which isn't enough – she'd been getting it every day at Princess Margaret School. It's difficult to find out about resources without PMS acting as central point.

(Parent, primary)

He's not getting as much hydro as he was – well, we call it swimming – he was swimming twice a week. He's now only swimming once a week and when PMS closes this year I think it's going to be highly unlikely that he gets any swimming, to be honest.

(Parent, secondary)

It will be noted that nearly all of the illustrative commentary here (which is representative of the parents' views generally) relates to the physical aspects of care, which appear in the case of some students to have declined in quantity since the inception of the project. These include the provision of hydrotherapy, about which several parents had concerns.

Although they are more than balanced by commentary about the adequacy of such provision, and by the substantial social and curricular benefits of inclusion, it is worth noting that the parents who were most concerned about the lack of, for example, physiotherapy, tended to be those with children who had the most serious physical disabilities.

As problems centered around inter-agency co-operation and the funding of services adjacent to education (such as speech therapy and physiotherapy) there are issues here to be resolved concerning the financing of a set of devolved services. Substantial multi-disciplinary co-operation is required at not only professional level but, perhaps more importantly, at administrative and policy-making levels.

A third set of comments related to the hypothetical children with whom the Inclusion Project would not be able to cope, in the same way that it occurred with the teachers. A typical comment from a secondary parent was, 'I wouldn't like to generalise about inclusion – it works wonderfully for [my child] but it wouldn't work for everyone.'

Amongst this complex set of attitudes and perceptions is a strong feeling as to the benefits in general of the project, though some parents had concerns about loss of therapies. It may be worth noting that this regret of the loss of health-related services is one of the consistent findings of integration studies of children and young people with physical disabilities.

RECOMMENDATIONS

A range of recommendations arise from this chapter on the process of change in the context of the literature review which preceded it. These recommendations have applicability for:

- other special school staff considering changes similar to that made in the Inclusion Project;
- other mainstream schools considering partnership in similar inclusion projects;
- LEAs; and
- national policy.

School culture

There are first recommendations concerning the ethos of the partner schools. A project cannot legislate for ethos; neither can it, if one is being realistic, do much to influence school culture from the outside. Nevertheless, there are points which can be kept in mind as Georgiades and Phillimore (1975) remind us when working with institutions such as schools. They say that it is important both to work with 'the healthy parts of the system' – in other words to seek out schools (or systems within schools) which are sympathetic to the change being proposed, and to 'cultivate the host culture' – to work with the system of the school and to seek to influence those who manage it.

These points are germane to the set of issues concerning the culture into which the Inclusion Project was moving. The attitude of staff and senior management was found to influence the acceptance of the project. Recommendations concerning school culture therefore include:

- negotiating for the co-ordinator to be on the senior management team of a partner primary school, or an appropriate management grouping of a secondary school (such as a head of years' group);
- suggesting and initiating continual review of schools' SEN policies, with such a review process involving senior management, governors and representatives from the inclusion project (see Tarr and Thomas, 1997);
- initiating a development forum with Inclusion Project staff together with key staff from partner schools. This would enable those who have not yet developed *flexible practice* to move in this direction;
- considering for future similar projects the benefits of more gradual change, especially if the effects of implementation mean that a particular school will be accommodating several students at one time.

Neighbourhood schools

The physical fabric of buildings can be a problem in embracing inclusion. However, on the basis of the limited sample of responses here, it appears that effecting change is more dependent on a sympathetic culture than on the physical fabric and design of buildings. While physical problems can be irritating and at times cause serious impediments to inclusion, ways round problems were often found if staff were supportive of inclusive ideals. The corollary of this is not to say that adaptations to buildings are unimportant, but rather that the benefits of neighbourhood schools (*vis-à-vis* 'resourced' schools) should be stressed in weighing the appropriateness of a particular school for a child.

Communication

- Written definition of roles and procedural guidelines are necessary for Inclusion Project and partner school staff. These will assist in determining not only appropriate pedagogic activity on the part of staff such as LSAs, but will also serve to guide staff inside and outside the Inclusion Project on who is responsible for what, and who is accountable to whom.
- Time for meetings should be timetabled for key staff. The budgetary implications of this should be accounted for through money-follows-child accounting systems.
- All staff in a school should use the same staffroom – there should not be a special staffroom or base for Inclusion Project staff.
- Mobile phones would provide a relatively inexpensive means of easing the accessibility of peripatetic co-ordinators.
- In secondary schools, where flexibility in the work of the LSA is especially important, pagers should routinely be available.
- Clear benefits have been demonstrated of keeping the 'teamness' of the Inclusion Project. The implication for future projects is that they should be kept to a small scale (as distinct from conflating the efforts of several closing special schools and producing a larger support service).

The work of LSAs

- It should be understood that one of the policy decisions behind an inclusion project is that its resources are delivered not merely to project students but also to other students in the host school. As part of this, it should be understood that it is legitimate and desirable for LSAs to work with a wider range of children.
- The team approach to the deployment of LSAs in the Inclusion Project was well received and should be considered in future projects.
- Pay scales for LSAs should be rationalised in such a way that there is a 'spine' on which all staff are paid.
- The common term LSA or ESA (Education Support Assistant) stresses the educational aspect of the assistant's role, and stresses the links between inclusion project assistants and host school assistants. Those terms thus seem preferable to SA (Support Assistant).
- The title LSA should be reinforced to partner school staff, so that the inaccurate and pejorative term 'carer' is not used.
- Prior to the implementation of a project, a programme of regular training for LSAs should be introduced and this should stress educational as opposed to care issues.

Continuing professional development

- One of the differences between inclusion and integration lies in the preparation of staff for the process. There should therefore be preparatory training of a practical nature backed up with reading material.
- There should be ongoing staff training of mainstream staff by Inclusion Project staff in the practicalities of making inclusion work.

'Purchaser–provider' relationship

- The purchaser (LEA) must make plans to shift sufficient funds from segregative services to make the provision of the above inclusive services a realistic proposition. The financial implications of inclusion are significant and an inclusive policy is a prerequisite for confidence in the ability of the purchaser to maintain the necessary level of services to support inclusion. (These services include a service manager, teacher-co-ordinators, LSAs, bought-in professional services and supply and 'cover' to provide non-contact time to hands-on staff for meetings, planning and training.)
- Contractual arrangements with the 'purchaser' of an inclusion service need to be secure at the outset of any project.

General

- A major organisational change such as this needs to be discussed carefully with staff; the idea cannot be successfully presented at a one-off meeting. A phased programme of introduction should be considered and even 'reverse integration' from the mainstream to the special school prior to the project as a preparation for staff and students of both schools.
- There is a good deal of evidence in this inclusion project of different attitudes and styles on the part of individuals involved in the project. Often, therefore, the appropriateness of particular ways of working for inclusion is predicated on the working preferences of individuals. Effort should therefore be expended in teaching staff about the ideals of inclusion and accompanying support practices before and during a project.
- There is strong support from schools for the active role taken by co-ordinators in the everyday work of the classroom. The role of the co-ordinator should continue to be primarily a hands-on one.
- As part of a new inclusion project, the active development of social and curricular strategies such as peer tutoring, buddy systems, circles of friends and co-operative learning should be considered from the outset.
- The benefits of maintaining additional therapeutic activities such as horse-riding should not be automatically assumed and should, in an inclusive environment, be assessed *vis-à-vis* the cost in curriculum lost.

- There should be a degree of 'slack' in the personnel management of the system to enable it to cover for sickness of staff without serious administrative problems.
- Parents should be encouraged to have direct contact with school, not principally with inclusion project staff.
- Some parents, particularly of children with more serious disabilities, regretted the loss of more regular hydrotherapy and physiotherapy. Ways of maintaining these by retaining central facilities should be considered in any new inclusion project.

10

HAVE CHILDREN BEEN INCLUDED IN THE CURRICULUM?

We began and ended our earlier chapter on the curriculum (chapter 3) with a discussion about what is meant by the curriculum and curricular inclusion. Our theme was that the curriculum is not usefully seen as a commodity which can be 'delivered' or 'accessed'. It is better seen, to quote from Swann, 'not as knowledge to be conveyed but as a set of teaching and learning relationships by which that knowledge is conveyed' (1988: 98). Some children will require experiences of one kind; some will respond better to experiences of another kind.

We emphasised also that there are no edicts which one can lay down about the appropriateness of the National Curriculum (NC) for all children. It is not an abrogation of the principle of inclusion to suggest that some children should have a different set of curricular experiences or even different curriculum content. It is no defeat to suggest that a child should be exempted from the NC.

And there are no special techniques or pedagogies which can be used with children who have difficulties which will magically provide the right experiences for them. The lesson of research over the past twenty years into children's learning is that good teaching is good teaching for all children.

It is on the basis of these assumptions that the analysis of children's curricular experiences in the Inclusion Project has been undertaken in this chapter.

A number of themes arose from the conjoint analysis of the literature and research data:

1 The extent of Inclusion Project students' presence/absence in classrooms. Reasons for any absence; effects of absence; access to the curriculum.
2 The nature of the focus of children's work as part of (a) the whole class; (b) groups; (c) as individuals. The inclusiveness of the related activities.
3 Facilitation of inclusion: by teachers and by learning support assistants.
4 The promotion of full access to the curriculum through (a) classroom management strategies and (b) differentiation.
5 The effects of promoting inclusion on the education of other pupils.

PHYSICAL PRESENCE AND ACCESS TO THE CURRICULUM

For many of the Inclusion Project co-ordinators, particularly those working with primary pupils, the establishment of a balance between students' presence in or absence from the classroom was a preoccupation throughout the year, and was further complicated by the strong views of the students and their classteachers on the issue.

There were some straightforward physical reasons why a child should have to be away from the classroom, such as toileting and physiotherapy. However, there was evidence that in two cases toileting was taking more time than it should, and there were suspicions that students might be using it as an excuse to avoid work. Attempts were being made to enable certain children to become sufficiently aware of the structure of the day to plan for themselves to ask for the toilet at break or lunchtime rather than during lessons. The disruption was serious enough in one student's case to prevent him from completing enough coursework to re-enter the GCSE and improve on the grade he obtained at special school.

Physiotherapy was another activity which took Inclusion Project students out of the classroom unless it could be somehow incorporated into work within it, as for example with Daniel's hand exercises, which the teacher felt would also be useful for other pupils. The development of in-class working by non-education staff such as physiotherapists was often remarked on for its benefits, but it depended to a great extent on the working preferences of the individual physiotherapists involved.

Secondary pupils were able to have some physiotherapy out of school hours and to fit the rest in with their subject timetables. For primary schoolchildren, with a more fluid structure to their week, there were often problems of missing part of a project or one stage of a learning process.

Withdrawal from the classroom for individual work was a regular feature of primary school life, sometimes to an adjoining room or to a central resource centre where other children had individual work sessions. The pupils seemed not to like being withdrawn and this ties in with other findings on withdrawal (Simmons, 1986). The actual site seemed to make no difference to Luke's and Caroline's resistance to withdrawal, suggesting that the real reasons for their reluctance lay elsewhere: the difficulty of the work, the pressure of one-to-one teaching, an unwillingness to leave the company of their peers and a stigma imposed by having their difference emphasised.

Teachers varied in their wish for withdrawal. Caroline's classteacher was resolute that Caroline needed to work on an individual programme for her basic skills as some other children did, even though the Inclusion Project co-ordinator was surprised at the amount of time Caroline was out of the classroom for this and other things. Luke's classteacher, on the other hand, became more and more unhappy with the amount that Luke was missing through his 'outside engagements', perhaps seeing that only partial access to class activities was leading to confusion.

Most primary Inclusion Project pupils also went horse-riding, and swimming at Princess Margaret School (which was still open at this time), in school time. This was causing a certain amount of controversy in all the schools because of the amount of whole-class work that was being missed as a result (and, at Heather Grove Primary, because some of the other children felt it was unfair that Inclusion Project pupils should be able to ride when they couldn't).

Inclusion Project students at the secondary school were exempted from some of the demands of the core curriculum, or the school's own requirements. This was not apparently an option for their non-disabled peers. Greg, for example, was allowed to take two GCSE courses in the area of technology, and no humanities subject at all; Jerry was allowed not to take French (which he hated); Mike was allowed not to take PE, which *he* hated. The flexibility that permitted notice to be taken of individual preference in this way could perhaps lead to envy of the students' special treatment, and it raises again the question of legal obligations to deliver the National Curriculum to all pupils (unless there is disapplication). The Meadow Hill Comprehensive SENCO felt that the school's curriculum as currently constituted could not promote educational inclusion for everyone who had the physical ability to be present in the classroom, commenting, 'My feeling was that if we had children who fell out of the learning curve of this school too far, I couldn't see that it would be a productive relationship for anyone'. These comments are a reflection of the constraints imposed by the compartmentalised secondary curriculum. Certain pupils at West Hill Primary, for instance, had severe learning difficulties yet were able to be included in the work and discourse of the class.

There is a distinction to be made here between serious learning difficulties and the literacy and numeracy difficulties experienced by Greg. The latter, though serious, were comparable with some other members of his year-group, and permitted him to work alongside them all the time with the help of an LSA. Even so, his mother was concerned that his involvement in some of the subjects was inappropriate. She was far from worried about him not having access to a full curriculum and commented that she felt that further compromises might have to be made on the curriculum front as a price to pay for Meadow Hill's continuing inclusion.

INCLUSIVE CLASSWORK, GROUPWORK AND INDIVIDUAL WORK

Classwork

However much teachers and Inclusion Project co-ordinators attempted to reduce the time spent by students in cupboards, resource centres or physiotherapy rooms, mere physical presence in the classroom, as noted above, was not necessarily an indication of involvement in the same aspects of the curriculum as the rest of the class. Luke, for example, often worked on his own programme with an LSA even though he was in the classroom:

> The only time I observed him actually doing the same as the others on this day was the Anglo-Saxon treasure hunt, to which he wasn't contributing much and from which he didn't appear to be benefiting except, that is, in terms of social contact.

> (Observation)

The same thing seemed to happen at West Hill Primary, again raising the question of the balance of individual progress in the basics against work in the group:

> Another assistant comes and talks to James. Shows a card with some signs on it. . . . The task is entirely different from that being asked of the rest of the class. . . . Tom returns to the class with two assistants. . . . Two assistants remove him from wheelchair and place him in a chair with a group of the children. But even though he is with a group he too is being asked to do an entirely different task from them.

> (Observation)

The work in question is clearly not just a differentiated version of that of the group but is of an altogether separate nature. Perhaps we should not be too indignant about this. Undertaking the same tasks as the rest of the children – or even differentiated activities – need not necessarily be the touchstone against which inclusive practice is measured (see Swann, 1988). The quality of inclusion is perhaps better measured by evidence of acceptance and appropriate activity, and by the quality of the teaching–learning experience.

However, if a child is capable of undertaking the same curriculum as the other children, then every effort should be made to integrate the work of the child with that of the class. It appeared that with careful planning and good liaison between classteacher and co-ordinator, individual work could be carried out in the context of the work undertaken by the rest of the class.

Groupwork

In all the schools there was evidence of teachers' appreciation of the value of groupwork for the Inclusion Project students (and their peers), particularly as a strategy for involving the more isolated pupils in a less one-sided learning process:

> Researcher: Have you found you've changed your teaching practice at all to accommodate Jerry?
>
> Teacher: Well, not enough really, because Jerry would benefit from more groupwork because he doesn't speak out in class – and when we do groupwork it's very successful, relatively. One day, for instance, we were doing some acting out of the play we'd been studying. Apparently he was full of it; he was quite thrilled. I'd like to do that more often, to give him the fun of it.

It was important that teachers planning to include Inclusion Project students in groupwork thought about how those students could contribute constructively, to avoid a merely token physical presence in the group. This could be hard in situations where the underlying concepts involved in a lesson were beyond the understanding of the Inclusion Project student:

> Luke in a group of three going round grounds (with LSA pushing), working out clues for Anglo-Saxon treasure hunt to give another group. Had to be translated into runes. Not something Luke could help with much, though putting the translation sheet on his lap so that he could try to point to needed symbol made him engage with the activity for some of the time. Alison [LSA] needed continually to remind the other kids to involve him and nag him herself to answer. Kerry (one of the group) tried to do this but then said to Alison, 'He doesn't want to.' Trying to get him to find the symbols slowed them down, and they hadn't finished by the time the teacher called them back to the classroom.

> (Observation)

Luke had more successful groupwork experiences than these, particularly in drama, where he was observed to engage well with both the other students and the substance of the work – perhaps because understanding did not necessarily have to take place at such an abstract level.

Deliberate efforts were made at all the primary schools to set up groups which might benefit the development of project students' basic skills while reinforcing those of other pupils as well. Caroline was often able to take part in academic group or partner work, such as maths and English. Towards the end of the year she shared her formerly individual maths sessions with another boy from her class (partly an attempt to lessen her resistance to these sessions), and worked with him on spelling exercises, since this was an area in which he also was shaky compared with most of the rest of the class. Caroline, like all the other pupils in her class, was part of a named group who sat together at one table and frequently worked on the same tasks, even if they were not doing so collaboratively.

At Meadow Hill Secondary, work with *student partners* was common, and valuable as a tool of curricular inclusion. However, partnering was informal and was not planned in sufficient detail to enable the label 'peer tutoring' to be given to it. Mike benefited from student partners in all subjects except CDT, with a consequent widening of his cultural horizons and expanded understanding of the work. Jerry and Greg were often unwilling to let the LSAs out of sight, but in lessons where this could be arranged there were obvious gains in terms of increased awareness of personal responsibility for performance and exposure to others' ways of thinking. In some cases there appeared to be a fine line between working as equal partners and working as supporter and disabled student – in other words, the able-bodied student adopted, or was forced into, the role of the LSA. Two observations of classes where Greg was persuaded to part with his LSA illustrate the difference between these roles:

English. Teacher discovered Greg had worked with Emma, and asked him to go and do so again – she said he should tell Emma what to write. . . . Emma quite helpful to Greg by reading and writing and *not* giving him all the answers. Greg also chatting with kids at another table . . . he pointed out to Emma that she'd missed a letter off one word (help not all one way).

Art. Greg working with Barry on their Mohican masks. The teacher glued on two of the three spikes to Greg's mask and then spent a lot of time explaining to Greg how to make the spikes stand up with papier-mâché. He suggested Barry helped – but Greg made Barry do the sticky bit he didn't like doing, while he held the spike. Barry said, 'You're moving it Greg!' Greg said, 'Don't go so mad! Just whack him in!' Barry very patient for a while, then said, in frustration, 'Can you do something, Greg?' Greg replied, 'Cor, you *are* in a mood!' (Typically for Greg, he recognised that Barry was upset but not that he himself was the cause of it and could do something about it.) They went on chatting while they worked, but Barry was getting more frustrated because Greg wouldn't keep the mask still . . . Barry, to cap it all, got mildly told off by the teacher for not making the paper wet enough – this made him really cross and he started slapping paste everywhere. . . . The teacher told them to pack up. They tidied up, with Barry again doing most of the work.

(Observation)

The amount of responsibility for Greg's work that Barry found himself taking on made this experience of working with a partner unsatisfying for both boys: Greg did virtually nothing and Barry couldn't get on with his own project. However, Greg may have learned something about the effect of his behaviour on others and Barry may have extended the boundaries of his own patience and tolerance.

The implications of this are around attempting to reduce the element of chance in determining the success or otherwise of partnering experiences. Chances of success could be increased by planning and structuring the partnering experience in such a way that peer-tutoring could be said to exist. The advice of, for example, Topping (1988) on structuring peer-tutoring would be valuable for further or extended use of this approach to groupwork. In brief, Topping gives ideas on:

- how partners can be matched;
- the nature of the materials being used;
- time, place and duration of peer-tutoring sessions;
- teaching techniques to be adopted;
- participant training methods;
- monitoring, evaluation and feedback.

There is much advice in the literature also on, for instance, co-operative groupwork for inclusion (see, for example, Putnam, 1993; Aaronson and Bridgeman, 1979). Group and partner work will be examined again in the context of teachers' attempts to promote curricular inclusion through classroom management techniques.

Individual work

Limitations on students' participation in curriculum tasks due to physical difficulties were mitigated to a greater or lesser extent by three things: technology, LSA help (to be discussed later; see p. 155 below) and the student's own initiative.

The latter, initiative, was most obvious in Mike's case; for example, because he was unable to get the lid off his calculator with his fingers he used his teeth. Technology was a help to Jerry, who eventually obtained a voice-activated computer to eliminate (in part) the need for a scribe, and to Luke, in the shape of a switched voice recorder, to give him a speaking part in drama productions, and a computer (with much useful software) which, however, rarely worked. This was a serious problem for staff at Oakwood Junior, as the SENCO explained, because it was Luke's only method of independent recording as well as being a source of useful staged practice in basic skills.

There were some instances of students' own inhibitions limiting their curricular inclusion. For example, Mike and Jerry were reluctant to volunteer answers to teachers' questions in class unless they were sitting at the front of the room and close enough to the teacher not to need to raise their voices – being afraid, presumably, of their peers' ridicule if they got the answers wrong. One of Mike's science teachers commented:

> I do notice he's fairly reluctant to volunteer answers to questions in front of other people, and that's despite me trying to take note of the fact that he's actually got his hand up or not. But he doesn't do a lot of oral participation even though you quite often think that he probably knows the answer.

All the students except Mike needed help with recording at some level, and there were sometimes problems with students dictating to scribes in voices which were either too loud or too soft compared with the surrounding noise of the classroom, resulting in either inhibition on the part of the student or frustration on the part of the LSA. Jerry noted this difficulty in his diary: 'I get on well with my helpers in school who help me mainly with my writing. The only problem with telling my helpers what to write is when the classroom is noisy and I can't make myself heard.'

There was also evidence of some students bringing strategies into play that would help them to avoid the really hard work of thinking: simple non-response in Luke's case, and a noticeable concentration on the easy minutiae of a task in Jerry's – to avoid having to concentrate on planning a difficult next stage or coming to grips with the whole picture. If this is the case, then it seems appropriate for priority to be given to strategies which will enable students to feel more confident in their expression; some of these are discussed in chapters 3 and 4 above.

Learning difficulties were another factor affecting participation in a given task. For example, Greg's difficulties with reading and writing meant that his contributions in these areas were less enthusiastic and more slowly executed than when an oral response was required. Despite this evidence that project students' participation in curriculum tasks was subject to some limitations relative to their disabilities, it was encouraging to see that, particularly in the primary schools, difficulties tended to be overcome by the expectation that children would join in with physical activities however they could:

> PE: Caroline found a space, as requested, and curled up, then uncurled, with the others. Asked to go tall slowly – Caroline demonstrated her ability to control the chair up and down. Jogging – LSA helped her move her legs and feet. Then running round room – Caroline went quite slowly – no one got run over. Stop-start game, where children had to make themselves into different shapes, tall, short, wide – they were told the shape before they started to run, so that they had to concentrate on remembering it as well as listening out for the command to stop. Caroline was able to do this competently on her own.
>
> (Observation)

FACILITATION OF INCLUSION: BY TEACHERS AND BY LSAs

The nature of the interaction between project student and LSA or teacher is crucial to the student's level of participation in the work of the class. This relationship – and more importantly, the pedagogic philosophy held by the teacher or LSA – are central to the success of the student's inclusion. There are expectations about *need* which promote and encourage particular ways of working. As Jordan (1994) notes, teachers have markedly different ways of conceptualising need and special need. Some adhere to medical-restorative notions. These notions are accompanied by expectations about the need for special expertise in instruction and for special pedagogy. Clearly these notions are inconsistent with inclusive practice and are inconsistent also with evidence on efficacy (as discussed in chapter 3; see also on the question of efficacy, Newcomer and Hammill, 1975; Arter and Jenkins, 1979; Brown and Campione, 1986; Wang *et al.*, 1995).

While these views on pedagogy and need are important, there are also constraints on curricular inclusion which arise from the support relationship: the physical difficulties of the students (which may make communication with them inconvenient), and/or assumptions about it being properly the job of an LSA to communicate with the included child. There are also assumptions about the exclusiveness of the relationship between the LSA and a target child.

There are, then, a mix of factors which may constrain curricular inclusion, as the following subsections illustrate.

Teachers

A teacher who regards the project student as the responsibility of the LSA may isolate the LSA–student pair from the rest of the class, precluding the student, perhaps, from benefiting from expert subject knowledge, and preventing the teacher from getting to know the student well enough to plan properly for his or her inclusion. There were few examples, fortunately, of this attitude, although students were often observed being reminded by LSAs to address questions directly to teachers and peers rather than to/through them. There were, though, also occasions on which this advice could well have been addressed to the teacher:

> Mrs Tupper [teacher] gave Ann [the LSA] the test and talked about [student] as though he wasn't there, apart from to say 'You'll just have five minutes [student's name].' . . . Later Mrs Tupper came in and asked the LSA, 'Can [student] come out at seven minutes past twelve, so I can talk to the class?'
>
> (Observation)

Part of this ignoring of the student seemed to represent a desire not to ignore the presence of the LSA and to make sure that someone understood the task. Some teachers were very good at addressing their discussion to the student concerned, for example this art teacher at Meadow Hill Comprehensive:

> Mrs Potter talked to Jerry about how hard you had to press to make wax-resist work, and how difficult white was to work with. (Noticeable that she didn't assume that because he couldn't do the actual pressing he ought not to be given a chance to understand the process.)
>
> (Observation)

One or two secondary subject teachers began the year appearing to feel, or saying they felt, that the project students were nothing to do with them:

> Mr Gates [teacher] came up to [student] and said, 'Everyone finds this confusing.' The LSA told me that she had thought this an unhelpful remark, and that Mr Gates was helping others but not [student] – that it was a pity teachers didn't teach the SIP pupils more. It was her perception that many mistook the facilitating role of the LSA for one of teaching, and were perhaps reluctant to appear to be teaching another adult, or to look as though they were assuming the adult hadn't understood.
>
> (Observation)

As noted in the previous chapter, however, many of these teachers had changed their attitude remarkably by the summer term. There were even occasions when secondary teachers appeared to be spending more time than was justified on the project student, bearing in mind the presence of the LSA.

At the primary schools, there was generally far more direct interaction from the start between teacher and pupil than in many of the secondary classes – partly, perhaps, because of the teacher's continual presence, which led more quickly to a comfortable and communicative relationship than did thrice-weekly subject lessons at secondary stage; and partly, also, because primary teachers regard their responsibility for their class members more holistically, embracing every aspect of their students' lives, whereas subject teachers may be more concerned with what relates to performance in their own subject. Some of the primary class teachers, however, also showed development in their confidence to work directly with project students over the year, as this observation at West Hill Primary in the summer term suggests:

> Assistant is still sitting with the other group . . . Daniel turning pages of book. . . . Teacher now works by asking him to put fingers on words and asking him to read. . . . Teacher insists on Daniel completing the

work she is asking him to do, asking him questions, prompting him. Clearly the input of the teacher adds something to the contribution of the assistant on her own. Teacher excellently manages juggling this work with Daniel with her management of the other children.

(Observation)

Occasional examples of this flexible interchange of roles between teacher and LSA were observed. Where it happened it appeared to work extraordinarily well, enabling a number of benefits:

- It provides variety for the student and enables him or her to benefit from the teacher's particular skills.
- It includes the student fully in the material being taught by the teacher.
- It signals to the class as a whole that the LSA does not work exclusively with the 'special' student and that that student is an integral member of the class.
- It frees the LSA to work with other students who can benefit from individual attention.
- It provides variety to the role of the LSA.

Formalising such an exchange of roles – as, for example, in 'room management' (see chapter 2 and Thomas, 1992) – may have benefits. Room management involves teacher and assistant planning tasks to be undertaken in a session and dividing their pedagogic activity between themselves as 'individual helper' and 'activity manager'. In this way roles can be shared systematically.

LSAs

Interaction between project student and LSA was complex, involving elements of physical support, mechanical support and learning support, depending on the area of the curriculum and on various characteristics of the student and LSA concerned. For example, Greg needed help with organisation of work and time, with scribing and with slowing himself down and giving himself time to think. His own assessment of the LSAs' value to him was purely in terms of psychological support:

Researcher: What sort of help is the most important to you?

Greg: Support assistants' courage [sic] – you know. Saying, 'OK, so she shouted, you don't need to get worried, you don't need to jump.'

LSAs were generally extremely skilled at judging the level of help that was appropriate and how to give it. This was a continuous process, as the demands of a single activity changed from the employment of one skill to another:

Frog masks for rainforest topic: The painting is going well. Luke holds the brush in his fist and Emma [LSA] guides it – Luke is definitely following with his eyes the movement of the brush. Emma encourages him from time to time, but doesn't nag. The amount of concentration, co-ordination and muscle power Luke needs must be immense. Emma tries to help him have more control when he dips into the tray for more paint. She seems very good at judging the right moment to do this, when he might be receptive. . . . She's very good at giving him the chance to do on his own the things she thinks he might be able to do, and to ask if he needs her help.

(Observation)

There were some issues regarding the interaction between LSAs and project students which seemed to be common to almost every situation. One was the constant need to encourage students' independence and greater responsibility in circumstances where the students themselves might find it easier to rely on adult help. For example, many LSAs were looking for ways to enable students to attract teachers' attention directly, rather than by using them (LSAs) as intermediaries. This involved alerting the teachers to potential difficulty: explaining, for instance, that Jerry needed to have eye contact with the teacher before he would ask or answer a question.

Running counter to these efforts was a less common form of interaction of which LSAs themselves may have been unaware. It arose mainly in the context of discussions between a scribing LSA and a student about how to tackle a task or whether an answer was right. LSAs would occasionally insist on their own way of doing something or their own answer (which turned out at least once during observation to be wrong) instead of writing down what the student had requested:

Next exercise Greg missed an answer – LSA wanted to go on to the next one; Greg wanted to put down what it ought to be: 'Put that down.' She didn't.

(Observation)

Such incidents occurred particularly in circumstances where the student's understanding of the subject appeared to be better than that of the LSA: Jerry was actually roused to self-assertion by his frustration on one such occasion.

One student's mother had worried that he would receive too much support (in fact he was rarely seen in the company of an LSA):

Researcher: Are you happy about support in the classroom?

Mother: Oh very. We are very pleased. He started off with a full-time assistant, which he doesn't need because he only needs somebody obviously for the things that he can't physically do, and to help him with his personal needs . . . he doesn't want an adult traipsing round following him all the time. So very pleased with it. Because that was one of the things that used to worry us when Mike was in mainstream schooling before: the fact that he always had an adult with him, even in the playground he had an adult with him. And it cramps your style!

Jerry echoed this comment (rather surprisingly, perhaps, considering how unwilling he seemed to be to do without an LSA), when he remarked that although he was happy about how the LSAs had worked with him 'it was a pain having to have a scribe all the time'. However, excellent relationships seemed to exist between almost all LSAs and students. Specific ways in which LSAs were able to contribute constructively to making the curriculum more accessible to project students will be explored in the section on differentiation (see p. 160 below).

There was occasional evidence of a lack of guidance for LSAs on how to interact with the class as a whole and whether to become involved in work with other children:

> Tom is being helped by assistant continuously; she does not help the others on the table, or reprimand them for noise. Seems a bit of a waste of her abilities, and perhaps rather restrictive for Tom who is being helped continuously. This is despite the fact that his table is one of the most troublesome of all.
>
> (Observation, primary)

As noted in Part I, it is inappropriate for LSAs to work exclusively with one child, and the training of LSAs for the new inclusive role can stress this fact. When LSAs did become more involved in the general groupwork it clearly paid dividends for all, as this observation later in the school year and with a different assistant indicates:

> Group certainly benefits from having the assistant on their table – she now prompts Tom through task. Quite a high level of noise and activity (non-directed) in the class, though not in Tom's group.
>
> (Observation, primary)

The willingness of LSAs to become thus involved, however, seemed to rest more on individual initiative than in general policy.

PROMOTING CURRICULAR INCLUSION

There were two main areas through which teachers and Inclusion Project staff sought to promote curricular inclusion: classroom management techniques and differentiation. The former was mainly the province of the class or subject teacher, and the latter a collaborative effort or a process of informal adaptation by LSAs.

Classroom management

The first line of approach for class and subject teachers was to ensure, as they would for any child in non-mixed-ability settings, that project students worked in groups where the level of ability matched their own as closely as possible. Previous knowledge of the child, if he or she was already in the school, was often available, and where it was not, as in the case of the Meadow Hill students, considerable discussion took place between subject heads and Inclusion Project staff as to which set would be most appropriate. Observation suggested that this preparation had been effective: all the secondary students appeared to be in GCSE groups that suited their ability. Assignment to working groups in the primary schools was flexible, and not necessarily related to chronological age.

Another important aspect of classroom management – important for all students – is the position of teacher and student relative to each other and to any teaching aids being used. Disabled students may not be able to move easily to see the board, or the teacher if the latter changes position. Some staff, such as the teacher below, were very aware of this:

> I tend to move around the room a fair bit when I'm teaching anyway. I sort of trot round the side and all the rest of it, but I don't ever go anywhere where Mike can't see – you know, stand right behind him or anything like that – whereas other people can just swivel in their chairs he can't do that so easily.
>
> (Teacher, secondary)

In contrast to this, there were, infrequently, situations in which the teacher seemed unaware of possible difficulties, as this observation demonstrates:

> Mike followed well and could see the board, but was never in the teacher's line of sight – she had her back half-turned to him. He didn't volunteer any answers, but she wouldn't see his hand up anyhow.
>
> (Observation)

In the relatively static environment of the secondary classroom, this kind of logistical problem could be fairly easily solved once the teacher realised its inhibiting effect. In primary classrooms, however, where children were constantly being asked to move from their table to the 'base' area and the teacher was often teaching from wherever she happened to be, making sure the project pupil could participate where required could be difficult. There were some occasions when Caroline ended up with her back to the scene of the action, but generally her classteacher gave the impression of being constantly aware of possible difficulties and strategies that could be used to overcome them.

Generally, staff felt that managing a classroom with a wheelchair-user in it was less problematic than they had expected. This was particularly the case at secondary level where there was more space in the classroom than there was at primary level. However, where two wheelchair-users were present in the classroom, as in one class at West Hill Primary, space did become tight and movement could become difficult for everyone in the class. In these circumstances, the reorganisation of the classroom may be considered, as for example described by Lucas and Thomas (1990) (see chapter 4 above).

One difficult question for classteachers was the extent to which they should have the same expectations of the disabled child as of any other. Many staff emphasised the importance of expectations of behaviour which were the same for all:

Researcher: How do you see the role of the subject teacher?

LSA: To treat them the same as the other children, but being aware that they have different needs: for example, Greg's interruptions. But they should tell him if it's not the right moment to interrupt all the same.

Tom and James's classteacher had been unsure originally whether conformity should be expected:

I must admit that at the very beginning I didn't tell Tom off. I didn't quite know what to do – you know, it was really a question of, 'What do I do now?' But now he gets treated exactly like everybody else. If he talks he gets told off. He gets red cards and green cards like everybody else.

(Teacher, primary)

It seems important that project children should be able to participate, at the level appropriate to them, in whatever reward schemes are in operation in their class. The teacher-co-ordinator at Oakwood Junior described how this would work for Luke, who, until the end of the summer term 1996, had had his own gold stars: 'There is now a class merit system which Luke is part of. The class sets its own targets for the week: Luke's is greater independence in drinking.'

Once bench-marks for general behaviour are established, it is necessary to look at how expectations of constructive participation in class are created. The approach of Caroline's classteacher can be used as a model of good inclusive practice, as these excerpts from a day's observations illustrate:

Show-and-tell: Meg [teacher] asked who wanted to show, and suggested Caroline raised herself up a bit so that the others could see what she was showing – reminded everyone to speak clearly.

PE: Emphasis on discussion rather than one partner telling the other what to do. Caroline working with Gareth. . . . They were all summoned into a circle and Meg asked for volunteers to demonstrate their games. Caroline very keen to be picked – put up her hand enthusiastically. When they were picked, Meg said, 'Who's going to do the talking?' Gareth said he was, but Meg said, 'Have you discussed it?' It transpired they hadn't, and when they did, Caroline managed to persuade him that she should.

These inclusive ways of working with Caroline quickly became part of everyone's routine, so that when the classteacher was ill and a supply was put into a situation of which she had no previous experience, Caroline, with the help of the LSAs, was able to fit naturally and productively into everything that went on, including PE. This contrasted with one particular observation at another school:

> This particular activity [in PE] not designed to include these children . . . [Inclusion Project child] joins in at the end but is conspicuously not included in the 'race', since the children have already done their cheering and [child's] trip along the course is all but an afterthought, ignored by the children.

The picture of non-inclusion illustrates the importance of teachers' designing all class activities with the disabled child's participation in mind. The task is not easy – particularly in PE, where there is a need for forward planning in every aspect of lesson preparation. There is clearly room here for the development of liaison between the co-ordinator–classteacher–LSA team in planning and developing appropriate activities. The implication is for further non-contact time to allow this.

Differentiation

Differentiation can apply to outcomes, particular children being expected to draw different things from the same activities, for instance the homonym exercise in which Caroline and John thought about the varied meanings of words that sound the same, whereas children who could read thought about the way this variation was reflected in the spelling of the words. This was an example of spontaneous adaptation by Pat, the LSA, rather than something planned for by the person devising the activity (the supply teacher).

Differentiation by activity aims at getting children to the same point by different means. For example, Luke and Greg were able to participate in the tests their peers were taking through the use of oral/gestural response and a scribe. Adapting the science test with Luke in mind led the classteacher to use the multiple-choice format she had designed for him with the rest of the class, benefiting also the other children with difficulties in literacy skills.

Usually, primary level differentiation was a combination of adapted outcome and activity after initial planning. Progress and further adaptation depended on the reaction of the student. Before the initial planning could take place, a thorough knowledge of the project student's current skill level was necessary (as in the assignment to groups, above). Some primary children's lack of concrete experience of the physical world had to be taken into account: Caroline and Luke, for instance, had not grasped the concept of 'weight', nor were they able to make sense of historical time because they had missed out on a view of the working of time in their everyday lives. Tom, at West Hill Primary, had a similar problem with history.

The importance of bearing in mind such gaps when planning activities is obvious, and may point the classteacher towards back-up work that might enable the child to participate in the future. For example, Caroline was given an adapted timetable format, which simplified the structure of the day into large, meaningful, chunks.

There was much evidence that as individual teachers' understanding of the project students' abilities and difficulties increased, they felt able to undertake more differentiation, basing this on their usual teaching practice and taking responsibility for directing the LSAs they had previously regarded as 'experts':

Alison [LSA] read to Luke from the work the class was doing, but it sounded difficult for him and she read it as though she didn't really expect him to take it in – it was about the geographical distribution of the Anglo-Saxon kingdoms. He then had to answer the questions on the map sheet – Polly [classteacher] suggested putting the answers on the E-tran frame [a vertical transparent frame on which pieces of paper could be stuck] . . . she said to Alison, 'Do you need to read the passage to him again? – And perhaps fewer choices on the frame? Four perhaps?'

(Observation)

As well as thorough knowledge of the child, one LSA suggested that identifying the educational aims of the activity was an essential precondition for good adaptation: 'The subject teacher's role is to lead the room, to include all the children in the room in what they're teaching, have clear learning objectives – they should ask LSAs to adapt work but not to differentiate, which needs specialist knowledge.'

This quotation introduces the much disputed issue of who should take responsibility for differentiation. There was evidence of contradictory views, particularly at Meadow Hill Comprehensive, where some teachers would have liked to take on more responsibility themselves. One said, 'Edward [LSA] has brought in a few tools, and little drills, but in an ideal world I'd like to make him [Mike] a whole set of tools myself.' Others – more likely to be subject specialists in secondary school – felt the responsibility was clearly that of the learning support staff as far as adapting the format of materials was concerned. In one class, a teacher had avoided the discussion of genetic disorders in science – notionally to 'protect' the project student, but perhaps to avoid careful thought about differentiation and teaching approach surrounding a difficult issue. This can be contrasted with some carefully prepared question-and-answer sessions which were given on the topic of disability in PSE. The successful outcome in the latter suggests that the missing of the subject in science options represented a missed educational opportunity. There is also evidence of a sympathetic yet inappropriate attitude to disability associated with protection and vulnerability.

The necessity for differentiated equipment has already been touched on briefly. This seemed to be better organised in the primary schools, where close liaison between classteachers and Inclusion Project staff allowed for the provision of such things as fat crayons for Caroline (very desirable objects to her peers who were stuck with the ends of thin, coloured pencils). There were instances at Meadow Hill Comprehensive where potentially useful technological aids were not being used – perhaps because they could not be afforded. In art, for instance, Jerry used mainly the ordinary brushes, pens and pencils his peers used, when he used them at all. It might have been possible for him to use one of the art software packages to produce some of the work required. At least the work would have been more 'his' than most of the assignments, even if the variety of media employed was more limited, and he would have been able to exercise his design and colour faculties to a higher level than was possible when directing someone else.

Lateral thinking can be more useful than expensive resources (such as software) in some circumstances: the teacher at Heather Grove Primary puzzling over how to include Caroline in class recorder sessions decided to put her in charge of providing a percussive backing. This would improve the overall class performance and give her the chance to play – which physical problems with handling a recorder had previously denied her.

Ways were also found of adapting features of school life other than class lessons so that project students could participate: for example, the use of a special route around Hinckley Point power station, with an accompanying friend, enabled Mike to go on an interesting, curriculum-related, trip he had missed out on at primary school. Trying to improve communication in the classroom was another way of adapting school life to foster the fuller involvement of the project student: there was some teaching of Total Communication in Luke's class towards this end, but although his peers appeared to enjoy learning it his own level of achievement in signing seemed to be too low for this to make much difference to his general participation.

Students did not always welcome supporters' attempts to make their lives easier through differentiation: Mike, for instance, had been lent a pocket-book by the Inclusion Project, but never used it, however tired his hands, because he didn't want to look different. He also rejected the help with homework which both Jerry and Greg benefited from, preferring to reinforce his inclusion by competing from, as he saw it, the same base-line as his peers.

THE EFFECT OF INCLUSION PROJECT STUDENTS' PRESENCE ON THE EDUCATION OF OTHER CHILDREN

As we remarked in the introduction to this section, no one interviewed felt that the students' presence was having an adverse effect on the education of other children, even if this was sometimes achieved at the expense of teachers' own time. Many of the strategies described in the sections above, on classroom management and differentiation, were reported to be helpful to other students in the group, particularly those with lower attainment, and the presence of an extra adult in the class was universally welcomed. As one primary teacher said, 'That's sort of a bonus because I get [names of two assistants] in there all the time. Although they're supporting Daniel it's another adult in the class, which is always useful.'

One of the primary teachers explained the specific ways in which she felt other children benefited from the presence of a disabled student:

It really adds something to the classroom. You get extra help: children learn to be more co-operative and helpful. . . . If Tom goes somewhere there's always someone there to open the door for him, and those kind of manners are almost second nature to them now. It makes school a more natural, warmer, more human place.

One secondary teacher put forward the view that project students were getting a disproportionate amount of support and that, although others were not actually suffering because of their presence, some of these could do with just as much help themselves: 'I find it a bit irritating that Jerry has these people dancing attendance on him. . . . Say I'm teaching and I say, "Three minutes to discuss this with your friends," and he discusses it with an educated adult. . . . It just annoys me.'

There was occasional evidence at the beginning of the school year, when the children were unfamiliar with each other, of a disruptive effect arising from the novelty of the inclusive experience:

Teacher tells children to 'stop and listen'. Knot of children are around Tom. James makes loud screech, seemingly involuntary – breaks the emerging order that is developing in the class.

(Observation)

However, this kind of incident diminished as the year wore on and as the classroom participants became more familiar with one another.

Envy by other Heather Grove Primary children of Caroline's horse-riding in school time has already been mentioned in the context of out-of-class activities. It is another, small, example of what could be seen as privileged treatment, as opposed to treatment strictly according to need, as any other child in the school would (ideally) receive. These are perhaps things the

Inclusion Project teams need to monitor, since the success of inclusion depends ultimately on equality of opportunity for all.

CONCLUSIONS AND RECOMMENDATIONS

The following advice summarises the main recommendations made in this chapter.

- Frequent joint planning sessions between class or subject teacher and co-ordinator will enable as much integration of the student's individual programme into general class or groupwork as possible. Non-contact time needs to be made available for this and the economic implications of this need to be considered alongside the macro-changes involved in redeveloping the school as a service. In other words, if 'money follows child' in this redelivery, a primary consideration in the structuring of a new service must be the provision of time for teams to plan and review.

- There should be a minimisation of withdrawal from the classroom – either for care or education – to avoid dislocation of classwork. This has implications for the co-ordination of services and communication of staff in the Inclusion Project and in partner schools. There is evidence of very different views on appropriate pedagogy based in turn on views about special need and special expertise. It may be that the provision of a short learning pack together with ongoing professional development on inclusion for all staff would assist in fostering appropriate methods and strategies. This goes also for physiotherapy (if there is physical room in the classroom), where classteachers remarked on the benefits of seeing the physiotherapist at work.

- Flexibility is needed in considering strict adherence to NC requirements, especially in the secondary school. If the school's curriculum organisation is not amenable to an integrated curriculum (as is the case in the vast majority of secondary schools) it may be possible through learning support departments to provide significant curricular adaptation and support to enable inclusion.

- Greater structuring of groupwork and student partnering to include co-operative groupwork and peer-tutoring would increase the chance of the success of peer partnerships and would ensure that the activities undertaken are appropriate in the context of the work being undertaken by the rest of the class.

- Teacher and LSA can be encouraged to exchange roles occasionally, in such a way that the teacher works intensively for periods with the included child while the LSA temporarily takes on the role of the 'activity manager'.

- LSAs can be encouraged to provide 'on-the-spot differentiation'.

- A radical physical rearrangement of the classroom resources and furniture may be helpful where space becomes restricted.
- More use could be made of IT and other aids to facilitate inclusion, especially in the secondary phase and for young people with more serious physical disabilities. There is a role for any inclusion project in providing a central databank and dissemination of information in this area.

11

SOCIAL INCLUSION

INTRODUCTION

A number of issues were raised in Part I of this book about social interaction in inclusive classrooms. These included:

- the social interaction of disabled and non-disabled students in an inclusive environment;
- the factors which influence the attitudes of non-disabled students to their disabled peers, and vice versa;
- the influence of integration on the development of disabled students' social skills and self-esteem;
- the organisation of classrooms and schools and its effects in promoting social inclusion.

It has been difficult isolating themes and tensions from the data about the social experiences of the children and young people, for the *prima facie* impression in examining the data is of the success of the project in promoting social inclusion. This impression is consistent across situations and almost unanimous as far as informants are concerned. However, the issues bulleted above serve as useful foci for the analysis which follows.

Given that so much of the following discussion refers to the individual children and young people of the project, it is worth referring the reader back to chapter 8, where case studies of these individuals are given.

Prior to the full analysis, sociograms for the classes of each of the primary pupils are given. The sociograms are of the primary pupils only, since their classes are more consistent than those of the secondary-age students, for whom year groupings break due to subject choice and setting. Pseudonyms have been given to all of the children.

Children were asked to say in confidence who they would like to sit next to or play with in each of the classes, and in general an unremarkable pattern of relationships emerges for the Inclusion Project students. Even where the students have severe disabilities (for example, in the cases of Tom and Joe) they emerge as well-integrated socially to their classes. For several of the children reciprocated choices are made: in other words, one child's choice is

166

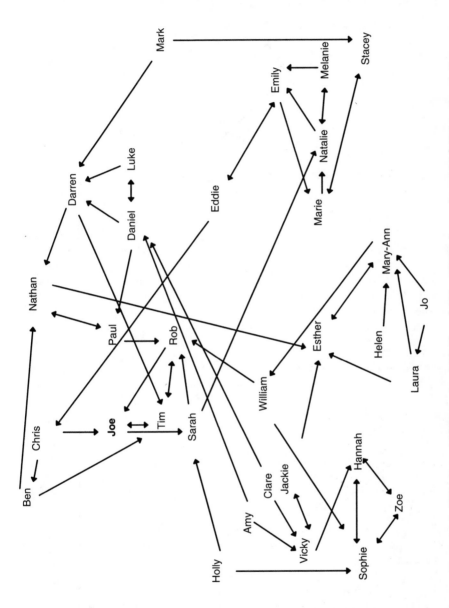

Figure 11.1 'Who I would like to sit with': Class 4, West Hill Primary, June 1996. SIP student is Joe

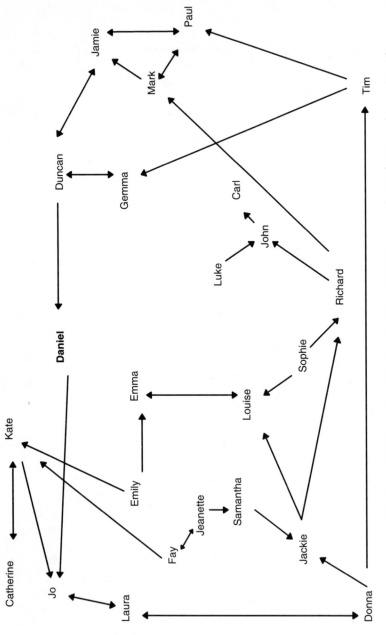

Figure 11.2 'Who I would like to sit with': Class 1, West Hill Primary, July 1996. SIP student is Daniel

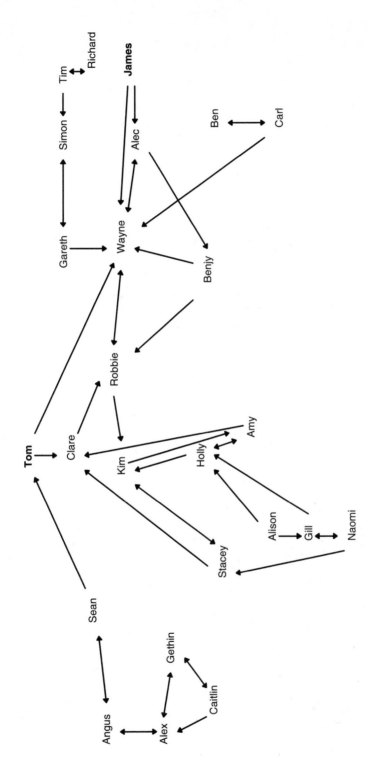

Figure 11.3 'Who I would like to sit with': Class 3, West Hill Primary, June 1996. SIP students are James and Tom

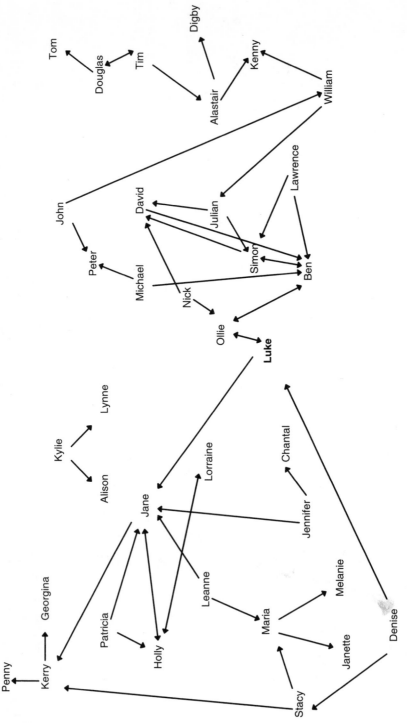

Figure 11.4 'Who I would like to play with': Class CL, Oakwood Primary, January 1996. SIP student is Luke

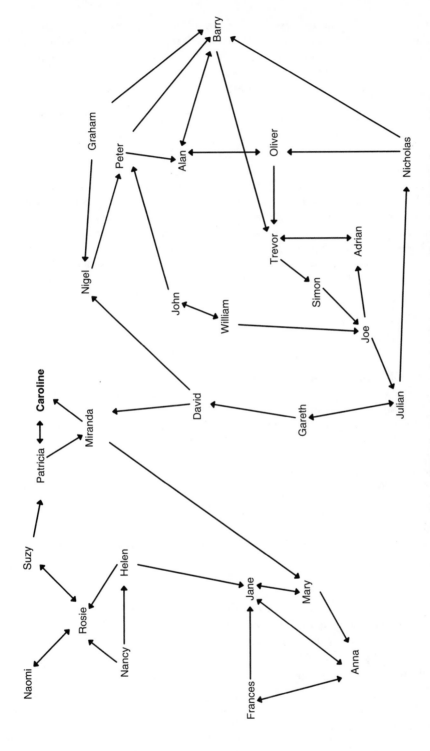

Figure 11.5 'Who I would like to play with': Class 2, Heather Grove, December 1995. SIP student is Caroline

'returned' by the chosen child. The findings here are thus in contrast to those of others such as Swanson (1996), who have found in the specific case of students with learning disabilities that these students have 'lower sociometric status than their nondisabled counterparts'. Given the learning difficulties of several of the pupils in this study, the results here are therefore encouraging and indicate the success of the inclusive arrangements.

The only child among the Inclusion Project students who emerges without any designated choices from the other children is James. However, this does not necessarily indicate isolation, and James's teacher reports that James is well liked, as indicated later in this chapter.

The sociogram is a crude instrument, depending as it does in large part on children's changing pattern of friendships. However, it gives a reasonably accurate picture of social relationships within a stable group such as a class year-group. The only place in which this has not been reflected in these sociograms is in the case of Tom, where his close friendship with Wayne is not apparent via a reciprocated choice. However, the friendship was recorded in a reciprocated choice made in an earlier sociogram undertaken by the classteacher, and the classteacher attests to the continuing strength of that relationship.

ANALYSIS

In the following analysis observations and reflections of project participants – students, parents and staff – are grouped into broad themes. Where appropriate, these are accompanied by pointers for further action. In particular, aspects of school and class organisation which appear to impinge on the social relations of participants are discussed in the context of descriptions of organisational practice which has been found to be beneficial in similar situations elsewhere. Other themes that emerge which have not figured significantly in the literature are the influence of the personality of the child involved, and the special pressures which may exist for non-disabled peers.

The themes that emerge are as follows:

1 **Benefits accruing inside and outside school from the experience of inclusion**
   mainstream versus segregated schools: students' views
   friends
   extra-curricular/community involvement
2 **Personality and its interaction with inclusion**
   student personality and its influence on the inclusion experience
   changes in personality under inclusion
3 **Attitudes of other pupils**
   primary
   secondary

stresses and strains for non-disabled students

changes in attitude

4 **Nature of relationships between Inclusion Project students and non-disabled peers**

opportunities for social contact

friends or acquaintances?

5 **Promoting social inclusion**

induction of students in transition from special to mainstream schools

support networks

opportunities for social mixing

the influence of 'hovering adults'.

These are taken in turn in the following sections.

Benefits accruing inside and outside school from the experience of inclusion

There are a number of findings concerning the consequences of inclusion for students' experiences generally and for their friendships and social contacts both inside and outside school.

Mainstream versus segregated: students' views

The section of the literature review on self-advocacy (chapter 6) reported two findings which are broadly confirmed by our investigations into how students feel about being in the mainstream. First, with only one exception, all the students who had transferred prefer to be in an inclusive rather than a segregated school (compare the similar results of Thomas, 1982; Anderson and Clarke, 1982). Second, the variety of responses to their new environment reflects their individuality as much as any survey of responses among able-bodied children would, with the implication that practitioners must understand the uniqueness of each student's experience before starting to plan future initiatives (see Potts, for example, 1992). Having said this, of the students in the study who had transferred from the special school, only one, the Year 10 student Greg, regretted the move.

Observation suggested that it was Greg's social naïveté with his peers which was making him unhappy, as well as, to a lesser extent, pressure of work. His diary entry for 29 September 1995 (one of only two he produced) records: 'The worke hear is VEARY hard! . . . live is very hard for me at the monmten.' He is certainly not the only one at Meadow Hill, or any other comprehensive, to be facing these problems: his inability to settle happily should not, therefore, be viewed as an argument for segregated schooling but perhaps for more sensitively inclusive settings and/or a greater range of inclusive settings.

The positive reactions of the students in the study to mainstream social life reflected the variety of individual personality and circumstance one would have expected. Both the other teenagers who went to Meadow Hill, Mike and Jerry, admitted to initial nervousness, but this appeared to wear off quickly in Mike's case:

> Researcher: Do you remember how you felt when you first came to Meadow Hill?
>
> Mike: Probably a bit nervous. A bit excited. I was a bit – I needed the care around me, but I don't want it round me now.

Jerry's reaction to life at Meadow Hill Comprehensive is an interesting example of the conflict that may arise between what people believe the disabled person to feel and what they themselves say they feel. Jerry, in his interviews and diary entries and in talks with his mother, insisted that he wanted to be in mainstream: 'I really like being with able-bodied students – I felt more separate at Princess Margaret's.' He added that the time in his life when he had felt most 'down' was when he realised that his illness had progressed to the point where he would have to go to special school. However, many of the LSAs working with Jerry appeared to think he wasn't happy in mainstream.

Both Jerry and Mike commented that they felt more grown-up at Meadow Hill Comprehensive, and more appropriately placed in relation to their intellectual equals:

> I [like] being with people my level . . . I mean they had a nice atmosphere there [PMS] but towards the end, when I came here for, like, a couple of days I came here, when I went back to PMS I thought – it just seemed babyish all of a sudden.

The primary schoolchildren were all happy in their mainstream settings according to their own, their teachers' and their parents' accounts, and our classroom observations. Some were vehement about not wanting to return to the special school.

Friends

With the exception of Greg, and to a lesser extent Jerry, all the students' reports of the friends they had made were confirmed by teachers' and parents' accounts, by classroom observation and, in the primary schools, by sociometric exercises.

Luke, the project pupil at Oakwood Junior, who had never been to the special school, identified a particular friend, Ollie, via his talking-book. This was a boy who had been in his class since he joined the school at four-and-a-half. Observation of Ollie's affection for, and understanding of, Luke confirmed the relationship. Caroline reeled off a long list of children she considered her friends, most of whom could be observed working with her, playing with her at break and/or featuring as reciprocal choices in the sociometric exercise:

Researcher: Who are your friends here?

Caroline: Miranda, Patricia and Helen, and Adrian and Simon, and I also like Helen.

Researcher: You said Helen.

Caroline: There's two Helens in the class – I also like Helen Graves. And there's William – I like him.

A teacher described the differing friendship patterns of Tom and James at West Hill Primary, illustrating again the importance of taking the individual into account when thinking about the promotion of social inclusion:

They have now each got their own little groups of friends. And they're now quite protective of each other. . . . James, I find, he gets on well with all of the class. He likes playing with everybody, whereas Tom is more selective; he just likes a couple of people and that's it – he doesn't want to move on to other people.

At the secondary level, Mike expressed his frustration with the limited social world of the special school (where he was still boarding during the study year):

I've got more friends now than I did at PMS . . . some of my friends, they come over to PMS in the evenings. But yeah, I think I've got better friends here. I mean, I had friends at PMS . . . the people that are boarding aren't really – you can't really talk to them. Because David will only say, 'I'll pinch your face,' and Martin will only smile at you.

Greg and Jerry both said that they had made friends, but this wasn't borne out by observation (see p. 177 below on the nature of their social interaction). Jerry seemed to have little understanding of how he might relate to other students as an equal, rather than as a dependant. Mike, by contrast, didn't want to be thought of by other students as anything but an equal. The same applied to Tom at West Hill Primary, who went to some lengths to separate himself from his disabled classmate. As the teacher observed, 'Tom really doesn't like being thought of as different – in fact, he doesn't like going anywhere near James at all. He really keeps as far apart as possible and just backs into his wheelchair if James is passing.'

The sociogram confirmed this finding: neither Tom nor James identified each other as friends. There was no evidence that any of the ex-special school children particularly wanted to associate with each other in the schools where this would have been possible, the lure of the able-bodied social world being apparently far greater than any possible benefits of solidarity with disabled peers. This contradicts the findings of Markides (1989) that disabled children, with a hearing impairment in the case of his study, tend to choose friends who have similar impairments – perhaps the crucial element here is the distinctive communication made possible by a common deaf culture.

The message is that generalisations about appropriateness of placement are dangerous when they are based on crude descriptors such as 'disability'; the social success of a placement will depend on numerous factors such as the nature of the child's disability, and perhaps more importantly the child's personality, age and maturity. However, more relevant as far as this study is concerned, preferences will be predicated on the success of the host establishment in promoting an inclusive culture; there is a danger in looking at the success or otherwise of social relationships to alight on 'within-child' factors. The section below on promoting social inclusion (p. 185) examines some of the ways in which the influence of any such within-child differences can be minimised.

Extra-curricular/community involvement

The students' views of social life are reflected in, and affected by, the range of their extra-curricular and community involvements. Luke, for example, despite identifying Ollie as a particular friend at least twice, tended to be negative about his school social life – telling the classteacher that he had no real friends. This was perhaps related to the fact that he had few opportunities to mix with his peers outside school hours until invited by the classteacher to join her drama club. Plans were also being made by the project to find a volunteer to take him to other community events where his peers would be present.

This is easier where the child attends a neighbourhood school: Caroline (Heather Grove Primary) had friends living near by and met the same groups of children in the community as in school. However, pupils attended West Hill Primary (which can be seen as a 'resourced' school) from a much wider radius and children were taken from their neighbourhood communities for school attendance; here, parents regretted the lack of community friendships, although one extremely strong friendship had been made where the boys visited each other's houses.

Mike (Meadow Hill), though he was not a local, managed to immerse himself thoroughly in extra-curricular activities such as stage management, running the stationery shop, prefect training and helping with the school magazine. He invited the friends he had made this way into his own (special school) community for activities there, such as snooker and a disco.

However, this did not alleviate his isolation during the holidays and at weekends when he was back at home, a considerable distance from Meadow Hill Comprehensive. Greg, who did not make a friend he could visit or phone, or become very much involved in extra-curricular activities, seemed to be relieved to get home each evening and put school behind him. Living in a village where there were no Meadow Hill pupils, but several members of his extended family on whom he could rely for a predictable and warm reception, may have been a help in enabling Greg to 'switch off' from his problems at school.

Personality and its interaction with inclusion

Personality characteristics and their influence on the inclusive experience

Crucial to the making of relationships in school, as elsewhere, are the personality characteristics of the students involved. In a newly inclusive classroom there may be substantial obstacles to be overcome by disabled students wanting to get to know their disabled peers. These may include:

- fear of the unknown;
- barriers presented by physical impediments;
- communication difficulties;
- the arrival of the student in an already established teaching group.

Add to this the difficulty for secondary students of being in a different group for virtually every subject, with different pupils in each, and some of the reasons why Greg and Jerry found the process of making friends such hard going can be appreciated.

In an ideal inclusive world, the onus would not be on the disabled student to overcome these obstacles, or the obstacles themselves would have ceased to exist as such; but the world the project students were entering was not ideal in this respect and therefore, particularly at secondary level, social success appeared to depend on the possession of unusually developed social skills.

Of the Meadow Hill students, only Mike exemplified these. He was outgoing, good at asking for help in a non-submissive way, good at smiling at people, and good at judging how much to join in with general classroom chat. He was also good at finding interesting things to do and getting involved in them: 'not a loud person, but a do-er', as the Meadow Hill co-ordinator described him.

Greg was also outgoing, but not often appropriately so, consistently misinterpreting others' actions and responding with misplaced aggression, or contributing to conversations in a manner which others found hard to take seriously. This typical observation illustrates some of the difficulties he had in relating to others:

177

Greg was sitting at a table with two boys. One of these reached over to Greg's pencil tin, a treasured possession because of the 'Harley' on the front, and Greg got aggressive, saying, 'Oi! Give that back!', but calming down when he realised the boy meant no harm.

Jerry, though very happy to respond to others' approaches, found it almost impossible to initiate any sort of interaction other than with the adults he knew from the special school, as these observations, made at break-time, show:

Jerry went to the hall to have a drink. No one, apart from the two LSAs, talked to him, and he made no attempt to join any of the groups of students around the hall (though able to do so). Didn't approach others, as others do in their wheelchairs.

The disentangling of cause and effect is, of course, difficult here. It may be that submissiveness or over-reaction are products of the restricted kind of socialisation experienced in a segregative environment – which these students had experienced until their recent placement in the mainstream. If this is indeed the case, the corollary is for early inclusion in order to provide the opportunity to develop appropriate social behaviour.

Observed changes in personality under inclusion

Children whose ability to articulate verbally and express their personality is severely limited by physical difficulties may find it less frustrating to adopt a passive, reactive role, in which their intentions cannot be misunderstood. Luke was one such child, though there was some evidence at the end of the year that, in response to continuous effort by the Inclusion Project team, Luke was beginning to take a more active role in initiating interaction and exerting himself to participate more in other ways. The change in Tom was more striking:

Tom seems very very happy. If you talk to the co-ordinator you realise how much difference there is between Tom then and Tom now he's included here. Then he was a very quiet little boy who didn't want to speak and didn't want to work and didn't like being there, at PMS, and now he's screaming across the playground to his girlfriend 'I love you [child's name]!'

Jerry's mother considered that he was becoming more assertive as a result of the wider range of teenage behaviour he was exposed to at Meadow Hill, though he only seemed comfortable with this new, or perhaps newly re-discovered, aspect of his personality at home, since it wasn't generally observable at school. She reported that he was much more confident, better at expressing himself, and 'different', in that he argued with her more.

Mike, who, as we have noted, came to Meadow Hill Comprehensive already equipped with good social skills, also began to become more assertive during the year, or rather, began to relax his slightly over-compliant image and adopt a more street-wise persona, with an increased use of very mild swearing and a more aggressive attitude towards the infamously stubborn fire doors.

We have already seen that Greg's mother felt he lost self-confidence during the year at Meadow Hill, possibly, if social comparison theory is to be believed, because he was constantly measuring himself against peers who were not receiving the amount of help that he was; but there was evidence of other changes which were very confusing for him and ultimately further destructive of his self-esteem. He seemed to suffer from a conflict between wanting to do what he knew from his upbringing was the right thing (there was lots of evidence at first that the bad behaviour of some pupils was a shock to him) and also wanting desperately to be liked and part of the gang. This, combined with a lack of social understanding, resulted in his being exploited by pupils encouraging him to smoke and take money from home to buy cigarettes. Again, his previous segregation doesn't seem to be the issue: this is the sort of situation that many able-bodied students get into and it reinforces the argument for a variety of inclusive educational provision and for more structures in place in the school's pastoral system (such as buddy systems, circles of friends, co-operative learning and other ways of linking students in natural, supportive relationships).

Attitudes of other pupils

This is the other side of the relationship equation and it can, as noted in the previous section, have an important bearing on the direction in which the disabled child's personality develops, and, concomitantly, the types of friendships or other interactions they become involved in.

Primary

> At first there were some very obvious characters who found it very hard to have him there and were very intolerant of him, not in a physical way but very dismissive with their body language and turning away and answering him, or not bothering to listen to him.
>
> (Teacher, primary)

This excerpt describes an exceptional state of affairs: there is far more evidence in this study that primary children are more positive in their desire to interact with their disabled peers than secondary pupils (although one must bear in mind that only one secondary school was involved in the project). This may be partly because of the greater plasticity and adaptability of the primary child. The world is newer to young children and they are therefore more open to exploring and accepting a wide range of ways of relating than secondary-age students, who may have already constructed for themselves firmer models of their social worlds.

Another observation at West Hill Primary reveals both the tentativeness of social contact among young children, but also its accepting and essentially catholic nature:

> Daniel playing in sand alongside a girl. He makes first approach to her. She looks at him and makes no response. Daniel puts hand in sand and the girl copies him; appears to be some co-operative play though there is no talking between them. Daniel clearly trying to make a tunnel and says something. Girl doesn't respond . . . Daniel says 'Will you help me?' to the girl, three times. She says something and does go to help him. Pushes him out of the way, gently, and makes a tunnel under his direction. After slow start they are now talking quite frequently about their construction, she telling him what to do and he responding.

> (Observation)

The natural inclusiveness of the girl's behaviour is interesting, given the problems which Daniel had experienced with some other children. The variability in behaviour among the children in response to Daniel is evidence of both a lack of concern to be seen 'doing the right thing' (or indeed knowledge about what the 'right thing' is) and of the plasticity in thinking in young children just referred to.

The following observation confirms the spirit of acceptance and assimilation which had developed among slightly older children in a culture of unequivocal inclusiveness (which existed in this school): 'Joe continually dribbling but others don't seem to notice or mind. Children talk to Joe quite spontaneously and naturally.' The explanation for the greater observed acceptance possibly also relates to the small size of the classes, the consistency of their membership and the opportunity afforded by the continual presence of one classteacher for the modelling of appropriate behaviour towards the disabled child. The ethos of the schools and their staff was also important: avowedly and determinedly accepting of difference.

There were numerous examples in the three primary schools of attitudes which had been established in the context of desirable behaviour overall but which were particularly helpful to the disabled child, for instance this observation on oral participation in Caroline's class: 'It's noticeable that though she speaks slowly, the other children are quite used to waiting patiently and quietly for her contribution'.

A classteacher commented on the extent to which disabled children in the class were seen as individuals by their peers:

The children call them Tom and James, but if you get parents coming in they might talk about the 'handicapped children' but the children don't refer to them in that way; they don't refer to 'the boy in the wheelchair'.

At Luke's school there was further evidence of the importance of adult modelling of behaviour in a legacy of rather patronising attitudes which had become established during the time before the Inclusion Project's involvement: the 'pet hamster' syndrome, evident in the babyish way some children talked to Luke, as though they thought he wouldn't understand them if they talked to him as they would to any other peer; and in the muffled 'Aaah's' which greeted his appearance on stage in the drama club production.

Secondary

Attitudes of students at the secondary school seemed to depend largely on individual personality, particularly where Mike and Jerry were concerned, rather than on any kind of established group behaviour, which, as already discussed, is harder to influence when groups and teachers are continually changing. The idiosyncratic nature of social acceptance also appeared to be due to the less unequivocal messages about inclusion which came from staff in this environment. This is not to say that staff were not sympathetic or helpful, merely that in the larger environment the possibility of distortion in the message about inclusion is greater due to the larger number of individuals involved and the greater difficulty of maintaining a 'party line' than in the closer environment, culture and community of a primary school.

The destructive effect of this kind of lack of accepted ways of showing sensitivity and appreciation is illustrated by the contrast between the reception given to similar events, 'show-and-tell' at Heather Grove (primary), and assembly at Meadow Hill (secondary):

Heather Grove Primary: Caroline introduced the Bambi she was given in hospital and talked about where it lived at home. She was articulate and audible and was clearly pleased at the Bambi's reception. . . . Another girl introduced a cuddly toy she was given when she was in hospital . . . the classteacher made the connection between the experience of Caroline and this girl and another girl who was currently in hospital . . . the teacher came up to Caroline afterwards and talked about the Bambi, how nice and soft it was.

(Observation)

Meadow Hill Secondary: He gave a talk on drag-racing, which he's fascinated by, in assembly: 'Nobody clapped me, Mum!' And he was so hurt by this, really, really hurt by this, and I just said, 'Well . . . not everybody is interested in drag-racing,' but it was, you know, not a ripple. And it was the first thing he said. He'd got all the stuff: I don't know how he actually did it in school but he'd taken a video and he knows quite a bit about it. . . . But he was very disappointed, very disappointed, that nobody clapped him.

(Parent, secondary)

Although the latter can partly be attributed to the greater embarrassment and self-consciousness usually seen in secondary pupils, it is also the case that staff attitudes are communicated to students, who assimilate them with great sensitivity. The parent's account reveals that, if nothing else, there was no system in place for taking positive action (such as a staff member initiating the applause).

Greg's fellow pupils may have found it harder to work out how to relate to him because his disability, unlike those of the other Inclusion Project students, was invisible but at the same time had more direct bearing on his social skills than those of Mike and Jerry. Greg's classteacher commented:

I'm just on the outside looking in but I just think that a lot of people in the class are very good with Greg, and they've incorporated, if you like, his 'nonsense', his badinage, his exaggeration. I think they've done quite well. I don't know how much Greg can change – I don't know whether he can control his behaviour or change it, but if he says, like he does, that he's been best mates with the lead singer in Blur, then they'll say something like, 'Oh yeah? What's his name then?', but they don't say it in a nasty way, and I think that's a miracle really.

There is some evidence that attitudes in this teacher's tutor-group were influenced both by Mike's presence and by the job-share of the teacher interviewed here (who had taught disabled children before) with the Inclusion Project co-ordinator. Between them, it is possible that they had begun to establish some kind of accepted behavioural norms in the way that the primary classteachers were able. Certainly, attitudes towards Greg elsewhere were not so kindly on the whole: students tended to tease him and egg him on to do things that were wrong, or would be amusing to them, whereas they saw more of a clear-cut role for themselves in relation to Jerry and Mike, either as a friend or as partner in class. Two students in particular stood out as keen to be involved in a 'helping' role, one who wanted to work with disabled people and adopted Jerry as a partner in science, and one who just wanted to help.

Stresses and strains for non-disabled students

Several teachers made the point that trying to relate constructively to a disabled child can sometimes be stressful for fellow pupils, who may themselves need carefully considered support. There was also evidence that the 'host' children may be asked to take on too much in the way of peer-tutoring, and this is something about which any inclusion project needs to guard. In the following example a girl had been asked to carry out a task with Luke which involved persuading him to communicate:

> The teacher returned and got a girl [Laura] who had finished all her work to read to Luke. . . . Laura was thinking about how to read to him and show him the pictures at the same time – she discussed this difficulty with another, more confident and outgoing girl [Clarissa], to whom she subsequently went for advice about using the talking-book. She's very hesitant, shy and uncertain herself, but even with Clarissa's help couldn't get Luke to tell them what he wanted to read . . . the co-ordinator returned and asked Luke to thank Laura for reading to him, using the 'thank-you' sign. Laura hovered, ill at ease . . . and went back to her table, visibly relieved.
>
> (Observation)

There was evidence that children found it easier to relate positively to Luke when working alongside him, rather than having responsibility for a joint activity with him, and that on these occasions they were able to notice, and take pleasure in, his achievements. For example, the boy painting at the same table as Luke suddenly announced, with a broad grin: 'I just hear him say "Yeah"!' While peer-tutoring (discussed in chapter 10) is therefore to be encouraged, there are limits to the extent of responsibility which children should be expected to carry.

Changes in attitude

There was little evidence anywhere that able-bodied students' attitudes changed much over the year, after the initial few weeks when they became established. It should be remembered that the three primary schools were already used to the presence of a disabled child when the project began – yet another possible reason for the greater warmth of welcome their pupils appeared to project.

The nature of relationships between Inclusion Project students and non-disabled peers

Opportunities for social contact

The importance of opportunities for informal interaction was emphasised by these West Hill Primary parents, among many others in the study:

> Most important is the ability [for him] to mix with other children – that has done more than all the other things put together. . . . At

school he has friends [but before] he was inward and introverted. Here he is like a different child.

A concern expressed by some secondary students' parents was that their children were more at ease interacting with grown-ups than with other children. This was particularly so in the case of Jerry, whose problems were compounded by his frequent physical isolation in the classroom, with only an LSA within speaking distance. Periods in class when a disabled child is unaccompanied may therefore be valuable socially for the very reason that they are, temporarily, free from the demands of LSAs and NC tasks, and are therefore available for other children to get to know better:

> Tom is in corner, two boys have talked with him. Now leave him. He shouts. Two others approach again and talk to him. . . . James is still in other corner, apparently only talking/messing around with a boy and a girl. They don't appear to be doing much that is constructive . . .
>
> (Observation)

but Tom and James here have spent ten minutes interacting informally, and unsupervised, with their friends, which is more than Jerry, for instance, might do in a week, due to the factors discussed in earlier sections.

The quality of interaction in class, however informal, is quite likely to be inhibited due to the presence somewhere of an adult, compared with what goes on at lunchtime and in the playground. Most of the physical contact and rough-and-tumble behaviour which primary children often manifest appeared to take place in these circumstances. Take this observation: 'Children line up to go out to play. Couple of other children quite rough with Daniel and actually hit him; he retaliates but doesn't over-retaliate.' It was also noticeable that the emotionally freer, physical, approaches made to Caroline by her peers tended to be in the absence of a teacher or LSA, as in this observation: 'William teased her in a friendly way and then went up and hugged her – they pretended to be biting chunks out of each other.'

Out in the playground, some of Caroline's interactions with other children were of a decidedly adventurous nature, giving her the opportunity to experience sensations of danger which one would imagine most adults try to protect her from:

> Playtime: exclusively with Tina [child from a lower year group] just going round the playground together, Tina partly operating the chair. Tina decided to try and steer the chair with her hat over her eyes – Caroline let her – they crashed into the side of one of the pre-fabricated buildings and examined it for damage. Whole incident unnoticed by LSA and dinner ladies.
>
> (Observation)

Friends or acquaintances?

This distinction is only relevant to the secondary pupils, since, as we have seen, all the primary Inclusion Project pupils had some warm and friendly social relationships at school. Mike's social interaction at Meadow Hill was also, as we have seen, often characterised by the demands of real friendship. One teacher observed: 'It's lovely to hear that Mike's got Johnny going off to play billiards with him. I mean they've really clicked, they're both in my tutor group – it's a real friendship, a friendship of equals.'

Greg, on the other hand, although in purely quantitative terms inter-acting more than either of his ex-special school colleagues, rarely seemed to establish identification or true communication with any one group, an observation confirmed by this comment from his year head and RE/English teacher: 'I sometimes watch him out the window and he seems to gravitate round from group to group, not hanging in for long periods of time.'

Jerry's English teacher explained why she felt his school relationships had all remained on the level of 'friendly acquaintance' and had not deepened into genuine friendships:

I think it's probably very difficult to get to know him. I think it would take a special effort rather than in the way that most friendships are formed. Friendships are formed by an odd word or a look, aren't they, I mean you click with that person. And I think the nature of Jerry's disability makes that difficult. . . . And comparing him to Mike, who's also in a wheelchair, I think it's in the nature of Jerry's disability that his face isn't expressive in the same way.

This last comment was only confirmed in observation in as much as Jerry doesn't offer a smile readily; but he was sometimes seen to smile in response either to a teacher's joke or to a comment of his girl science partner. Eye contact was also felt by some staff to be important in improving the quality of students' interactions: this was one of the goals set for Luke at Oakwood Junior. Where young people appear not to have developed important and discrete social skills (such as eye contact or smiling), the use of behavioural techniques (as described by, among others, McBrien and Foxen, 1981) can be successful and should be considered.

Promoting social inclusion

What can we conclude from the previous discussions about the factors which are most important in promoting social inclusion? How were these reflected in the practice of the Inclusion Project teams? What else could the staff involved be doing to improve the social lives of those students who find this aspect of school difficult?

Induction of students in transition from special to mainstream schools

The secondary students who transferred from the special school were nervous to begin with and found their new school, to a greater or lesser extent, a shock:

> At first I was really surprised by how noisy it is in class. Princess Margaret School was really quiet most of the time. . . . My biggest fears have been that I would get lost as it is such a big school. . . . I found big classes with people I didn't know made me feel shy and nervous.

Part of the reason this student didn't know any of the other students was that he didn't come from the local area. One of the West Hill Primary teachers explained how she felt this might affect Daniel's social life in school:

> I was worried about the friendship groups that might not happen . . . about friends coming back to the house, you know . . . but [Daniel's house] is not local to the school and other children have to make a special effort to go.

Joe's parents confirmed that this was a major worry for them as well:

> Our choice would have been a local village school – not West Hill. He would have made friends in his local area here if he had gone to this [local] school. We go to the village and kids don't know Joe; they don't know him or talk to him.

Caroline's mother suggested that because her daughter attended the village primary and was well known in the three local villages, she would have a big advantage socially at secondary school. Certainly, as the introductory chapter implied, if inclusion is interpreted as having a community element, it would seem to be essential that children joining mainstream at the beginning of their educational career should have a plan that enables them to progress right through with their local peers.

Bearing in mind that not being at a local school where they know people is yet another obstacle in the way of some students' social progress, what could be done to ensure greater confidence at the start of the school year? The Inclusion Project staff arranged one or two day visits for the Meadow Hill Comprehensive students in the previous term, but these were evidently not frequent enough for them to feel entirely comfortable with the new prospect.

Ideally, it seems as though many more regular visits, perhaps every week for the term before full-time entry, would be beneficial both to the students transferring from special education and to the mainstream students and staff. All involved would then have plenty of time to think and talk about their reactions, educate themselves about the implications of a changing environment, and develop particular points of social contact which the new students would be able to rely on in their first few weeks: people they had already struck up a relationship with, whom they could look forward to meeting again. Reverse visits can also be arranged, whereby students from the mainstream visit the special school by way of preparation.

It is important not to forget that staff may be transferring from special to mainstream education as well, and may suffer from a similar sense of social dislocation: one of the LSAs remarked that it was important to her that the new school should be welcoming and that other staff should be interested in why the transfer had taken place.

Another aspect of this familiarisation process is the opportunity it gives mainstream teachers to get to know their new students, plan how to include them both socially and otherwise, and think about how to model behaviour towards them in such a way that a tone is set for the class as a whole.

Two alternative conclusions emerge from this micro-analysis of the social relations developed by the children in the Inclusion Project partner schools, given that the children in primary schools seemed to relate better socially than those in the secondary school. One conclusion is that there are features of secondary school organisation which make it inherently unresponsive to inclusion: it is too large for good communication and its subject-oriented structure makes it insensitive to the particular needs of children with disabilities.[1] An alternative conclusion is that secondary schools are certainly more complex and difficult to effect change in, yet there are many organisational innovations which can be introduced which can stimulate social interchange and facilitate acceptance of students with disabilities. (These are discussed below and are reiterated in the conclusion to this chapter.)

Support networks

How could secondary schools attempt to promote social inclusion by emulating some of the features of primary school life that seemed to be helpful? One issue which could be addressed where possible is maintaining the consistency of teaching groups. While impossible beyond Year 8, it might be possible to ensure that students with disabilities were with a consistent group of pupils in Y7 and Y8. This would have important organisational and curricular implications which a school might be unwilling to consider. However, the pastoral benefits – not just for disabled students, but for all – may make such a change worthy of consideration.

If money had been available to fund a 'circle of friends' co-ordination post, as the project managers had originally envisaged, it is possible that more could have been done at Meadow Hill Comprehensive to alleviate Greg's and Jerry's social difficulties. As it was, the over-stretched Inclusion Project co-ordinator herself made many attempts, with help from LSAs, to promote

Jerry's social inclusion, most of which he resisted at first. Two ideas which looked potentially successful were: (1) a plan to recruit other students, instead of LSAs, to accompany him from lesson to lesson and to lunch, and to help him in the lift; (2) the PSE question-and-answer sessions on disability which were held in small groups and gave Jerry's registration peers the opportunity to find out more about his life, and Jerry the chance to explain how he felt about things to a few people at a time. The registration classteacher who helped to instigate this, explained how they had gone about it:

> It started off from a general thing about disability that the PMS staff got started with the initial ideas. And then with my own tutor-group Jerry took a group of about six of them for about half an hour each week where he talked some more about his own problems, and they were then able to ask him questions themselves. . . . His counsellor came and worked with him at the same time, so he was there for support.

Opportunities for social mixing

Enlightening though this may have been in terms of educating the other students about disability, it did not lessen Jerry's observed isolation, perhaps partly because few of his peers were in the same subject groups as him. Less formal and structured opportunities may be more valuable in promoting individual relationships of equality where both parties talk about their feelings incidentally.

How did Inclusion Project staff attempt to provide more of these informal opportunities for social mixing, and were there things they did that inadvertently prevented it? Physical position in class is, as we have seen, important in providing access to informal conversation and gossip. This CDT teacher explains the problems in his workshop:

> The people who they sit next to they get on well with; and they move around the class, specially Greg: he's very inquisitive and he's not afraid to go over and have a look at other people's work. Mike not so much so, maybe because of his lack of mobility. Also, he sits on one of the side desks in Design and Technology because his wheelchair can fit under there and he's a bit isolated there . . . so I wouldn't expect Mike to have as many friends as Greg.

On the researcher's subsequent visit to the class Mike was sitting at a table with everyone else, rather low down but coping nevertheless; it was not clear whether he, the teacher or an LSA had initiated this change, but it made an observable difference to the level of his social involvement. Jerry's physical isolation in class (except in science), usually on his own at the back of the room, has been mentioned elsewhere.

One of the most important parts of the day for gossip and general sociability in any school is lunchtime. It was noticeable that in all the schools visited, the project children tended to sit together. Greg and Mike soon went off on their own ploys after the first few weeks, but in the primary schools the habit continued, or, in the case of Heather Grove, began to establish itself with the arrival of another wheelchair-user. The following observations are illustrative:

> Lunch. Classes rotate sittings but Luke goes in straight away, because of the length of time it takes to give him his lunch – overlaps with his own class at some point, but sideways on to end of table so not able to interact socially much even if he happens to be sitting near someone he knows.

> Jerry entirely on his own at end of table: rota system means others coming and going but Jerry needs whole lunch period ('or longer' according to an LSA) to eat his lunch. No one talked to him. . . . I discussed with various SIP staff where the year 11s went at lunchtimes: wherever it was, it wasn't the dining room. . . . Some year 11s have passes to go out, some are in the courtyard, some in the prefects' room and some in the classrooms, where, however, you're not allowed to eat.

The influence of 'hovering adults'

Another aspect of the promotion of social inclusion is the extent to which staff, usually LSAs, are able to stand back in social situations and allow students to interact with their peers uninhibited by an adult presence. While there was plenty of evidence, particularly in later interviews, that LSAs recognised the importance of such backing-off, there were also several examples of situations where valuable social experience was missed because of unnecessary adult attention:

> Dress rehearsal. There were four groups, each performing a creation story – Luke's was Scandinavian. While waiting to go on stage, the children stood or sat around and chatted; one or two came up and talked to Luke. The LSA decided Luke should be occupied and found two books to read to him, which effectively cut him off from further social interaction until it was time to perform.
>
> (Observation)

The result of this as far as social inclusion is concerned was two-fold: (a) it cut Luke off from further development of his relationship with Drama Club colleagues in the kind of joint enterprise situation where much interaction and growth of comradeship takes place, and (b) it emphasised his differentness, as someone who couldn't be expected to wait like the others but had to be entertained. LSAs at Oakwood Primary made a determined effort to leave

Luke alone in the playground after the first few months, with the result that children came up and involved him in their games on all the occasions observed.

At the secondary level, an adult presence sometimes had the effect of making a student behave more childishly than when he was on his own with his peers:

> Two others came to use the drawing boards on Mike's side of the room, but because he is constantly working with the LSA and has his back to the rest of the room he is very much closed off. He needed help from the LSA to draw lines, manipulate the set square etc. and immediately seemed to become less mature in behaviour, hanging the set square on his nose a couple of times.
>
> (Observation)

Finally, there were aspects of classroom life or ethos that were subtle contributors to the process of social inclusion and could be built on elsewhere, for example, making the classteacher the first point of contact for parents, rather than the Inclusion Project teacher-co-ordinator. This happened only at Heather Grove Primary, where Caroline's mother already knew the school staff well because they were part of her local community.

Other small yet important details that could be changed to make the disabled child feel more comfortable include:

- the positioning of the project newcomer's name in the correct alphabetical place in the register instead of stuck on at the end for administrative convenience (and therefore always read out last);
- the entry of all pupils into ramped classrooms via the ramp rather than the steps: on the observation days Luke and Caroline lined up with their peers in the playground and then went in separately up the ramp.

Points such as these, trivial though they seem, contribute significantly to the new child's experience at school and to the constructions the host children make around their presence. If administrative systems appear to 'speak' difference, then children can be forgiven for maintaining notions about the abnormality of the newcomer.

CONCLUSIONS AND RECOMMENDATIONS

To conclude, the evidence of this chapter suggests a number of points to consider in the promotion of social inclusion:

- Families should be able to choose a well-supported and accessible place at a school in their home neighbourhood. The *neighbourhood* school (as distinct from the resourced school) is especially important for the development and maintenance of close relationships in the child's local community.

- Regular, frequent, pre-entry visits to the chosen mainstream school may be useful. 'Reverse' visits may also be useful, that is from the mainstream school to the special school (see Walter, 1997, discussed in chapter 4 above).
- Intensive contact with a limited group of peers may be desirable for some pupils. The informal social contact which comes over lunch and other unstructured activity can usefully be encouraged and enhanced.
- Staff supporting pupils should seek opportunities to leave pupils alone with their peers, even if this means that they themselves work with another child or on another task. The recommendation made in previous chapters is therefore reinforced – that support staff should be seen as primarily the support of an individual but also as providing learning support to the rest of the class.
- Routine aspects of classroom practice, and the general ethos of the classroom, should be examined to see whether changes could make the disabled child feel more at home. Tutor-group activities can help students with disabilities, as can other kinds of positive action: promoting buddy systems, circles of friends, co-operative learning. Attention to apparently small administrative matters (such as the child's correct alphabetical placement at registration) will also be helpful in promoting social inclusion.
- There is some indication that some students might benefit from social skills training (in, for example, the use of a smile or eye contact). Behavioural methods in this area are sophisticated and successful and their use with selected students would be helpful.
- An inclusive culture communicates itself from the staff to the students in a school, and is crucial for the social acceptance of children who are different. For this reason it is important that the culture of the school is well understood and policy on equal opportunities and diversity unequivocal. The evidence is that if such a culture is positively promoted and continually reinforced in the school's communications, meetings and activities it will benefit the acceptance of children who are different.

12

OVERVIEW AND CONCLUSIONS

In this book we have attempted to fuse a discussion about the ideals behind inclusion with a picture of an inclusion project in practice. Our aim in the two parts of the book has been to straddle the theory–practice divide, seeking at all times to look both to theory and practice – to keep in mind the strong principles behind the move to inclusion whilst observing and noting the practical challenges to be met. We have therefore tried to inform the theoretical discussion with our research findings, and to examine those findings in the context of the theoretical discussion. We have intended in this process to examine difficulties and challenges in the light of others' experiences and to make recommendations on the basis of that examination. Those recommendations are summarised below. The recommendations from Part I are general ones, while those from Part II relate both to inclusion in general and specifically to the introduction of inclusion projects.

SUMMARY AND RECOMMENDATIONS FROM PART I

A number of recommendations stemmed from the discussion in Part I. These include the following:

General issues

- There is a general acceptance in the research literature that all teachers are qualified to teach children with special needs. Although some children certainly need additional support, there is no special pedagogy which has been shown to be especially useful with children who have disabilities or learning difficulties.
- Successful inclusive schools have a culture of acceptance articulated through leadership which is seen to be supportive of inclusion.
- Inclusion needs a well-co-ordinated array of services to succeed.
- For inclusion to succeed, staff have to be able to work together and support each other in team teaching and other collaborative arrangements.

192

- Internationally, inclusion has worked best where there are financial systems in place for ensuring that the process is fully funded through policy which has redirected funds from segregative to inclusive provision.
- The problems of co-ordinating educational, social and medical services in dispersed inclusive services suggest that unified SEN budgets and single children's departments are preferable to the existing array of separate spending departments.

Support

- It is consistent neither with the ethos of inclusion nor with the evidence as to its efficacy in practice that supporters should work only with designated children. Supporters (LSAs or specialist teachers) should be able flexibly to provide support to anyone who appears to need it insofar as this does not result in the neglect of the designated child or children.
- An inclusive ethos implies that all children should be educated together for curricular and social reasons. There is little evidence that withdrawing them for particular periods is beneficial.
- The research evidence is that there is invariably inadequate communication between team participants in support arrangements. Communication and planning would improve if the supporter were to be seen working as part of a team with line-management responsibilities to the classteacher.
- Expectations of LSAs are often made on judgements about their role which centre around care. These may be appropriate in some cases, but not in all, and even when children do have care needs, the job of the LSA in a school must be centred on educational needs rather than care needs.
- The inclusion co-ordinator has a clear role in facilitating these developments. While most integration schemes do not have anyone in this role, there is an analogue here in the Inclusion Project in the role of the teacher-co-ordinator.

Curriculum

In inclusion projects, the development of an inclusive curriculum has been addressed in a variety of ways, including:

- altering the format of the lesson;
- changing the arrangement of groups;
- changing the ways instruction is delivered;
- adapting goals ('differentiation by outcome');
- using different materials;
- providing alternative tasks ('differentiation by activity').

Social

Promoting social relationships in inclusive schools depends on positive action. Social relationships cannot be expected merely to happen. Such positive action may include the provision of:

- carefully structured joint activities;
- opportunities for co-operation in classwork;
- altered classroom layout and organisation;
- systems for facilitating peer co-operation within the school. Strategies such as peer-tutoring, buddy systems, circles of friends, co-operative learning and other ways of connecting students in supportive relationships are needed.

In addition, ways should be found of:

- enabling students of different abilities to work together;
- presenting information on disabilities;
- arranging social events for all students;
- staff acting as models of accepting and welcoming behaviour.

The physical environment

Here, the benefits of a number of features of provision emerge from the literature:

- Children benefit from placement with others in their year-group – not in a separate unit;
- Neighbourhood school attendance is preferable to 'resourced' school attendance;
- Simple low-tech solutions to physical problems are often as effective as expensive structural changes;
- Ingenuity, knowledge of pupils' needs and staff goodwill appear more than adequately to compensate for deficiencies in physical provision.

SUMMARY AND RECOMMENDATIONS FROM PART II

School culture

A project cannot legislate for ethos; neither can it, if one is being realistic, do much to influence school culture from the outside. Nevertheless, there are points which can be kept in mind, as Georgiades and Phillimore (1975) remind us, when working with institutions such as schools. They say that it is important:

- to work with 'the healthy parts of the system' – in other words, to seek out schools (or systems within schools) which are sympathetic to the change being proposed;

- to 'cultivate the host culture' – to work with the system of the school and to seek to influence those who manage it.

These points are germane to the set of issues concerning the culture into which the Inclusion Project was moving. The attitude of staff and senior management was found to influence the acceptance of the project.

Recommendations concerning school culture therefore include:

- negotiating for inclusion co-ordinators to be on the *senior management teams* of partner primary schools, or appropriate management groupings in secondary schools (such as a heads of year-groups);
- suggesting and initiating *continual review* of schools' SEN policies, with such a review process involving senior management, governors and representatives from the inclusion project;
- initiating a *development forum* with inclusion project staff together with key staff from partner schools. This would enable those who have not yet developed flexible practice to move in this direction;
- considering the benefits of more *gradual change* for future similar projects, especially if the effects of implementation mean that a particular school will be accommodating several students at one time.

Neighbourhood schools

The physical fabric of buildings can be a problem in embracing inclusion. However, on the basis of the findings reported in this book, it appears that effecting change is more dependent on a sympathetic culture than on the physical fabric and design of buildings. While physical problems can be irritating and at times cause serious impediments to inclusion, ways round problems were often found if staff were supportive of inclusive ideals. The corollary of this is not to say that adaptations to buildings are unimportant, but rather that the benefits of neighbourhood schools, which may not be ideally resourced or planned (vis-à-vis 'resourced' schools), should be stressed in weighing the appropriateness of a particular school for a child.

Communication

- Written definition of roles and procedural guidelines are necessary for inclusion project and partner school staff. These will assist in determining not only appropriate pedagogic activity on the part of staff such as LSAs, but will also serve to guide staff inside and outside any inclusion venture on who is responsible for what, and who is accountable to whom.
- Time for meetings should be timetabled for key staff. The budgetary

implications of this should be accounted for through money-follows-child accounting systems.

- All staff in a school should use the same staffroom – there should not be a special staffroom or base for inclusion project staff.
- Mobile phones would provide a relatively inexpensive means of easing the accessibility of peripatetic co-ordinators.
- In secondary schools, where flexibility in the work of the LSA is especially important, pagers should routinely be available.
- Clear benefits have been demonstrated of keeping the 'teamness' of the Somerset Inclusion Project. The implication for future projects is that they should be kept to a small scale (as distinct from conflating the efforts of several closing special schools and producing a larger support service).

The work of LSAs

- It should be understood that one of the policy decisions behind an inclusion project is that its resources are delivered not merely to project students but also to other students in the host school. As part of this, it should be clear that it is legitimate and desirable for LSAs to work with a wider range of children than simply the 'target' children.
- The team approach to the deployment of LSAs in the Inclusion Project was well received and should be considered in future projects.
- Pay scales for LSAs should be rationalised in such a way that there is a 'spine' on which all staff are paid.
- The common term LSA or ESA (Education Support Assistant) stresses the educational aspect of the assistant's role, and stresses the links between inclusion project assistants and host school assistants. Those terms thus seem preferable to SA (Support Assistant).
- The title LSA should be reinforced to partner school staff, so that the inaccurate and pejorative term 'carer' is not used.
- Prior to the implementation of a project, a programme of regular training for LSAs should be introduced, which should stress educational as opposed to care issues.

Continuing professional development

- One of the differences between inclusion and integration lies in the preparation of staff for the process. There should therefore be preparatory training of a practical nature backed up with reading material.
- There should be ongoing professional development for mainstream staff provided by inclusion project staff in the practicalities of making inclusion work.

'Purchaser–provider' relationship

- The purchaser (LEA) must have made plans to shift sufficient funds from segregative services to have made the provision of the above inclusive services a realistic proposition. The financial implications of inclusion are significant and an inclusive policy is a prerequisite for confidence in the ability of the purchaser to maintain the necessary level of services to support inclusion. (These services include a service manager, teacher-co-ordinators, LSAs, bought-in professional services and supply and 'cover' to provide non-contact time to hands-on staff for meetings, planning and training.)
- Contractual arrangements with the 'purchaser' of an inclusion service need to be secure at the outset of any project.

The curriculum

- Non-contact time needs to be made available for frequent joint planning sessions between class or subject teacher and co-ordinator.
- There should be a minimisation of withdrawal from the classroom – either for care or education – to avoid dislocation of classwork.
- Groupwork and student partnering can be structured to include co-operative groupwork and peer-tutoring, though the latter must be well thought out and organised: there is evidence that ad hoc peer-tutoring may not be helpful.
- Teachers and LSAs can use systems (such as 'room management') to structure their co-operative work.
- LSAs can provide 'on-the-spot differentiation'.
- Imaginative use can be made of IT and other aids to facilitate inclusion, especially in the secondary phase and for young people with more serious physical disabilities.
- Unified policy should be established on marking and amanuenses. Such a policy may be used within a particular project, or on a wider scale – perhaps regionally.
- The benefits of maintaining additional therapeutic activities such as horse-riding should not be automatically assumed and should, in an inclusive environment, be assessed vis-à-vis the cost in curriculum lost.

Social

- Families should be able to choose a well-supported and accessible place at a school in their home neighbourhood. The neighbourhood school (as distinct from the resourced school) is important for the development and maintenance of close relationships in the child's local community.

- If children are transferring from special to mainstream school, regular, frequent, pre-entry visits to the chosen mainstream school may be useful.
- The informal social contact which comes over lunch can usefully be encouraged.
- Staff supporting pupils should seek opportunities to leave pupils alone with their peers, even if this means that they themselves work with another child or on another task.
- Routine aspects of classroom practice (for instance, the placing of the child's name in alphabetical order on the register) should be examined to see whether changes could make the included child feel more at home.
- There is some indication that some students might benefit from social skills training in simple, discrete skills.
- An inclusive culture communicates itself from the staff to the students in a school, and is crucial for the social acceptance of children who are different. For this reason it is important that the culture of the school is well understood and policy on equal opportunities and diversity unequivocal.

General

- There is strong support from schools for the active role taken by inclusion co-ordinators in the everyday work of the classroom. The role of the co-ordinator should be primarily a hands-on one.
- Parents should be encouraged to have direct contact with their child's school, not principally with project staff.

THE FUTURE?

We asked at the outset of this book why, given the moral imperative for inclusive schools and the empirical evidence in their favour, inclusion had not caught on faster. The answer surely lies in a mixture of conservatism, inertia and fear of the unknown. The inclusion project analysed here shows that with vision and careful planning special schools can successfully change their work in such a way that they can enable their mainstream partners to include children with even serious disabilities. One of our clearest findings has been that while many mainstream staff were highly sceptical about the inclusion project before it started, they had changed their views entirely after several months of seeing it in practice and were fulsome in their support for inclusion.

Inclusion will certainly happen increasingly over the first part of the twenty-first century. Even if schools and administrators are not convinced by the ethical arguments or empirical evidence in its favour, it seems likely that they will have to respond to an increasingly anti-discriminatory legislative environment backed by vigorous rights movements across the world. The de-segregationist and anti-discriminatory environment is now international and it seems impossible that its direction will be reversed. Governments, administrators and schools thus face a clear choice: to fight a rearguard action in maintaining an existing establishment of segregated provision, or to implement planned programmes of inclusion wherein special schools are transformed to inclusion services.

If they choose the first of these alternatives, they will perpetually be stretching resources, making ends meet and mainstreaming individual children only where it is 'economically efficient' (or only where parents are sufficiently assertive or litigious). At the same time they will be maintaining a special sector which becomes increasingly expensive as it accommodates a dwindling population of more difficult-to-place children. 'Inclusion' in such circumstances will be underfunded. The inevitable result will be the repeated breakdown of individual placements as schools struggle in vain to meet children's needs.

The second alternative, however – the implementation of planned programmes of inclusion – offers the chance to shift appropriate resources to make inclusion work. As the findings reported here have shown, such well-resourced inclusion can work, though the enterprise is a developmental one and there are continually lessons to be learned. The education system is at the beginning of a new inclusive adventure and it will take decades to develop practice. But there can be no doubt that a non-segregated, diverse population of children and young people in schools will produce schools which are more sensitive and more people-orientated. And it will produce a younger generation which is more tolerant and accepting of difference. In inclusive schools, all will thrive.

Appendix

MORE INFORMATION ON INCLUSION
Addresses and websites

Two lists are given here to provide further information and to promote discussion about inclusion. The first list is of addresses of organisations (all in the UK) which provide advice and guidance on inclusion and related issues. It has been adapted from the list produced by the Centre for Studies on Inclusive Education (whose address is given in the list) and is reproduced with their kind permission.

The second is a list of Internet websites about inclusive education, disabilities and other related subjects. It is based on one compiled by David Skidmore of the University of Reading, who has given us his kind permission to reproduce it. The list was last updated in November 1996 and comprises a mix of US, Canadian and UK sites. For updates on the list see the address at the foot of the list. This list was compiled from information supplied by various members of the inclusive education discussion list, whose contributions are gratefully acknowledged. However, no endorsement of sites is implied by their incorporation here. If you wish to join the inclusive education list – which is a free, international discussion and question and answer forum on inclusion via e-mail – see the instructions at the bottom of the second list.

ADDRESSES

Help and advice: key organisations

Advisory Centre for Education (ACE)
Aberdeen Studios
22–24 Highbury Grove
London N5 2DQ
Tel: 0171 354 8321 (free telephone advice between 2 and 5 pm, Monday to Friday)
Publishes guides for parents on the education system, the *ACE Special Education Handbook*.

Alliance for Inclusive Education
Unit 2, 70 South Lambeth Road
London SW8 1RL
Tel: 0171 735 5277 Fax: 0171 735 3828
A network of individuals and groups working to change law, policy and
practice so that all disabled children are included in mainstream schools
and colleges. It offers information, advice and training, leaflets and
reports etc.

Campaign for State Education (CASE)
158 Durham Road
London SW10 0DG
Contact: Margaret Tulloch. Tel: 0181 944 8206
A national organisation with local associations and individual national
membership. Campaigns for a first-class state education service
throughout life. Publishes *Parents and Schools*.

CSIE (Centre for Studies on Inclusive Education)
1 Redland Close
Elm Lane
Redland
Bristol BS6 6UE
Tel: 0117 923 8450 Fax: 0117 923 8460
A national, independent educational charity giving information about inclu-
sive education. It is committed to working towards an end to segregated
education for all disabled children.

Council for Disabled Children
8 Wakley Street
London EC1V 7QE
Tel: 0171 843 6000
Has a free information service and a range of free publications, including a
list of organisations concerned with specific disabilities and other leaflets.
Promotes collaborative work between different organisations providing
services and support for children and young people with disabilities and
special educational needs. For a full list send a large s.a.e.

Disability Equality in Education
78 Mildmay Grove
London N1 4PJ
Tel: 0171 254 3197
Provides disability awareness training and publications.

Education Otherwise
PO Box 7420
London N9 9SG
Tel: 0891 518303

Self-help organisation offering support, advice and information to families practising or contemplating home-based education as an alternative to schooling.

Network '81
1–7 Woodfield Terrace
Chapel Hill
Stansted
Essex CM24 8AJ
Tel: 01279 647415

A national network of parents' groups supporting families with disabled children; offers advice and information by telephone and through links with local groups and individuals; issues publications including guides to law, organises conferences and training days. Network '81 is run by and for parents. Advice help line weekdays, 10 am–2 pm.

Parents for Inclusion
Unit 2, Ground Floor
70 South Lambeth Road
London SW8 1RL
Tel: 0171 735 7735 Fax: 0171 735 3828

Organisation for parents of children with special needs to help each other by forming local groups, mainly in the London area. Helps parents with the assessment and statementing procedure and runs training days. Write or telephone between 10 am and 12 noon on Wednesdays (term-time only).

SKILL (National Bureau for Students with Disabilities)
336 Brixton Road
London SW9 7AA
Tel: 0171 274 0565 Fax: 0171 274 7840

Organisation concerned with developing opportunities in further, higher and adult education, training and employment for young people and adults with special educational and training needs throughout the UK. Information service, 1.30 pm–4.30 pm, Mon–Fri (0171 978 9890). Send s.a.e. for publications list and information.

Statutory organisations and quangos

Commission for Racial Equality (CRE)
Elliot House
10/12 Allington Street
London SW1E 5EH
Tel: 0171 828 7022 Fax: 0171 630 7605

Council on Tribunals
22 Kingsway
London WC2B 6LE
Tel: 0171 936 7045

Department for Education and Employment (DfEE)
Sanctuary Buildings
Great Smith Street
London SW1P 3BT
Tel: 0171 925 5000

Equal Opportunities Commission (EOC)
Overseas House
Quay House
Manchester M3 3HN
Tel: 0161 833 9244 Fax: 0161 835 1657

Office for Standards in Education (OFSTED)
Alexandra House
33 Kingsway
London WC2B 6SE
Tel: 0171 421 6800

Special Educational Needs Tribunal
71 Victoria Street
London SW1H OHW
Tel: 0171 925 6925

Welsh Office
Education Department
Government Buildings
Ty Glas Road
Llanishen
Cardiff CF4 5WE
Tel: 01222 761456

Expert witnesses

Independent Panel for Special Education Advice (IPSEA)
4 Ancient House Mews
Woodbridge
Suffolk IP12 1DH
Tel: 01394 382814

Operates a daily advice line on LEA duties, parents' rights and children's
entitlements. Has a network of volunteer professional advisers offering
free second professional opinion and support. IPSEA also runs the Free
Representation Service (FRS) for parents appealing to the SEN Tribunal.
Publishes a newsletter and other information on changes in the law and
important legal judgements. IPSEA would like to hear from potential
volunteers for FRS or advice line.

Legal advice

The Children's Legal Centre
University of Essex
Wivenhoe Park
Colchester
Essex CO4 3SQ
Tel: 01206 873820 or 872466

An independent national body concerned with laws and policies which affect
children and young people in England and Wales. It provides a free
advice and information service by phone and by letter.

Disability Law Service (Network)
16 Princeton Street
London WC1R 4BB
Tel: 0171 831 8031

Further organisations

The ACE Centre Advisory Trust
Waynflete Road
Headington
Oxford OX3 8DD
Tel: 01865 63508 Fax: 01865 750188

Provides advice on information technology for pupils and students with
disabilities and other special needs.

Barnardos
Tanners Lane
Barkingside
Ilford
Essex IG6 1QG
Tel: 0181 550 8822

Barnardos has 125 years' experience of working with children and young
  people. The organisation runs residential special schools, homes and
  community projects and has wide interests in education.

British Council of Organisations of Disabled People
Litchurch Plaza
Litchurch Lane
Derby DE24 8AA
Tel: 01332 295551 Fax: 01332 295580
Minicom 01332 295581

A national organisation of disabled people representing 116 disabled
  people's organisations. Works to promote and protect disabled people's
  human and civil rights, including campaigning for comprehensive anti-
  discrimination legislation. Offers speakers, workshop facilitators and
  materials for workshops/conferences involving disabled people.
  Publications list, information leaflets, also individual membership.

The Children's Society
Edward Rudolf House
Margery Street
London WC1X OJL
Tel: 0171 837 4299

Aims to offer a comprehensive child care service to any child or any family
  in need, whether spiritual, physical or emotional.

Down's Syndrome Association
155 Mitcham Road
London SW17 9PG
Tel: 0181 682 4001

Information, advice and support for families and professionals associated
  with children who have Down's Syndrome. Resource centre in London
  and nationwide network of branches and self-help support groups.
  Publications lists.

Friends for the Young Deaf
East Court Mansion
College Lane
East Grinstead
West Sussex RH19 3LT
Tel: 01342 312639
Focuses on the integration needs of young deaf people; works to develop
    their skills through co-operation and integration between deaf and
    hearing people. Offers training workshops, holiday and sports events,
    information leaflets.

National Confederation of Parent/Teacher Associations
2 Ebbsfleet Industrial Estate
Stonebridge Road
Gravesend
Kent DA11 9DZ
Tel: 01474 560618
Provides model constitutions.

The National Deaf/Blind and Rubella Association (SENSE)
11–13 Clifton Terrace
Finsbury Park
London N4 3SR
Tel: 0181 961 7795
Offers nationwide family advisory service and rehabilitation and training
    centre for young deaf/blind adults. Quarterly magazine and publications
    list.

National Deaf Children's Society
15 Dufferin Street
London EC1Y 8PD
Tel: 0171 250 0123
Advocacy and counselling for parents with deaf children. Publications list
    available.

People First
Instrument House
207 Kings Cross Road
London WC1X 9DB
Tel: 0171 713 6400 Fax: 0171 833 1880
A self-advocacy organisation run by and for people with learning difficulties.
    Has a range of publications, runs conferences and offers training.

Pre-School Learning Alliance (PPA)
69 Kings Cross Road
London WC1X 9LL
Tel: 0171 833 0991

Helps playgroups and parents understand and provide for the needs of young children. Promotes community-based provision for under-fives. Wide range of publications on play, training and how to run a group.

Rathbone C.I.
1st Floor
Excalibur House
77 Whitworth Street
Manchester M1 6EZ
Tel: 0161 236 5358

The National Rathbone Society merged with Community Industry in 1995. A national charity working for and on behalf of people with learning difficulties. Runs a learning difficulty help-line, offers free leaflets and a newsletter.

Royal Association for Disability and Rehabilitation (RADAR)
12 City Forum
250 City Road
London EC1V 8AF
Tel: 0171 250 3222, 0171 250 0212

Aims to improve the environment for disabled people and acts as a co-ordinating body with over 400 member associations. Publications list.

Royal National Institute for the Blind (RNIB)
224 Great Portland Street
London W1N 6AA
Tel: 0171 388 1266

Gives information on all aspects of the education of visually handicapped people, courses, special schools and colleges, individual advice and support. Wide range of leaflets available on request.

Royal National Institute for the Deaf (RNID)
19/23 Featherstone Street
London EC1Y 8SL
Tel: 0171 296 8000

Offers information on all aspects of hearing loss. Student and parent advocacy and counselling. Communications Support Service. Publications list.

Royal Society for Mentally Handicapped Children and Adults (MENCAP)
123 Golden Lane
London EC1Y ORT
Tel: 0171 454 0454

Provides support, information and advice for individuals with learning difficulties and their families in the UK. Has national, regional and local membership. Offers FE colleges, training and other services. Leaflets available.

SCOPE
12 Park Crescent
London W1N 4EQ
Tel: 0171 636 5020

Provides and promotes facilities for the treatment, training, education and residential care of children and adults with cerebral palsy. Publishes the monthly *Disability Now* and a wide range of publications. Send s.a.e. for list.

INTERNET WEBSITES

ACE Centre, UK. Provides advice on IT for disabled children
http://www.rmplc.co.uk/eduweb/sites/acecent/index.html

The ARC (used to be the Association for Retarded Citizens)
http://www.metronet.com/~thearc/welcome.html

The ARC update on Education Report Card
http://www.metronet.com/~thearc/report/inclusup.html

Autism Resources
http://web.syr.edu/~jmwobus/autism/

Canada's Schoolnet
http://schoolnet2.carleton.ca/
also run as a newsgroup by Keenan Weller at
kwellar@schoolnet.carleton.ca

Center on Human Policy, Syracuse University
http://web.syr.edu/~thechp

Centre for Studies on Inclusive Education (CSIE), UK
http://ep.open.ac.uk/wgma/CSIE/csiehome.html

CHADD, Children and Adults with Attention Deficit Disorder
http://www.chadd.org/

Council for Exceptional Children, legislative updates, University of Virginia. Legislative issues that affect the special education field
http://curry.edschool.Virginia.EDU/curry/dept/cise/ose/info/cecupdate.html

Department of Education (USA)
http://www.ed.gov/

Down's Syndrome
http://www.nas.com/downsyn/
http://wvlink.mpl.com/users/casten_t/downsyn1.html

Education of visually impaired students
http://www.pleasant.org/pleasant/sarah/teach/blind-ed.html

ERIC Clearing House US Dept of Ed – Together we can. A guide to creating an interagency system of education and human services.
http://eric-web.tc.columbia.edu/families/TWC/

Fagile-X syndrome
http://www.worx.net/fraxa

Family Village Inclusion Resources, USA. Home page, articles, opinion and information on inclusion. Very comprehensive
http://www.familyvillage.wisc.edu/edu_incl.htm

Fetal Alcohol Syndrome
http://fohnix.metronet.com/~thearc/faslist.html

Guide to Learning Disabilities (and others)
http://www.fln.vcu.edu/ld/ld.html

Hearing Impaired Links Page
http://tardis.pacificu.edu/~brentb/deaf.html

Inclusion Press, Canada. Marsha Forest and Jack Pearpoint, Kichner, Ontario
http://www.inclusion.com

Institute on Community Integration, University of Minnesota
http://134.84.215.89/pub/

Interpreters for the deaf
http://www.sheridanc.on.ca/~cowley/asl-eng.html

Japan Down Syndrome Network
http://ss.niah.affrc.go.jp/~momotani/dowj1-e.html

Job Training Partnership Act (JTPA) US Dept of Ed
http://www.clark.net/pub/cfpa/execsumm/cb-inclu.html

Kansas Project, Best Practices for Inclusion
http://www.valdosta.peachnet.edu/coe/coed/sped/camp/proj/abstract.html

Mental Health. Index for psychology, support, and mental health issues, resources, and people on the Internet
http://www.coil.com/~grohol/

Midwest Conference on Inclusive Education, March 1996
http://www.esu3.k12.ne.us/esunotice/inclusive.html

Montana Office of Public Instruction
http://151.7.114.15/opi/opi.html

National Institute on Life Planning, Sonoma, CA
http://www.sonic.net/nilp/

National Resource Directory
http://www.portal.com/~cbntmkr/php.html

School Psychology Resources Online
http://mail.bcpl.lib.md.us/~sandyste/school_psych.html

Special Education Law
http://access.digex.net/~edlawinc

Special education resources
http://www.pleasant.org/pleasant/sarah/teach/sped.html

The special needs Internet project, UK
http://www.tcns.co.uk/waacis/

TIES (Teachers in Inclusive Settings) USC Fresno
http://beaches.soehd.csufresno.edu/soehd/ctet/ties.html

UK resources on Down's syndrome
http://ep.open.ac.uk/wgma/Chris/UKDSinfo.html

University of Maine: community inclusion projects
http://130.111.120.13/~cci/ccid.html

Welcome to the Family Education Network
http://www.familyeducation.com

Williams Syndrome
http://www.sos.on.ca/~pmackay/williams.html

Yahoo, Society and Culture: Disabilities. Wide range of disability information
http://www.yahoo.com/Society_and_Culture/Disabilities/

The address for updates on this list is
http://www.mailbase.ac.uk/lists/inclusive-education/files/inclusion_sites.txt

To join the inclusive education list – which is a discussion and question and answer forum about inclusion via e-mail, follow these instructions. On e-mail, address a message to:

mailbase@mailbase.ac.uk

containing the following one-line message:

join inclusive-education Firstname Lastname (*substituting your own first and last names*).

NOTES

1 INCLUSIVE EDUCATION: THE IDEALS AND THE PRACTICE

1 In some US school districts a quarter of the budget is spent on special education (see Wang *et al.*, 1995). Internationally, around eight times as much money is spent on a special school pupil as on a mainstream pupil (OECD, 1994), though this average figure disguises the fact that in the USA fifteen times as much is spent on special school pupils. In the UK, 4.5 times as much is spent on each special school pupil as on each mainstream pupil, and the multiplier is rising consistently and significantly (Audit Commission/HMI, 1992a).

2 In Sweden, a pioneer in inclusion, integration of deaf children was superseded by a segregative policy for these children. A Swedish report to the OECD stated, 'The principle of integration has been discussed most energetically in this area . . . The possibility to participate and develop a positive self-image in a sign language environment has been viewed as a goal overriding integration' (OECD, 1994: 33).

3 'Cultural capital' is a term coined by the French sociologist Bourdieu to refer to the accumulated resources and insignia which can be 'cashed in' for society's goods and services (see, for example, Bourdieu and Passeron, 1977; Bourdieu, 1984).

4 As in Bourdieu's (*ibid.*) 'symbolic capital'. There is surely a sense in which different language and symbol systems develop in different kinds of school. If children do not have the 'right' language because they have attended a special school, they will be unable to exchange this 'symbolic capital' for other kinds of capital. Exclusion from the wider culture is the consequence.

5 This is especially so as recent evidence still attests to the interdependency of supposed 'factors' such as race and special needs. Lipsky and Gartner (1996) cite research showing that black students are far more likely to be labelled 'retarded' in the US (equivalent to the British 'moderate learning difficulties') than are white students – who are more likely to be categorised as 'learning disabled'.

6 The Audit Commission/HMI (1992a) found that 39 per cent of parents of children in special schools wanted a change of school for their children, as compared with 11 per cent whose children were in the mainstream.

2 USING SUPPORT IN INCLUSIVE CLASSROOMS

1 There is some evidence, though, that children whose first language is not English prefer and may benefit from intensive language tuition in withdrawal sessions

(Tatelman, 1996). There are also many in the deaf community (see, for example, Mason, 1994) who assert the right to a separate education system.

3 CURRICULAR INCLUSION

1 It should be noted that the validity of the results obtained from facilitated communication have been seriously questioned by, amongst others, Cummins and Prior (1992) and Hastings (1996).

4 SUPPORTIVE CLASSROOM ENVIRONMENTS FOR SOCIAL INCLUSION

1 The distinctions between neighbourhood schools and resourced schools are discussed in chapter 1.

7 RESEARCHING INCLUSION, AND METHODS USED IN THIS RESEARCH

1 There has been a tendency in the academic discussion of inclusion to prefer to discuss paradigms rather than paraprofessionals. It is a danger of which we are aware, yet it is important to frame the intellectual context of the debate on research methodology in what is a politically charged area.
2 A quasi-experiment is an experiment using 'naturally existing' conditions. In other words, conditions (experimental and control groups) are not devised and subjects randomly assigned, as would be the case in a 'true' experiment. Rather, naturally existing examples of the conditions in question are sought and the individuals who are associated with the conditions are used as 'subjects'.
3 Hammersley (1992) contends that case studies offer only a 'weaker' claim to generalisability than does research based on large representative samples. This weaker claim does not, however, mean that results are not therefore generalisable.

8 THE PLACE AND THE PEOPLE

1 At the time of the project, Steve Connor was the assistant divisional director for Barnardos responsible for the school.
2 Vivian Upton was the deputy head of the school, to become deputy principal in charge of the Inclusion Project.
3 Classteacher – to become a teacher-co-ordinator in the SIP.
4 West Hill was the first primary school to become involved.
5 Paul Upton was the headteacher of West Hill School.
6 Martin Babb was the PMS social worker.

9 THE PROCESS OF CHANGE

1 It should be re-emphasised in doing this, that this research makes no pretence to conform to the expectations of nomothetic research methodology. The categories which are ultimately derived from the data are not watertight or mutually exclu-

sive and there are many instances in which a comment or observation may be categorised in a variety of ways. The aim, however, recognising all of this, is to provide a gestalt of the data and the interpretations made from it.

2 In other words, resourcing a school so that it is particularly well equipped to accommodate children with certain kinds of disability. Doing this means that some children will not necessarily attend their neighbourhood school.

3 In fact, swimming and physiotherapy were provided at PMS only twice a week at most.

11 SOCIAL INCLUSION

1 A corollary to this conclusion might be that schools which hold to the philosophy of the Small Schools movement (see Hodgetts, 1991) are naturally inclusive and more appropriate for the needs of some students than large comprehensives.

BIBLIOGRAPHY

Aaronson, E. and Bridgeman, D. (1979) 'Jigsaw groups and the desegregated classroom: in pursuit of common goals', *Personality and Social Psychology Bulletin*, 5, 4, 438–46.

Ainscow, M. (1995a) Education for all: making it happen. Keynote address to the International Special Education Congress, Birmingham, UK.

—— (1995b) 'Education for all: making it happen', *Support for Learning*, 10, 4, 147–55.

Ainscow, M., Booth, T. and Dyson, A. (1995) 'Tales of innocence and experience from Richard Lovell Community High School', in J. Allan, *Inclusion and exclusion: an international comparison*, Cambridge: unpublished symposium proceedings.

Alderson, P. (1995) *Listening to Children: Children, Ethics and Social Research*, London: Barnardos.

Anderson, E.M. and Clarke, L. (1982) *Disability in Adolescence*, London: Methuen.

Anderson, L.W. and Pellicer, L.O. (1990) 'Synthesis of research on compensatory and remedial education', *Educational Leadership*, 48, 1, 10–16.

Armstrong, D., Galloway, D. and Tomlinson, S. (1993) 'Assessing special educational needs: the child's contribution', *British Educational Research Journal*, 19, 2, 121–31.

Arter, J.A. and Jenkins, J.R. (1979) 'Differential diagnosis – prescriptive teaching: a critical appraisal', *Review of Educational Research*, 49, 4, 517–555.

Audit Commission/HMI (1992a) *Getting in on the Act: Provision for Pupils with Special Educational Needs: The National Picture*, London: HMSO.

—— (1992b) *Getting the Act Together: Provision for Pupils with Special Educational Needs: A Management Handbook for Schools and LEAs*, London: HMSO.

—— (1994) *The Act Moves On: Progress in Special Educational Needs*, London: HMSO.

Baker, E.T., Wang, M.C. and Walberg, H.J. (1995) 'The effects of inclusion on learning', *Educational Leadership*, 52, 4, 33–5.

Ballard, K. (1995) 'Inclusion, paradigms, power and participation', in C. Clarke, A. Dyson and A. Millward (eds) *Towards Inclusive Schools?*, London: Fulton.

Bayliss, P. (1995) 'Reluctant innovators: meeting special educational needs in a middle school', *Support for Learning*, 10, 4, 170–6.

Bear, G., Clever, A. and Proctor, W. (1991) 'Self-perceptions of nonhandicapped children and children with learning disabilities in integrated classes', *Journal of Special Education*, 24, 4, 409–26.

Bennett, N. and Blundell, D. (1983) 'Quantity and quality of work in rows and classroom groups', *Educational Psychology*, 3, 2, 93–105.

Best, R. (1991) 'Support teaching in a comprehensive school: some reflections on recent experience', *Support for Learning*, 6, 1, 27–31.

214

Beveridge, S. (1996) 'Experiences of an integration link scheme: the perspectives of pupils with severe learning difficulties and their mainstream peers', *British Journal of Learning Disabilities*, 24, 9–18.

Biklen, D. (1990) 'Communication unbound: autism and praxis', *Harvard Educational Review*, 60, 3, 291–394.

—— (1993) *Communication Unbound: How Facilitated Communication is Challenging Traditional Views of Autism and Ability/Disability*, New York: Teachers College Press.

Biklen, D., Saha, N. and Kluwer, C. (1995) 'How teachers confirm the authorship of facilitated communication: a portfolio approach', *Journal of Association for Persons with Severe Handicaps*, 20, 1, 45–56.

Bines, H. (1986) *Redefining Remedial Education*, Beckenham: Croom Helm.

Birch, H.G., Richardson, S.A., Baird, D., Horobin, G. and Illsley, R. (1970) *Mental Subnormality in the Community: A Clinical and Epidemiological Survey*, Baltimore: Williams and Wilkins.

Booth, T. (1992) 'Under the walnut tree: the Grove Primary School', in T. Booth, W. Swann, M. Masterson and P. Potts (eds) *Learning for All 2: Policies for Diversity in Education*, London: Open University Press/Routledge.

—— (1995) 'Mapping inclusion and exclusion: concepts for all', in C. Clarke, A. Dyson and A. Millward (eds) *Towards Inclusive Schools*, London: David Fulton.

—— (1996) 'A perspective on inclusion from England', *Cambridge Journal of Education*, 26, 1, 87–98.

Booth, T. and Booth, W. (1996) 'Sounds of silence: narrative research with inarticulate subjects', *Disability and Society*, 11, 1, 55–69.

Bourdieu, P. (1984) *Distinction*, London: Routledge and Kegan Paul.

Bourdieu, P. and Passeron, J-C. (1977) *Reproduction in Society, Education and Culture*, London: Sage.

Broomhead, R. and Darley, P. (1992) 'Supportive parents for special children: working towards partnership in Avon', in T. Booth, W. Swann, M. Masterson and P. Potts (eds) *Learning for All 2: Policies for Diversity in Education*, London: Open University Press/Routledge.

Brown, A.L. and Campione, J.C. (1986) 'Psychological theory and the study of learning disabilities', *American Psychologist*, 41, 1059–68.

Burgess, R.G. (1982) 'The unstructured interview as an observation', in R.G. Burgess, *Field Research: A Sourcebook and Field Manual*, London: George Allen and Unwin.

—— (1984) *In the Field*, London: George Allen and Unwin.

Cashdan, A., Pumfrey, P.D. and Lunzer, E.A. (1971) 'Children receiving remedial treatment in reading', *Educational Research*, 13, 2, 98–103.

CEC (1994) '12 Principles for Successful Inclusive Schools', *CEC Today Newsletter (Council for Exceptional Children)*, May.

Chinapah, V. (1989) 'Mainstream schooling for the physically handicapped: how can counselling help?' *International Journal for Advancement of Counselling*, 12, 223–36.

Chiu, L. (1990) 'Self-esteem of gifted, normal and mild mentally handicapped children', *Psychology in the Schools*, 27, 2, 263–8.

Christophos, F. and Renz, P. (1969) 'A critical examination of special education programs', *Journal of Special Education*, 3, 4, 371–80.

Clarke, C., Dyson, A., Millward, A. and Skidmore, D. (eds) (1995) *Innovatory Practice in Mainstream Schools for Special Educational Needs*, Newcastle: University of Newcastle upon Tyne for the DfE.

Clough, P. (1995) 'Problems of identity and method in the investigation of special educational needs', in P. Clough and L. Barton, *Making Difficulties: Research and the Construction of SEN*, London: Paul Chapman Publishing.

Cohen, E.G. (1976) 'Problems and prospects of teaming', *Educational Research Quarterly*, 1, 2, 49–63.

Cohen, L. and Manion, L. (1985) *Research Methods in Education* (2nd edn), Beckenham: Croom Helm.

Cole, D. and Meyer, L. (1991) 'Social integration and severe disabilities: a longitudinal analysis of child outcomes', *Journal of Special Education*, 25, 3, 340–51.

Combes, A. (1995) 'Taking pupils with special needs out of mainstream: a change in thinking', *Support for Learning*, 10, 4, 161–3.

Copeland, I. (1995) 'The establishment of models of education for disabled children', *British Journal of Educational Studies*, 43, 2, 179–200.

——(1996) 'Integration versus segregation: the early struggle', paper presented to the Annual Conference of the British Educational Research Association, Lancaster.

Cowne, E. (1996) *The SENCO Handbook: Working Within a Whole-school Approach*, London: David Fulton.

Cox, D. (1996) 'Design and technology at Foxyards Primary School', in P. Widlake (ed.) *The Good Practice Guide to Special Educational Needs*, Birmingham: Questions Publishing Co.

Cronbach, L.J. (1982) *Designing Evaluations of Educational and Social Programmes*, San Francisco: Jossey Bass.

—— (1987) 'Issues in planning evaluations', in R. Murphy and H. Torrance (eds) *Evaluating Education: Issues and Methods*, London: Harper and Row.

CSIE (1992) *Bishopswood: Good Practice Transferred*, Bristol: Centre for Studies on Inclusive Education.

—— (1995) *Checklist for Inclusion: Developing Schools' Policies to Include Disabled Children*, Bristol: Centre for Studies on Inclusive Education.

—— (1996) *Developing an Inclusive Policy for your School: A CSIE Guide*, Bristol: Centre for Studies on Inclusive Education.

Cummins, R.A. and Prior, M.P. (1992) 'Autism and assisted communication: a response to Biklen', *Harvard Educational Review*, 62, 2, 228–38.

Delefes, P. and Jackson, B. (1972) 'Teacher pupil interaction as a function of location in the classroom', *Psychology in the Schools*, 9, 119–23.

DES (1978) *Special Educational Needs*, Report of the Committee of Enquiry into the Education of Handicapped Children and Young People, Cmnd 7212, London: HMSO.

DeVault, M.L., Harnischfeger, A. and Wiley, D.E. (1977) *Curricula, Personnel Resources and Grouping Strategies*, St. Ann, Mo.: ML-GROUP for Policy Studies in Education, Central Midwestern Regional Lab.

DfE (1994) *The Code of Practice on the Identification and Assessment of Special Educational Needs*, London: HMSO.

Doble, J.M. (1986) 'Integration of physically handicapped pupils in a comprehensive school', M.Ed. thesis, University of Edinburgh.

Donkersloot, P. (1991) 'Humberside Initiative: County Education Service for Disability', *Head Teachers' Review*, Spring, 7–10.

Dorn, S., Fuchs, D. and Fuchs, L.S. (1996) 'A historical perspective on special education reform', *Theory into Practice*, 35, 1, 12–19.

Dunn, L.M. (1968) 'Special education for the mildly mentally retarded: is much of it justifiable?', *Exceptional Children*, Sept., 5–22.

Durkheim, E. (1933) *The Division of Labour in Society*, London: Collier-Macmillan.

Dyson, A. and Gains, C. (eds) (1993) *Rethinking Special Needs in Mainstream Schools: Towards the Year 2000*, London: David Fulton.

Edmonds, R. (1979) 'Effective schools for the urban poor', *Educational Leadership*, 37, 1, 15–23.

Eichinger, J. (1990) 'Goal structure effects on social interaction: nondisabled and disabled elementary students', *Exceptional Children*, 56, 5, 408–16.

Elliot, J. and Adelman, C. (1976) *Innovation at the Classroom Level: A Case Study of the Ford Teaching Project*, Milton Keynes: Open University Press.

Farrell, P. and Scales, A. (1995) 'Who likes to be with whom in an integrated nursery?', *British Journal of Learning Disability*, 23, 156–9.

Ferguson, P.M. (1992) 'The puzzle of inclusion: a case study of autistic students in the life of one high school', in P.M. Ferguson, D.L. Ferguson and S.J. Taylor (eds) *Interpreting Disability: A Qualitative Reader*, New York: Teachers College Press.

Ferguson, P.M., Ferguson, D.L. and Taylor S.J. (eds) (1992) *Interpreting Disability: A Qualitative Reader*, New York: Teachers College Press.

FEU (1990) *Developing Self-advocacy Skills with People with Disabilities*, London: Further Education Unit.

Field, M. (1988) 'The integration of physically handicapped pupils into mainstream secondary schools', *Pastoral Care*, Sept., 22–31.

Fleming, H., Dadswell, P. and Dodgson, H. (1990) 'Reflections on the integration of children with learning difficulties into secondary mathematics classes', *Support for Learning*, 5, 4 180–5.

Fletcher, S.L. (1995) 'Integration: children of all abilities working together in an inclusive classroom', in P. Gammage and J. Meighan (eds) *Early Childhood Education: The Way Forward*, Derby: Education Now Books.

Fletcher-Campbell, F. (1994) *Still Joining Forces? A Follow-up Study of Links between Ordinary and Special Schools*, Slough: NFER.

—— (1996a) *The Resourcing of Special Edcuational Needs*, Slough: NFER.

—— (1996b) 'Just another piece of paper? Key Stage 4 accreditation for pupils with learning difficulties', *British Journal of Special Education*, 23, 1, 15–18.

Flynn, G. (1993) 'Leadership forum: inclusion, reform and restructuring in practice', paper presented to the Annual Convention of the Council for Exceptional Children, April 5–9, San Antonio, CA.

Ford, A., Davern, L. and Schnorr, R. (1992) 'Inclusive education: "Making sense" of the curriculum', in S. Stainback and W. Stainback (eds) *Curriculum Considerations in Inclusive Classrooms: Facilitating Learning for All Students*, Baltimore: Brookes.

Forest, M. and O'Brien, J. (1989) *Action for Inclusion: How to Improve Schools by Welcoming Children with Special Needs into Regular Classrooms*, Toronto: Inclusion Press.

Foucault, M. (1980) 'Two lectures', in M. Foucault, *Power/Knowledge: Selected Interviews and Other Writings*, Hemel Hempstead: Harvester Wheatsheaf.

—— (1981) 'Questions of method: an interview with Michel Foucault', *Ideology and Consciousness*, 8 (Spring), 3–14.

Fox, G. (1996) 'Managing special needs assistants', *Special Children*, March, 45–51.

Frederickson, N. and Woolfson, H. (1987) 'Integration: the social dimension', *Educational Psychology in Practice*, 3, 2, 42–8.

Fulcher, G. (1989) *Disabling Policies*, London: Falmer.

—— (1993) 'Schools and contests: a reframing of the effective schools debate?' in R. Slee (ed.) *Is there a Desk with my Name on it? The Politics of Integration*, London: Falmer.

Fullan, M. (1993) *Change Forces*, London: Falmer.

Galloway, D. (1983) 'Disruptive pupils and effective pastoral care', *School Organisation*, 13, 245–54.

Galloway, D.M. and Goodwin, C. (1979) *Educating Slow Learning and Maladjusted Children: Integration or Segregation?*, Harlow: Longman.

Garner, P. and Sandow, S. (eds) (1995) *Advocacy, Self-advocacy and Special Needs*, London: David Fulton.

Geen, A.G. (1985) 'Team teaching in the secondary schools of England and Wales', *Educational Review*, 37, 1, 29–38.

Georgiades, N.J. and Phillimore, L. (1975) 'The myth of the hero-innovator and alternative strategies for organizational change', in C.C. Kiernan and F.P. Woodford (eds) *Behaviour Modification with the Severely Retarded*, Amsterdam: Associated Scientific Publishers.

Gerber, M.M. (1996) 'Reforming special education: beyond "inclusion"', in C. Christensen and F. Rizvi (eds) *Disability and the Dilemmas of Education and Justice*, Buckingham: Open University Press.

Gibb, C. and Donkersloot, P. (1991) 'Planning de-segregation', *British Journal of Special Education*, 18, 1, 33–5.

Glaser, B.G. and Strauss, A.L. (1967) *The Discovery of Grounded Theory: Strategies for Qualitative Research*, New York: Aldine.

Greenwood, S. (1995) 'Involving the child: some thoughts on a code of good practice for secondary school', *Support for Learning*, 10, 4, 177–80.

Guralnick, M., Connor, R.T., Hammond, M., Gottman, J.M. and Kinnish, K. (1995) 'Immediate effects of mainstreamed settings on the social interactions and social integration of preschool children', *American Journal on Mental Retardation*, 100, 4, 359–377.

Hall, J. (1992) 'Segregation by another name?', *Special Children*, April, 20–23.

Hall, L.J. (1994) ' A descriptive assessment of social relationships in integrated classrooms', *Journal of Association for Persons with Severe Handicaps*, 14, 4, 302–13.

Hallinger, P. and Murphy, J. (1986) 'The social context of effective schools', *American Journal of Education*, 94, 3, 328–55.

Hammersley, M (1992) *What's Wrong with Ethnography?*, London: Routledge.

Hargreaves, D.H. (1982) *The Challenge for the Comprehensive School*, London: Routledge and Kegan Paul.

Hastings, R. (1996) 'Does facilitated communication free imprisoned minds?', *The Psychologist*, 9, 1, 19–24.

Hatton, E.J. (1985) 'Team teaching and teacher orientation to work: implications for the preservice and inservice education of teachers', *Journal of Education for Teaching*, 11, 3, 228–44.

Hegarty, S. (1993a) 'Conclusion', in M. Ainscow (ed.) *Towards Effective Schools for All*, Stafford: NASEN.

—— (1993b) 'Reviewing the literature on integration', *European Journal of Special Needs Education*, 8, 3, 194–200.

Hegarty, S., Pocklington, K. and Lucas, D. (1981) *Educating Pupils with Special Needs in the Ordinary School*, Windsor: NFER-Nelson.

Hendrickson, J.H., Shokoohi-Yekta, M., Hamre-Nietupski, S. and Gable, R.A. (1996) 'Middle and high school students' perceptions on being friends with peers with severe disabilities', *Exceptional Children*, 63, 1, 19–28.

Higgins, P.C. (1992) 'Working at mainstreaming', in P.M. Ferguson, D.L. Ferguson and S.J. Taylor (eds) *Interpreting Disability: A Qualitative Reader*, New York: Teachers College Press.

Hodgetts, C. (1991) *Inventing a School*, Hartland: Resurgence.

Houston, L. (1995) 'Experiences in inclusive education', *Bridges*, 2, 2, 21.

Hrekow, P. and Barrow, G. (1993) 'Developing a system of inclusive education for pupils with behavioural difficulties', *Pastoral Care*, June, 6–13.

Hutton, W. (1995) *The State We're In*, London: Jonathan Cape.

Inglese, J. (1996) 'Special teachers? Perceptions of the special expertise required for effective special educational needs teaching and advisory work', *Support for Learning*, 11, 2, 83–7.

Jacklin, A. and Lacey, J. (1991) 'Assessing integration at Patcham House', *British Journal of Special Education*, 18, 2, 67–70.

—— (1993) 'The integration process: a developmental model', *Support for Learning*, 8, 2, 51–7.

James, A. and Prout, A. (1990) 'A new paradigm for the sociology of childhood? Provenance, promise and problems', in A. James and A. Prout (eds) *Constructing and Reconstructing Childhood: Contemporary Issues in the Sociological Study of Childhood*, London: Falmer.

Janney, R., Snell, N.E., Beers, M.K. and Raynes, M. (1995) 'Integrating students with moderate and severe disabilities into general education classes', *Exceptional Children*, 61, 5, 425–39.

Jesson, D. and Gray, J. (1991) 'Slants on slopes: using multi-level models to investigate differential school effectiveness and its impact on schools' examination results', *School Effectiveness and School Improvement*, 2, 3, 230–71.

Johnson, D.W., Johnson, R.T. and Holubec, E.J. (1986) *Circles of Learning: Cooperation in the Classroom*, Edina: Interaction Book Company.

Johnson, D.W., Johnson, R.T. and Maruyama, G. (1983) 'Independence and interpersonal attraction among heterogeneous and homogeneous individuals: a theoretical formulation and a meta-analysis of the research', *Review of Educational Research*, 53, 1, 5–54.

Johnson, R.T. and Johnson, D.W. (1994) 'An overview of cooperative learning', in J. Thousand, R. Villa and A. Nevin (eds) *Creativity and Collaborative Learning: A Practical Guide to Empowering Students and Teachers*, Baltimore: Paul H Brookes.

Jones, A.V. *et al.* (1983) 'Integration of handicapped pupils into normal school and particularly into science lessons', *Education Science*, 105, 31–2.

Jones, C. (1987) 'Working together: the development of an integration programme in a primary school', *Cambridge Journal of Education*, 17, 3, 175–8.

Jordan, A. (1994) *Skills in Collaborative Classroom Consultation*, London: Routledge.

Jordan, L. and Goodey, C. (1996) *Human Rights and School Change: The Newham Story*, Bristol: CSIE.

Jupp, K. (1992) *Everyone Belongs*, London: Souvenir Press.

Kay, J. (1996) *The Business of Economics*, Oxford: OUP.

Kidd, R. and Hornby, G. (1993) 'Transfer from special to mainstream', *British Journal of Special Education*, 20, 1, 17–19.

Kishi, G.S. and Meyer, L.H. (1994) 'What children report and remember: a six-year follow-up of the effects of social contact between peers with and without severe disabilities', *Journal of Association for Persons with Severe Handicaps*, 19, 4, 277–89.

Kitzinger, J. (1990) 'Who are you kidding? Children, power and the struggle against sexual abuse', in A. James and A. Prout (eds) *Constructing and Reconstructing Childhood*, London: Falmer.

Lalkhen, Y. and Norwich, B. (1990) 'The self-concept and self-esteem of adolescents with physical impairments in integrated and special school settings', *European Journal of Special Needs Education*, 5, 1, 1–12.

Levine, D.U. and Lezotte, L.W. (1995) 'Effective schools research', in J.A. Banks and C.A. Banks (eds) *Handbook of Research on Multicultural Education*, Nebraska: Macmillan.

Lewis, A. (1995a) 'Views of schooling held by children attending schools for pupils with moderate learning difficulties', *International Journal of Disability, Development and Education*, 42, 1, 57–73.

—— (1995b) *Children's Understanding of Disability*, London: Routledge.

—— (1996a) 'Developing spoken language: making school experience meaningful', in P. Widlake (ed.) *The Good Practice Guide to Special Educational Needs*, Birmingham: Questions Publishing Co.

—— (1996b) 'Summative National Curriculum assessments of primary aged children with special needs', *British Journal of Special Education*, 23, 1, 9–14.

Leyden, G. (1996) ' "Cheap labour" or neglected resource? The role of the peer group and efficient, effective support for children with special needs', *Educational Psychology in Practice*, 11, 4, 49–55.

Lipsky, D. and Gartner, A. (1987) 'Capable of achievement and worthy of respect', *Exceptional Children*, 54, 1, 69–74.

—— (1996) 'Inclusion, school restructuring and the remaking of American Society', *Harvard Educational Review*, 66, 4, 762–96.

Lovey, J. (1995) *Supporting Special Needs in Special School Classrooms*, London: Fulton/Roehampton Institute.

Loxley, A. and Thomas, G. (1997) 'From policy to the real world: an international comparison of special needs administration', *Disability and Society*, 12, 2, in press.

Lucas, D. and Thomas, G. (1990) 'The geography of classroom learning', *British Journal of Special Education*, 17, 1, 31–4.

Madden, P. (1995) 'Why parents: how parents. A keynote review', *British Journal of Learning Disabilities*, 23, 3, 90–3.

Mapp, S. (1995) 'Joint effort', *Community Care*, 11–17 May, 16–17.

Maras, P. and Brown, R. (1992) 'Mainstream children's attitudes to disability', *Education Section Review*, 16, 2, 72–6.

Markides, A. (1989) 'Integration: the speech intelligibility, friendships and associations of hearing-impaired children in secondary schools', *Journal of British Association of Teachers of the Deaf*, 13, 3, 63–71.

Mason, D. (1994) 'Inclusive education leaves deaf children outsiders', *WFD (World Federation of the Deaf, Helsinki) News*, 4 (Dec.), 22.

Mason, M. (1995) *Invisible Children: Report of the Joint Conference on Children, Images and Disability*, London: Save the Children and the Integration Alliance.

Mason, M. and Rieser, R. (1995) 'Altogether better', in *'Special Needs' to Equality in Education*, London: Charity Projects/Comic Relief.

McBrien, J.A. and Foxen,T.H. (1981) *The EDY In-service Course for Mental Handicap Practitioners*, Manchester: Manchester University Press.

McBrien, J. and Weightman, J. (1980) 'The effect of room management procedures on the engagement of profoundly retarded children', *British Journal of Mental Subnormality*, 26, 1, 38–46.

McCracken, G.D. (1988) *The Long Interview*, Beverly Hills: Sage.

Meekosha, H. and Jacubowicz, A. (1996) 'Disability, participation, representation and social justice', in C. Christensen and F. Rizvi (eds) *Disability and the Dilemmas of Education and Justice*, Buckingham: Open University Press.

Meijer, C.J.W., Pijl, S.J. and Hegarty, S. (eds) (1994) *New Perspectives in Special Education*, London: Routledge.

Mercer, J.R. (1970) 'Sociological perspectives on mild mental retardation', in H.C. Haywood (ed.) *Sociocultural Aspects of Mental Retardation*, Englewood Cliffs, NJ: Prentice-Hall.

Miller, E. (1996) 'Changing the way we think about kids with disabilities: a conversation with Tom Hehir', in E. Miller and R. Tovey, *Inclusion and Special Education*, HEL Focus Series No. 1, Cambridge, MA: Harvard Educational Publishing.

Mittler, P. (1995) 'Raising expectations', *SLD Experience*, 12, 3.

—— (1996) 'Preparing for self-advocacy', in B. Carpenter, R. Ashdown and K. Bovair (eds) *Enabling Access*, London: David Fulton.

Moger, M. and Coates, P. (1992) 'Why integration matters: a report on the partnership between a special school and a comprehensive school', *Links*, 17, 2, 8–10.

Moore, A (1996) 'Making National Curriculum history more accessible', in P. Widlake (ed.) *The Good Practice Guide to Special Educational Needs*, Birmingham: Questions Publishing Co.

Moore, J., Carpenter, B. and Lewis, A. (1987) ' "He can do it really!": an account of partial integration in a first (5–8) school', *Education 3–13*, June, 37–43.

Mortimer, H. (1995) 'Welcoming young children with special needs into mainstream education', *Support for Learning*, 10, 4, 164–9.

Mortimore, P., Sammons, P., Stoll, L., Lewis, D. and Ecob, R. (1988) *School Matters: The Junior Years,* Exeter: Open Books.

Moss, J. (1987) 'Functional integration: the best of three worlds', *Journal of British Association of Teachers of the Deaf*, 11, 1, 15–21.

Neisser, U. (ed.) (1986) *The School Achievement of Minority Children*, Hillsdale: Lawrence Erlbaum.

New Brunswick (1994) 'Best practices for inclusion', unpublished paper, Student Services Branch, New Brunswick Department of Education, Fredericton, New Brunswick.

Newcomer, P.L. and Hammill, D.D. (1975) 'ITPA and academic achievement', *Reading Teacher*, 28, 731–42.

Newman, T. and Roberts, H. (1996) 'Meaning well and doing good: interventions in children's lives', in P. Alderson, S. Brill, I. Chalmers, R. Fuller, P. Hinkley-Smith, G. Macdonald, T. Newman, A. Oakley, H. Roberts and H. Ward, *What Works? Effective Social Interventions in Child Welfare*, London: Barnardos.

Newton, C., Taylor, G. and Wilson, D. (1996) 'Circles of friends: an inclusive approach to meeting emotional and behavioural needs', *Educational Psychology in Practice*, 11, 4, 41–8.

Nind, M. and Hewett, D. (1994) *Access to Communication*, London: David Fulton.

Nolan, A. and Gersch, I. (1996) 'More than an extra pair of hands', *Special Children*, March, 10–15.

Norwich, B. (1993) 'Towards effective schools for all: a response', in M. Ainscow, *Towards Effective Schools for All*, Stafford: NASEN.

Oakley, A. (1996) 'Who's afraid of the randomised control trial?', in P. Alderson, S. Brill, I. Chalmers, R. Fuller, P. Hinkley-Smith, G. Macdonald, T. Newman, A. Oakley, H. Roberts and H. Ward, *What Works? Effective Social Interventions in Child Welfare*, London: Barnardos.

O'Brien, J. and Forest, M. (1989) *Action for Inclusion: How to Improve Schools by Welcoming Children with Special Needs into Regular Classrooms*, Toronto: Inclusion Press.

OECD (1994) *The Integration of Disabled Children into Mainstream Education: Ambitions, Theories and Practices*, Paris: Organisation for Economic Co-operation and Development.

OFSTED (1996a) *Exclusions from Secondary Schools*, London: The Stationery Office.

—— (1996b) *The Implementation of the Code of Practice for Pupils with Special Educational Needs*, London: HMSO.

Oliver, M. (1992) 'Changing the social relations of research production', *Disability, Handicap and Society*, 7, 2, 101–114.

—— (1995) 'Does special education have a role to play in the twenty-first century?', *REACH: Journal of Special Needs Education in Ireland*, 8, 2, 67–76.

Orlowska, D. (1995) 'Parental participation in issues concerning their sons and daughters with learning disabilities', *Disability and Society*, 10, 4, 437–56.

Outhwaite, W. (1985) 'Hans-Georg Gadamer', in Q. Skinner (ed.) *The Return of Grand Theory in the Human Sciences*, Cambridge: Canto.

Parlett, M. and Hamilton, D. (1987) 'Evaluation as illumination', in R. Murphy and H. Torrance (eds) *Evaluating Education: Issues and Methods*, London: Harper and Row.

Paul, P.V. and Ward, M.E. (1996) 'Inclusion paradigms in conflict', *Theory into Practice*, 35, 1, 4–11.

Pickering, I. (1996) 'Look who's talking hi tech', *Special Children*, Feb., 28–30.

Pijl, S.J. (1995) 'The resources for regular schools with special needs students: an international perspective', in C. Clarke, A. Dyson and A. Millward (eds) *Towards Inclusive Schools?*, London: Fulton.

Pijl, S.J. and Meijer, C.J.W. (1994) 'Introduction', in C.J.W. Meijer, S.J. Pijl and S. Hegarty (eds) *New Perspectives in Special Education*, London: Routledge.

Plender, J. (1997a) *A Stake in the Future: The Stakeholding Solution*, London: Nicholas Brealey Publishing.

—— (1997b) 'A stake of one's own', *Prospect*, Feb., 20–4.

Porter, G. (1995) 'Organization of schooling: achieving access and quality through inclusion', *Prospects*, 25, 2, 299–309.

Postman, N (1995) *The End of Education: Redefining the Value of School*, New York: Alfred A. Knopf.

Potts, P. (1982) *Origins*, Milton Keynes: The Open University Press.

—— (1992) 'Introduction: finding a voice', in T. Booth, W. Swann, M. Masterson and P. Potts (eds) *Curricula for Diversity in Education*, London: Routledge.

Pugach, M.C. and Johnson, L.J. (1990) 'Meeting diverse needs through professional peer collaboration', in W. Stainback and S. Stainback (eds) *Support Networks for Inclusive Schooling: Interdependent Integrated Education*, Baltimore: Paul H. Brookes.

Putnam, J. (1993) 'The movement toward teaching and learning in inclusive classrooms', in J. Putnam (ed.) *Cooperative Learning and Strategies for Inclusion*, Baltimore: Paul H. Brookes.

Putnam, J., Spiegel, A.N. and Bruininks, R.H. (1995) 'Future directions in education and inclusion of students with disabilities: a Delphi investigation', *Exceptional Children*, 61, 6, 553–76.

Rawls, J. (1971) *A Theory of Justice*, Oxford: Clarendon Press.

Reynolds, D. (1995) 'Using school effectiveness knowledge for children with special needs: the problems and possibilities', in C. Clarke, A. Dyson and A. Millward (eds) *Towards Inclusive Schools?*, London: Fulton.

Reynolds, M.C. (1988) 'A reaction to the JLD special series on the Regular Education Initiative', *Journal of Learning Disabilities*, 21, 6, 352–6.

Reynolds, M.C., Wang, M. and Walberg, H. (1987) 'The necessary restructuring of special and general education', *Exceptinal Children*, 53, 1, 391–7.

Rieser, R. and Mason, M. (1990) *Disability Equality in the Classroom: A Human Rights Issue*, London: Inner London Education Authority.

Rizvi, F. and Lingard, B. (1996) 'Disability, education and the discourses of justice', in C. Christensen and F. Rizvi (eds) *Disability and the Dilemmas of Education and Justice*, Buckingham: Open University Press.

RNIB (1995) *Including Visually Impaired Children: Developing a School Special Educational Needs Policy to Facilitate the Successful Integration of Visually Impaired Children*, London: RNIB.

Roaf, C. (1988) 'The concept of a whole school approach to special needs', in O. Robinson and G. Thomas (eds) *Tackling Learning Difficulties*, London: Hodder and Stoughton.

—— (1992) '*Le mot juste*: learning the language of equality', in T. Booth, W. Swann, M. Masterson and P. Potts (eds) *Curricula for Diversity in Education*, London: Routledge.

Roaf, C. and Bines, H. (1989) 'Needs, rights and opportunities in special education', in C. Roaf and H. Bines (eds) *Needs, Rights and Opportunities: Developing Approaches to Special Education*, London: Falmer.

Rutter, M., Maughan, B., Mortimore, P. and Ouston, J. (1979) *Fifteen Thousand Hours: Secondary Schools and their Effects on Children*, London: Open Books.

Salisbury, C., Gallucci, C., Palombaro, M.M. and Peck, C.A. (1995) 'Strategies that promote social relations among elementary students with and without severe disabilities in inclusive schools', *Exceptional Children*, 62, 2, 125–37.

Sammons, P., Nuttall, D. and Cuttance, P. (1993) 'Differential school effectiveness: results from a re-analysis of the Inner London Education Authority's Junior School Project Data', *British Educational Research Journal*, 19, 4, 381–405.

Samson, A. (1986) *The Full-time Integration of Some Special School Pupils into Comprehensive Schools*, unpublished MSc dissertation, Manchester: Manchester University.

Sapon-Shevin, M. (1992) 'Celebrating diversity, creating community: curriculum that honors and builds on differences', in S. Stainback and W. Stainback (eds) *Curriculum Considerations in Inclusive Classrooms: Facilitating Learning for All Students*, Baltimore: Paul H. Brookes.

Saur, R.E., Popp, M.J. and Isaacs, M. (1984) 'Action zone theory and the hearing impaired student in the mainstreamed classroom', *Journal of Classroom Interaction*, 19, 2, 21–5.

Scott, P. (1996) 'LEAs and the development of the special education system in the UK', unpublished PhD thesis, Milton Keynes: Open University.

Scruggs, T.E. and Mastropieri, M.A. (1996) 'Teacher perceptions of mainstreaming/inclusion, 1958–1995: a research synthesis', *Exceptional Children*, 63, 1, 59–74.

Sebba, J. and Ainscow, M. (1996) 'International developments in inclusive schooling: mapping the issues', *Cambridge Journal of Education*, 26, 1, 5–18.

Sebba, J. and Ainscow, M. (eds) (1995) 'Understanding the development of inclusive schools', *Newsletter no.1: University of Cambridge Institute of Education*, September.

Shelling, G. (1996) 'Key concerns of people who have received special education: implications for inclusion', unpublished MA thesis, Oxford: Brookes University.

Sheppo, K.G. (1995) 'How an urban school promotes inclusion', *Educational Leadership*, 52, 4, 82–4.

Simmons, K. (1986) 'Painful extractions', *Times Educational Supplement*, 17 Oct.

Skinner, Q. (ed.) (1985) *The Return of Grand Theory in the Human Sciences*, Cambridge: Canto.

Skrtic, T.M. (1991) 'The special education paradox: equity as the way to excellence', *Harvard Educational Review*, 61, 2, 148–206.

Slee, R. (1995) 'Inclusive education: from policy to school implementation', in C. Clarke, A. Dyson and A. Millward (eds) *Towards Inclusive Schools?*, London: Fulton.

Spalding, B. and Florek, A. (1988) 'One school's approach to integration: developing a community philosophy and utilising an "in house" educational psychologist', *Support for Learning*, 3, 1, 27–34.

Stainback, S. and Stainback, W. (1990) 'Inclusive schooling', in W. Stainback and S. Stainback, *Support Networks for Inclusive Schooling: Interdependent Integrated Education*, Baltimore: Paul H. Brookes.

Staub, D. and Peck, C. (1995) 'What are the outcomes for nondisabled students?', *Educational Leadership*, 52, 4, 36–40.

Steinberg, A. and Tovey, R. (1996) '"Research says . . . ": a cautionary note', in E. Miller and R. Tovey (eds) *Inclusion and Special Education*, HEL Focus Series No. 1, Cambridge, MA: Harvard Educational Publishing.

Strain, P.S. and Kerr, M.M. (1981) *Mainstreaming of Children in Schools: Research and Programmatic Issues*, London: Academic Press.

Stukat, K-G. (1993) 'Integration of physically disabled students', *European Journal of Special Needs Education*, 8, 3, 249–68.

Swann, W. (1988) 'Learning difficulties or curricular reform: integration or differentiation?', in G. Thomas and A. Feiler (eds) *Planning for Special Needs: A Whole School Approach*, Oxford: Basil Blackwell.

Swanson, H.L. (1996) 'Meta-analysis, replication, social skills, and learning disabilities', *Journal of Special Education*, 30, 2, 213–21.

Tamaren, M.C. (1992) *I Make a Difference! A Curriculum Guide Building Self-esteem and Sensitivity in the Inclusive Classroom*, Novato, CA: Academic Therapy Publications.

Tarr, J. and Thomas, G. (1997) 'The quality of special educational needs policies: time for review?', *Support for Learning*, 12, 1, 10–14.

Tatelman, I.C. (1996) *Support Teaching Versus Intensive Language Teaching: An Evaluation of Two Approaches to TESL*, unpublished MPhil thesis, Oxford: Brookes University.

Tawney, R.H. (1964) *Equality*, London: George Allen and Unwin.

Thomas, D. (1982) *The Experience of Handicap*, London: Methuen.

Thomas, G. (1985) 'Room management in mainstream education', *Educational Research*, 27, 3, 186–93.

—— (1986) 'Integrating personnel in order to integrate children', *Support for Learning*, 1, 1, 19–25.

—— (1991) 'Defining role in the new classroom teams', *Educational Research*, 33, 3, 186–99.

—— (1992) *Effective Classroom Teamwork: Support or Intrusion?*, London: Routledge.

—— (1995a) 'From a school to a service: new proposals for the evaluation of Barnardo's inclusive education project in Somerset schools', internal report to Barnardo's.

—— (1995b) 'Special needs at risk?', *Support for Learning*, 10, 3, 104–12.

—— (1997) 'What's the use of theory?', *Harvard Educational Review*, 67, 1, 75–105.

Thousand, J.S. and Villa, R.A. (1990) 'Sharing expertise and responsibilities through teaching teams', in W. Stainback and S. Stainback (eds) *Support Networks for Inclusive Schooling: Interdependent Integrated Education*, Baltimore: Paul H. Brookes.

Tizard, J., Schofield, W.N. and Hewison, J. (1982) 'Collaboration between teachers and parents in assisting children's reading', *British Journal of Educational Psychology*, 52, 1–15.

Tomlinson, S. (1982) *A Sociology of Special Education*, London: Routledge.

—— (1996) 'Conflicts and dilemmas for professionals in special education', in C. Christensen and F. Rizvi (eds) *Disability and the Dilemmas of Education and Justice*, Buckingham: Open University Press.

Topping, K. (1988) *The Peer Tutoring Handbook*, Beckenham: Croom Helm.

Troyna, B. and Vincent, C. (1996) '"The ideology of expertism": the framing of special education and racial equality policies in the local state', in C. Christensen and F. Rizvi (eds) *Disability and the Dilemmas of Education and Justice*, Buckingham: Open University Press.

Udvari-Solner, A. and Thousand, J. (1995) 'Effective organisational, instructional and curricular practices in inclusive schools and classrooms', in C. Clarke, A. Dyson and A. Millward (eds) *Towards Inclusive Schools?*, London: Fulton.

Vaughan, M. (1989) 'Parents, children and the legal framework', in C. Roaf and H. Bines (eds) *Needs, Rights and Opportunities: Developing Approaches to Special Education*, London: Falmer.

Vaughan, M. and Shearer, A. (1986) *Mainstreaming in Massachusetts*, Bristol: CSIE.

Vislie, L. (1995) 'Integration policies, school reforms and the organisation of schooling for handicapped pupils in Western societies', in C. Clarke, A. Dyson and A. Millward (eds) *Towards Inclusive Schools?*, London: Fulton.

Wade, B. and Moore, M. (1993) *Experiencing Special Education: What Young People with Special Educational Needs Can Tell Us*, Milton Keynes: Open University Press.

Walker, D. (1995) *Postmodernity, Inclusion and Partnership*, unpublished MEd dissertation, Milton Keynes: Open University.

Walsh, B. (1993) 'How disabling any handicap is depends on the attitudes and actions of others: a student's perspective', in R. Slee (ed.) *Is There a Desk with My Name on it? The Politics of Integration*, London: Falmer.

Walter, R.E. (1997) Personal communication. Also: web site at http//rmplc.co.uk/eduweb/sites/meldreth/

Wang, M.C., Reynolds, M. and Walberg, H. (1987) *Handbook of Special Education: Research and Practice*, vol. 1: *Learner Characteristics and Adaptive Education*, Oxford: Pergamon.

—— (1995) 'Serving students at the margins', *Educational Leadership*, 52, 4, 12–17.

Ware, L. (1995) 'The aftermath of the articulate debate: the invention of inclusive education', in C. Clarke, A. Dyson and A. Millward (eds) *Towards Inclusive Schools?*, London: Fulton.

Weatherley, R. and Lipsky, M. (1977) 'Street level bureaucrats and institutional innovation: implementing special educational reform', *Harvard Educational Review*, 47, 171–97.

Wedell, K. (1994) 'Conclusion', in I. Lunt and J. Evans, 'Allocating resources for special educational needs provision', *NASEN Special Educational Needs Policy Option Group*, Policy Options for Special Educational Needs in the 1990s, Seminar Paper 4, Stafford: NASEN.

Weinstein, C.S. (1979) 'The physical environment of the school: a review of the research', *Review of Educational Research*, 49, 4, 577–610.

West, A. and Sammons, P. (1996) 'Children with and without "additional educational needs" at Key Stage 1 in six inner city schools: teaching and learning processes and policy implications', *British Educational Research Journal*, 22, 1, 113–27.

Wheldall, K. (1988) 'The forgotten A in behaviour analysis: the importance of ecological variables in classroom management with particular reference to seating arrangements', in G. Thomas and A. Feiler (eds) *Planning for Special Needs: A Whole School Approach*, Oxford: Basil Blackwell.

Wilson, D. (1990) 'Integration at John Watson School', in D. Baker and K. Bovair (eds) *Making the Special Schools Ordinary*, vol. 2, London: Falmer.

Wolery, M., Gessler-Werts, M., Caldwell, N.K., Snyder, E.D. and Lisowski, V. (1995) 'Experienced teachers' perceptions of resources and supports for inclusion', *Education and Training in Mental Retardation and Developmental Disabilities*, 30, 1, 15–26.

Wolfensberger, W. (1990) 'Human service policies: the rhetoric versus the reality', in L. Barton (ed.) *Disability and Dependency*, London: Falmer.

Woronov, T. (1996) 'New research supports inclusion for physically disabled: vocational ed prevents dropping out', in E. Miller and R. Tovey (eds) *Inclusion and Special Education*, HEL Focus Series No. 1, Cambridge, MA: Harvard Educational Publishing.

York, J. and Tundidor, M. (1995) 'Issues raised in the name of inclusion: perspectives of educators, parents, and students', *Journal of Association for Persons with Severe Handicaps*, 20, 1, 31–44.

Young, I.M. (1990) *Justice and the Politics of Difference*, Princeton, NJ: Princeton University Press.

INDEX